THE BIRTH
OF THE
BRITISH MOTOR CAR
1769–1897

Volume 3
THE LAST BATTLE
1894–97

By the same author
A Toy for the Lion (Kimber)
Adventurer's Road (Cassell)
The Trailblazers (Cassell)
Five Roads to Danger (Cassell)
The Wild Roads (Jarrolds)
The Age of Motoring Adventure (Cassell)
Car Badges of the World (Cassell)
The Motor Book (Methuen)
The Second Motor Book (Methuen)
Automobile Treasurers (Ian Allan)
The World's Motor Museums (Dent)
European Cars 1886–1914 (Ian Allan)
The Vintage Car 1919–1930 (Batsford)
Sports Cars 1907–1927 (Blandford Press)
Sports Cars 1928–1939 (Blandford Press)
Passenger Cars 1863–1904 (Blandford Press)
Passenger Cars 1905–1912 (Blandford Press)
Passenger Cars 1913–1923 (Blandford Press)
Racing Cars and Record Breakers 1898–1921 (Blandford Press)
Sprint: Speed Hillclimbs and Speed Trials in Britain 1899–1925
  (David & Charles)
Isotta-Fraschini: The Noble Pride of Italy (Ballantine)
Contributor to G.N. Georgano: *The Complete Encyclopedia of Motor
  Cars* (Ebury Press)

THE BIRTH
OF THE
BRITISH MOTOR CAR
1769–1897

Volume 3
THE LAST BATTLE
1894–97

T. R. Nicholson

© T.R. Nicholson 1982

9/00008.975

First published 1982 by
THE MACMILLAN PRESS LTD
London and Basingstoke
Companies and representatives
throughout the world

Volume 3   ISBN 0 333 28563 8

Volume 1   ISBN 0 333 23764 1
Volume 2   ISBN 0 333 28561 1
The set   ISBN 0 333 32717 9

Typeset and printed in Hong Kong

Contents

List of Plates

1

The New Contender, 1894–5

From 1894 onwards, the new generation of motor cars began to appear on Britain's roads. The earliest harbinger of the type most representative of the latest arrivals – foreign-designed petrol vehicles – was probably already in the country. At an unknown date, a Roger-Benz of 1888 type, now in the Science Museum, London, was imported into Britain. It is of the first type offered for sale by Mannheim, and it is unlikely that it would have been brought in after more advanced models were made available in 1893. But there is no certainty of this, so the place of this vehicle in history remains conjectural. Early in 1891 Frederick Simms planned to bring a car – presumably a Daimler – to England, but did not do so. Alfred Harmsworth, the future Lord Northcliffe, had ridden in a steamer at the 1889 Paris International Exhibition, and in a petrol car in Paris in 1893. Though later an enthusiastic owner-driver, he did not buy a car at this time. John Henry Knight, too, visited Paris in 1893, and rode on a Serpollet steamer. More notable altogether was a distinguished visitor to Bad Homburg in the same year, to whom the French chocolate millionaire Gaston Menier gave a ride in his Serpollet. The Prince of Wales had shown interest in Rickett's steamers as a young man, and now had his first recorded ride on a motor car.

As we have seen, a variety of indigenous electric vehicles, and also Roots's kerosene tricycle, made their forays in this period, while the Serpollet visiting Donkin's premises may have strayed into the neighbouring Bermondsey streets. But as far as the up-and-coming petrol car was concerned, Britons took their pleasures abroad. Sure signs of a strong and general revival of interest in motor cars, and in relieving them of their legal disabilities, began to appear only in 1894.

New British vehicles constituted one of these portents, if an insignificant one. The most prominent were still propelled by electricity, which is no surprise. They continued to be of all types, private and public. Walter Bersey ran a parcels van in the City of

London from early March 1894. It covered about 1000 miles in 11 months, earning good opinions from the press for its handiness, and bad ones from crossing-sweepers, bus drivers and cab drivers, who saw their livelihoods in danger. Its designer claimed firmly that running costs were half those of a horsedrawn van. Press estimates of its range varied wildly between 25 and 50 miles. The *Sun's* representative, who was given a ride, called the van "a triumphant success". Radcliffe Ward's Bersey-designed electric bus attracted notice; by mid-August 1894 it was said to have run 3000–4000 miles in the capital. Ward also ran an electric cab in London at about this time. The words of the horse cab driver who handled it must have confirmed his colleagues' worst fears, for he described the machine as easy to learn and to control.

Bersey and Ward had been involved with electric vehicles for years; not so Garrard & Blumfield of Coventry, who – like so many others – began to experiment with cars after making a name in the cycle industry. In June 1894 Charles Garrard's four-wheeled electric phaeton underwent a successful road trial between Coventry and Birmingham, a distance of 18 miles, at speeds of up to 10 m.p.h. It then ran about in the Birmingham streets. The *Cyclist* was inspired to prophecy – "The Carriage of the Future", it cried. The device was a mixture of crudity and advanced thinking. The frame was tubular, naturally enough, and large-section, small-diameter pneumatic tyres were fitted – the first to appear on a British car. But the coil springs protected only the passengers – the motor and the quarter-ton of fragile batteries (the latter amounting to half the weight of the vehicle) were unsprung. C.R. Garrard later worked for the Société des Cycles Gladiator and for Humber & Company, and eventually made a name for himself as a designer of exceptionally efficient petrol engines for Talbot cars.

Electricity remained the motive force of the hour, with confident supporters. In May 1894 the electrical trades members of the City of London Chamber of Commerce – prompted, no doubt, by constructors – wrote to the Commissioner of the Metropolitan Police to ask if, in his view, electric vehicles were locomotives in law. If he said no, his officers could hardly bring charges under the Acts. Not surprisingly, the Commissioner said that they were locomotives; but those who had raised the question declared that they would ask the Board of Trade for a ruling. Their confidence seemed justified. Electrics were so un-obtrusive that, in the five years to May 1896, Walter Bersey was not once prosecuted, active though he was; and by the same year Radcliffe Ward was working his bus with the tacit consent of the London County Council.

Among native constructors, the partisans of other forms of motive power were few. *Engineering* reiterated its earlier praise for the Serpollet boiler, and continued to do so into 1895. At the 1894 Stanley Show, James Roots showed a four-stroke kerosene engine for road vehicles. More significant for the future was the activity of another experimenter with internal combustion, Frederick William Bremer. This young Walthamstow engineer had started work in 1892 on a three-wheeled vehicle designed around a gas engine. While building, it evolved into the first British motor car to reflect Continental trends in design. By the time of its first outing on a public road in December 1894, it was a four-wheeler clearly inspired by Mannheim's Benz. A rear-mounted, water-cooled petrol engine with a single horizontal cylinder and automatic inlet valve drove through belt primary and chain final drive. There were two speeds; ignition was by coil and battery; and a differential was fitted. The wire-spoked wheels were shod with rubber tyres. The little car's most original feature was probably its wick carburettor with float feed and hot-water heating to aid vaporisation. Bremer had little money, so had to make most of the parts except for the wheels, tyres and chassis. The flywheel was a grindstone, and the insulation of the sparking plug was a clay pipe stem.

The car was not finished until January 1895. Its longest expedition was to Epping and back. Such trips were made very early on Sunday mornings, so as to escape the attention of the police. In spite of this precaution, Bremer once met a mounted policeman; but the horse bolted with its rider, so saving a confrontation. Like so many other innovators, Bremer lost interest in his creation once it was complete. Because it attracted no attention at the time, no promoter took it up. Nothing more was heard of it until 1912, by which time it was an antique.

These initiatives merely reflected the growing interest in motor cars; they could not fuel it, because they did not make cars available. Most were misdirected, and, besides, no one in Britain was going to build cars for sale until the law was changed. The same could not be said for two entirely new trends – the actual availability of practical motor cars on the Continent, and an increasing interest in them among influential British visitors that culminated in the first importation of one of the new generation of vehicles. Availability was crucial – for the first time, would-be motorists in Britain did not have to rely on the occasional products of native experimenters. By 1894–5 production of Panhard, Peugeot and Benz had got into its stride, although demand still exceeded supply; foreigners who were willing to wait, however, would get their motor cars.

It was to be expected that Sir David Salomons would be among the earliest of these pioneers. As "a frequent visitor to Paris" he had his interest in motor cars re-awakened there, and in 1894 visited the city with the intention of buying a car.[1] Whether he did so is not known; it is certain only that he did not bring one to England at this juncture. In 1894, too, a boy of 17, just up at Cambridge, had his first ride in a car in Paris – the Hon. Charles Stewart Rolls, third son of Lord Llangattock. Soon Rolls would be as prominent a figure in the motor car movement as Salomons.

Some time in 1894 the Hon. Evelyn Ellis of Datchet, Berkshire, bought a Panhard-Levassor in Paris, becoming probably the earliest English visitor to acquire one of the new petrol cars. But its time was not yet – Ellis kept his car in France, for use there. Ellis, the sixth son of Lord Howard de Walden, was the largest shareholder in the Daimler Motor Syndicate after Simms. His holding increased from 50 shares on the establishment of the business in 1893 to 105 in August 1894. By that time Simms had 220 out of the 600 shares taken up, so between them they controlled the business. Ellis was a director of the syndicate from August 1893 or earlier. By mid-1895 he kept a man-hauled estate fire engine with a Daimler pump and four Daimler-powered motor launches at his Thames-side home.

In Paris, one Englishman was actually engaged in selling motor vehicles, though not to his compatriots. This was Herbert Osbaldeston Duncan, a cycling journalist and keen racing cyclist. At various times he had represented Humber & Company and Rudge & Company in France, but in 1894 had entered into partnership with Louis Suberbie, formerly of the Gladiator cycle concern, to make the Hildebrand & Wolfmüller motor bicycle under licence. He was soon, as it transpired, to abandon the French connected for an English one.

Two other visitors to the Continent in 1894 later co-operated to lay one of the very first stones in the edifice of the British motor trade. Walter Arnold, now aged 75 years, and his brother George were partners in the firm of William Arnold & Sons, agricultural engineers and traction engine contractors of East Peckham in Kent – a considerable business. Walter Arnold's earliest traceable connection with motor cars was as a spectator at the 1894 Paris–Rouen trials. His friend Henry Hewetson was a tea broker of Catford. Visiting Mannheim with Arnold in 1894, he rode in a Benz, and visited the Benz works. In August Hewetson ordered a car of his own. In November he took delivery of it – the earliest documented importation of one of the new generation of motor cars.

Hewetson was well aware of the restrictions on such vehicles, and by openly driving about without a man in front, at above the legal limit, he deliberately flouted them. By courting police attention, he hoped to make publicity for the cause of the motor car. In doing so he perpetuated a technique pioneered by Sir Thomas Parkyns, and common to most of the first motorists. His method was first to ignore the restrictions altogether, then, when the police began to take an interest in his activities, to make the regulations look foolish. He arranged for a boy on a bicycle to ride ahead to warn of policemen, while another boy rode on the car, dismounting on a signal from the cyclist to walk in front with a red flag. Hewetson may have been aware of a by-law regarding a flag, or he may merely have believed, as did many others, that statute still demanded one. Whichever was the case, his flag consisted of a piece of red ribbon tied to a pencil, on the grounds that its size was not specified.

This modest budding of interest in the new, Continental breed of motor car was said later to date from the occasion when the vehicles first became news in France and in Britain – the Paris–Rouen contest of July 1894. Since none of the Englishmen named attributed any such significance to the event, one must be cautious in making the link, but as the one development more or less coincided with the other, the unprecedented publicity accorded to the *Concours des Voitures sans Chevaux* may well have aroused enthusiasm which might otherwise have remained dormant.

Engineering put it with cynical succinctness: "The ball was set rolling by a Paris journal in search of an advertisement." The publication referred to was *Le Petit Journal*, a mass-circulation newspaper for which, in 1896, 4 million readers were claimed. One of its editors, the brilliant and dynamic Pierre Giffard, had already been responsible for inspiring the Paris–Brest–Paris cycle race of 1891 and other sensational sporting events. *Le Petit Journal's* "trademark" was enthusiastic espousal of all forms of open-air exercise, the more spectacular the better, in the interests of boosting circulation. Motoring was not as out of place in such company as it would seem today, for, with motor cars at their then stage of development, it was hard, rough, slow work.[2] In 1892, while retaining his post with *Le Petit Journal*, Giffard became founder-editor of *Le Vélo*, a new cycling journal to cater for the sport-mad French. Nothing on the scale of Giffard's earlier promotions had been seen before, so now he would organise the world's first major demonstration of the latest means of locomotion, the motor car. It was appropriate that Rouen should be the destination – the world's first road race for cyclists had been run on the same route in 1869.

Giffard announced the coming Paris–Rouen contest in December 1893. It was emphasised that there would be no racing: this was a *concours* – a test, or rather a series of tests, with the object of discovering and encouraging the most promising design of vehicle. There were by now several "systems" on offer. Was the Panhard-Peugeot or the Roger-Benz recipe best? But what about steam or electric propulsion? And the endless permutations of engine position, change-speed and power transmission arrangements, and two, three or four wheels? No one could be sure, because they had not yet been subjected to prolonged, arduous and public comparative trials. The culmination of the tests, the 79-mile journey to Rouen, should provide some answers, even if no average speeds over 12 k.p.h. would be recognised. Safety, ease of control and low running costs would be the major criteria.

The very new growth of interest in motor cars in France was reflected in the number and origin of the entries. The final count, at the end of April 1894, was 102 vehicles from 93 individuals or firms. Only a minority existed outside the imagination of their entrants – the rest were the inspiration of publicity-seekers or over-optimistic experimenters. Only two entries came from Germany, and just one from Britain – the Garrard & Blumfield electric, which did not reach the start. All the rest were French.

Although the event was postponed seven weeks because most entrants were not ready, only 21 turned up to take part in the eliminating trials, which began on 19 July. These were held over six routes, each between 30 and 35 miles long, to avoid inviting public hostility with too great a concentration of cars in one place. To qualify, each car had to cover its course in four hours – the competitors had objected to a time limit of three hours. All succeeded in passing the eliminating trials, so qualifying to start for Rouen on 23 July.

Almost all the cars were from established manufacturers. This was a reflection not so much on the hopefuls as on the old hands. After all, by this time upwards of 300 practical passenger vehicles had been built in France by constructors such as Panhard & Levassor, Peugeot, Roger, De Dion, Serpollet and the Bollée family, or by their imitators. The great majority were three years old or less, and were running in the Paris area, so one is left with the conclusion that drivers lacked confidence in the reliability of their cars, or in their own driving ability, or both. Five of the starters were Peugeots, four were Panhards, and seven were steamers. Among them were a De Dion tractor hauling a victoria, a Scotte with a Field boiler, a Le Blant with a Serpollet boiler, and three Serpollets proper.

The De Dion tractor was fastest, covering the distance to Rouen at an average speed of $11\frac{3}{5}$ m.p.h., but two people were needed to drive it, and a Peugeot (averaging $11\frac{1}{2}$ m.p.h.) and a Panhard were declared joint winners on overall merit. Second and third places went to steamers. Fourth place was also shared, between two Daimler-engined petrol cars, while Emile Roger won fifth prize for his design improvements. The Scotte, which burst a tube – a failing at the end of steam's story, as at the beginning – gained a consolation prize. Of the 21 entrants, 17 vehicles completed the course; the four failures were all steamers. There was a lesson here, obscured by the success of the De Dion: for long-distance work over give-and-take roads, the simpler, lighter, stronger petrol cars were best.

The Paris–Rouen trial was at least as prominent a landmark in British as in French motoring history. The reason was that it prompted the nation's leading engineering journal to embrace the cause of the motor car with an enthusiasm that brought to the machine the publicity that it needed. The initiative of the *Engineer*, though taken over by others, opened a campaign that ended with the liberation of the motor car from the most onerous of the restrictions on it. At this time, William Worby Beaumont was one of the editors of the *Engineer*, and soon revealed himself as a dedicated partisan of the motor car. It is not unreasonable to suppose that the driving force behind the *Engineer*'s campaign came from him. Certainly he had the right background – he was a grandson of William Worby, the most notable pioneer of agricultural self-movers; he had been trained at the factory that made the Lenoir gas engine in England; and he was himself a patentee of variable-speed gears.[3]

At the end of March 1894 the *Engineer* became "the first journal in England to tell the world what was being done in France". A "special commissioner" – perhaps Beaumont – was sent over to investigate.[4] The journal's involvement opened with a detailed account of the regulations of the "international automobile carriage competition", of which, according to the organisers, the purpose was "to supersede almost entirely horse draught for street vehicles in towns and cities". An extended account of the background and build-up to the Paris–Rouen run appeared a few days before it took place, and a report of it followed. The "special commissioner", who clearly carried weight, was shown over the Panhard works, and described Panhard's and Peugeot's current offerings. For the first time, British readers were given a detailed description of the new machine, and its capabilities. The "very unpleasant" smell of a motor car and its "great vibration" when idling were not glossed over; but it was observed that "the petroleum carriages can go as fast as an ordinary cyclist cares to travel".[5] They were able to do so because of the lack of crippling restrictions. "The authorities in the United Kingdom", concluded the reporter, "appear to do what they can to hinder the use of such carriages, whereas in France . . . everything possible seems to be done to encourage their use".

The *Engineer* returned to the subject in an editorial later in the year. This helped to perpetuate the belief that the red flag was part of statute, and made other mistakes in describing the law, but it attacked effectively as well. For instance, the writer drew attention to the inconsistency which was allowing electric vehicles to run in the streets unmolested.[6] There was need to encourage cheap transport of all kinds, so the restrictions on traction engines should be relaxed as well.

For the time being, the *Engineer* campaigned almost alone. In April *Engineering*, while once again bemoaning the existing legislation, did not foresee its repeal, and saw no future for motor vehicles. The Paris–Rouen contest received a brief notice, but at this time *Engineering* was not interested in motor cars – an attitude shared by almost every other British publication.

However, a dramatic change in public as well as private attitudes was on the way. As we shall see, the *Engineer* intensified its campaign, and was joined by other institutions and individuals; but the real transformation in the prospects of the motor car happened when the main initiative for changing the law was taken over by the government. It now acquired an impetus that earnest editorials in technical journals could not hope to match. The vicissitudes of politics permitting, there was clearly going to be new legislation – when government Bills regulating self-propelled road vehicles had been presented in the past, they had invariably become law in one form or another. The only uncertainty was the direction this legislation would take.

With the spotlight about to switch to Parliament, another brief look at its character will help to explain what was due to happen in that area. The trends of the 1860s and 1870s continued, their direction unchanged. The "urbanisation" of Parliament, and the progressive, if hesitant and partial, liberalisation of opinion among its members advanced hand in hand. This said, the picture was as complex as ever. In the House of Commons elected in 1892, 163 Conservatives were landowners and 298 were engaged in finance, industry and commerce – the land had lost its dominant position in that party. Among the Liberals, a mere 51 were landowners, while 297 were in business and other professions.[7] As a broad generalisation, then, "trade" outnumbered "land" by between two and three to one. But as before, these figures are deceptive. They relate only to the major interest of each M.P. Many who were mainly businessmen also owned land, and many who were landowners had business interests as well, so interests were divided. Furthermore, the landowners – though reduced both proportionately and in total numbers – remained the largest single interest group in the Commons, with nearly half of the seats.[8] Theirs was also the most coherent, and therefore the most effective, of these groups, informal though it was. As for the Lords, they were, as always, dominated by the landed interest. This continuing, if weakened, hold was a clear element in the picture.

It was now more than ever unsafe to equate the Liberal label firmly with liberal views and the Conservative label with conservatism, particularly where a non-party political issue such as roads and vehicles was concerned. Progressive views on social and economic questions were as likely – or more likely – to be held by a Conservative as by a Liberal. This might be a matter of conviction, of expert knowledge, or of interest – or of a happy combination of these. For instance, a landowner conservative in politics and in most other respects might well favour a liberalising – even a Liberal – measure if it promised to improve the condition of arable farming. Conversely, an otherwise liberal-minded landowner might speak and vote against his party's measure if he grew animal feed or bred horses, and felt that the Bill would reduce demand for both. The bonds of party discipline, grown much stronger since the 1870s, were not invoked over non-partisan issues, or if the government was not in danger.

Such circumstances did not, however, save a non-partisan Bill from attacks designed simply to embarrass or blackmail the party behind it, irrespective of its merits. For example, the Irish Nationalist members regarded the measures of either major party as fair game. In general, they obstructed all legislation not Irish in content because they wanted legislation for Ireland, and all Irish legislation because they were against it.

The truth of all this would be reflected faithfully in the debates to follow, inside and outside Parliament, on the subject of the motor car. But amid all the difficulties of forecasting the reception and ultimate fate of some measures, it is still true to say that the climate for Bills of political, social and economic liberalisation was steadily improving.

Along with home rule for Ireland, imperial affairs, and worldwide Anglophobia, the linked issues of free trade and the agricultural depression exercised the minds of legislators. As we have seen, British industry was under attack in home and overseas markets from newly efficient and booming foreign industries. Measures that would foster industrial growth would be welcome. By the 1890s the traditional strength of British agriculture, its arable land under wheat, had been destroyed by falls in price. To make matters worse, the harvest weather in 1892, 1893 and 1895 had been particularly bad in the grain-growing areas of the east and south. A Royal Commission on the state of agriculture,[9] appointed in 1893, sat throughout the period under consideration, and produced interim reports in February 1896. Both the majority and the minority reports were in general agreement on causes and the kind of remedies required, which included reduced rates and land tax to encourage investment, and government loans to farmers for agricultural improvements.

Any promising remedies were eagerly investigated. One was the light railway, which was seen as an economical means of transporting farm produce to local markets, to ports or to the main line for distribution nationally. It performed the function of a branch line, but whereas ordinary branch lines were notoriously uneconomic to build and run, the light railway was in theory quickly built, and cheaply constructed and operated, thanks to the use of lightweight track and rolling stock, only the most basic of buildings, and the minimum standards in signalling and manning. In the last quarter of the 19th century and the first few years of the 20th, light railways were "vigorously advocated as the answer to rural transport problems both in Europe and in ... the developing colonies overseas".[10] But there were contrary arguments. For instance, costs were still heavy and delays long while the promoters of a light railway still needed an Act of Parliament, had to buy land like any other railway company, and were subject to the same operating regulations.

In December 1894 the Board of Trade – the department of state responsible for railways – called all interested parties to a conference on light railways. A committee from this conference, chaired by the eminent jurist and political theorist James Bryce, reported to the House of Commons in January 1895 in favour of relaxing regulations in favour of light railways, and making them easier to construct. The committee members included three names that became familiar in the context of road vehicles – Sir Albert Rollit, Alexander Siemens and Henry Hobhouse.

This activity culminated in the government-sponsored Light Railways Bill of 1896. The measure aimed to foster light railways by allowing them to be built with as little delay, trouble and expense as possible. To this end, the authority of the Board of Trade would supersede that of Parliament – no Act to build a line would henceforth be needed. Treasury grants or loans, up to a total of £1 million at any one time, were made available for construction. But the Bill hedged its financial inducements about with restrictions that still left most of the financing in the hands of the constructor. To qualify for a loan, the builder – whether private or a local council – had to raise at least half the capital needed in the usual way, by a share issue. Furthermore, not more than half of these shares could be owned by a council; the rest had to be privately acquired. The disincentives to invest were heavy. The truth of this only appeared with the passage of years, though even at the time the prospects of light railways were widely regarded as poor.[11] The Bill's critics pointed to the example of Ireland, where state-supported light railways had already been a financial failure. Traction engines had not performed an economic miracle, either. As ever, their main use was as mobile farm power units.[12]

It was against this background of heated but inconclusive debate on transport economies that a campaign on behalf of the motor car began in Parliament. From the beginning, it had powerful support. In 1894–5 George John Shaw-Lefevre[13] held office in the Liberal cabinet as President of the Local Government Board, the body responsible at state level for roads administration. Currently M.P. for Bradford Central, he was a dedicated, high-principled man of radical leanings who had been a member of every Liberal government since 1866, except that of 1885. He had been Parliamentary Secretary at the Board of Trade, an Under Secretary at the Home Office, and First Commissioner of Works for the Metropolis. Shaw-Lefevre's knowledge of agriculture was formidable. He had been a member of the Privy Council's agriculture committee, and was chairman of the 1893–6 Royal Commission on agriculture. On these matters and many more he was a prolific writer. There were few more deeply respected Parliamentarians.

In view of Shaw-Lefevre's interests, it is not surprising that the traction engine lobby found in him a sympathetic listener to its complaints. In December 1894 he received a deputation from the National Traction Engine Owners' and Users' Association, an interest group founded in the previous year to fight for changes in Highways Acts insofar as they affected traction engines. The petition that the deputation presented complained of the impossibility of through road traffic under the 1878 Act, with the mandate it gave for inconsistency in local authority by-laws and for a £10 licence fee per county. The President of the Local Government Board was sympathetic, and promised the deputation a Bill to create uniformity in regulations.

But Shaw-Lefevre realised that another, very different kind of vehicle should be catered for in any forthcoming change of law. The event that brought about this enlightenment seems to have been a visit to Paris early in 1895. Shaw-Lefevre was struck by the "not inconsiderable number" of cars in the streets. Visiting a car factory – probably Panhard & Levassor on the Avenue d'Ivry, the biggest and certainly the best-known Paris constructor – he made his official position known, and was taken for a drive in crowded streets. He became convinced that cars were perfectly controllable, and that horses were no more frightened of them than of other vehicles. He was also, obviously, so impressed by them that he was certain they would come to Britain. At a time when the motor car was an almost unknown quantity outside France, this showed remarkable prescience.

Propelled thus by a double impulse, Shaw-Lefevre now acted. In an official letter of 20 March 1895 he told the County Councils Association of the traction engine operators' complaint, asking the Association's advice on how the restrictions on those vehicles should be modified, and on the feasibility of levying a single licence fee valid for the whole country. In the same letter he pointed out that the regulations on traction engines were unnecessary for motor cars, and that industrial enterprise in Britain had been stifled while that of France forged ahead. This was a shrewd argument, playing on public awareness of the technological and industrial progress of other countries at Britain's expense. It was later taken up enthusiastically by others, who pointed out how Coventry, in decline in the 1860s, was given a new lease of life by the establishing of the cycle industry there. By 1895–6 it employed between 5000 and 6000 people in that city alone, and 25,000 in the country as a whole. Shaw-Lefevre prepared to rectify the situation by exempting vehicles not used for traction from the Acts, and he asked for the County Councils Association's views on this plan.

The Association appointed a committee to examine Shaw-Lefevre's letter. It reported that it was undecided on the matter of traction engine regulations, but that "subject to satisfactory safeguards as to weight, there is no objection to exempt single carriages which are not propelled by steam from the restrictions of the Locomotive Act". The words "single carriages . . . not propelled by steam" were intended to make sure that traction engines were excluded from the dispensation; by definition, they always towed another vehicle when on the road. On 17 May the Association added a recommendation that the weight limit for exemption should be 2 tons. Any vehicle weighing more must remain subject to the Acts.

These were epoch-making words indeed. Impressed by Shaw-Lefevre's evidence, the local authorities that made the by-laws had agreed that traction engines and motor cars were sufficiently distinct to be treated differently. The first battle in the campaign had been won.

At the time Shaw-Lefevre betrayed no sign of seeing events in such a dramatic light. His approach was low-key. The questions of traction engine and motor car regulation belonged together, and should preferably be dealt with at the same time. He left the impression that neither was more important than the other. However, since the County Councils Association asked for more time to consult its members about traction engines, it was sensible, he said, to dispose of the one matter that had been agreed, leaving the other until the Association had reached a decision on it.

The news that a Bill was on the way was revealed on 2 May. Dadabhai Naoroji, a Parsee of advanced Liberal views who represented Finsbury Central, stood up in the Commons to deplore the restrictions on motor cars – including, he said, the red flag – and to press for their free use "if unobjectionable to the public". Shaw-Lefevre replied that he was about to introduce a Bill; and on 17 June he did so. The Locomotives on Highways Bill contained one clause only. This was concerned principally with laying down that existing legislation governing locomotives on highways should not apply to any mechanically propelled vehicle of under 2 tons in weight that was not used for drawing another vehicle. The Bill mirrored the County Councils Association's views, except that their proposed exclusion of steam from exemption was dropped. This would have left the steamers of Serpollet and De Dion still regulated as traction engines. At a blow, and in a minimum of words, all the regulations that restricted the use of motor cars would be removed.

A rider to the Bill extended the power of local authorities to cover locomotive wheel width and design in relation to weight – without pointing out that with local authority control over vehicles under 2 tons removed, this power did not extend to them. Sir David Salomons was among those confused by the Bill's combination of succinctness and inconsistency. It is hard to explain why the rider was not kept back for inclusion in the promised traction engine Bill, where it belonged.

The Bill had influential friends, other than the President of the Local Government Board. Sir William Harcourt, Chancellor of the Exchequer, Leader of the House and a former Home Secretary, was "greatly interested" in the Bill, and later, as will be seen, concerned himself more intimately with motor cars. This radical reformer of independent, abrasively expressed views was regarded as the custodian of the Liberal conscience. Sponsoring the Bill with Shaw-Lefevre were the Postmaster-General, Sir Arnold Morley, and Sir John Hibbert, who though not a minister, was of altogether heavier metal. He was Financial Secretary to the Treasury, and had served on several Royal Commissions; most relevantly, he had been Parliamentary Secretary to the Local Government Board, and was currently Chairman of the County Councils Association. His support showed Parliament that the county authorities were behind the Bill.

Shaw-Lefevre did not expect the Bill to create debate – "it was not, he hoped, of a controversial nature". He again emphasised the inapplicability of existing law to motor cars, and added a few new arguments. The Paris–Bordeaux race just concluded – which Shaw-Lefevre referred to disingenuously as "a trial run" – had shown that petrol cars could maintain average speeds of 15 m.p.h. and remain in the complete control of their drivers. "Light carriages of Paris type" would still be subject to the regulations governing ordinary horse carriages, and to any additional ones the Local Government Board saw fit to impose.[14] Supervision would be there, but it would be exercised uniformly across the country by the central government. Uniformity of regulation was now essential, for as was later said, "these cars would very likely cross the boundaries of three counties in a single day."[15] Shaw-Lefevre made no emotive appeal to Parliament on the need to foster a new British industry, or on any other grounds of public interest; he deliberately concerned himself only with the reasonableness or otherwise of the law.

Shaw-Lefevre claimed later that his muted, almost offhand treatment of the issue was tactical – that to avoid alarming horse interests, he had refrained from stating his true belief, that the days of the horse were numbered. This sounds plausible. If he had cared as little for the motor car as his behaviour suggested, he would surely have held up his Bill until the County Councils Association had made up its mind about traction engines, rather than give cars a Bill of their own. Equally, he would hardly have bothered to assemble such powerful backing for his Bill. Furthermore, why call for support for British industry in a letter to local government officers, and not publicly before Parliament? Coming from a man who had sat in Parliament long enough to hear every debate on self-propelled vehicles since 1865, the suggestion that the new measure was non-controversial was disingenuous. It is much more likely that this old campaigner felt genuinely for the state of British industry, and kept his two-edged weapon sheathed. The rise of any new industry usually had a deleterious effect on existing ones – or at least caused fears that it would. If he had studied his history of the Bills that had failed, he would have noticed a common factor – that many of their partisans had made the mistake of inviting antagonism from entrenched interests, instead of trying to disarm them.

None of this is to suggest that Shaw-Lefevre regarded the traction engine's case as less important. To do so would be strange, given his known concern for agriculture and for transport. There is every reason to suppose that the main concern of the Bill that he had wanted to introduce would have been to answer the operators' plea to ease restrictions on these vehicles, as promised. The actual Bill reads very much like a clause lifted out of a wider measure. In particular, the intent of the rider, that applied only to vehicles over 2 tons, would have been much clearer in a context dealing with other traction engine regulations. The wording concerning motor vehicles would have constituted an additional, and apparently subordinate, part of the Bill. Quite apart from the intrinsic merits of the traction engine measures, they would have served the purpose of "carrying" the one liberating motor cars. Attention would have been concentrated on them, rather than – as happened – on the question of motor vehicles alone.

As matters stood, Shaw-Lefevre did his best to defuse the issue. His attempt to secure a quick, quiet passage for the Bill began well. Two members asked questions that proved only that they had not read the Bill. This lack of response to a Bill on its first reading signified little – full debate was reserved for the second reading. Even so, the *Engineer* was delighted, and showed it with less reserve than the cautious Shaw-Lefevre. The effect of a measure to exempt light self-propelled vehicles, "which ought to have been done long ago", should be "at once to open a new field for industrial enterprise". Indeed, "the demand for a really satisfactory road locomotive cannot fail to be enormous".

In the event, neither caution nor enthusiasm was rewarded. The Bill was due to have its second reading on 25 June, but on the 21st Lord Rosebery's government was defeated on a motion of confidence, and three days later resigned.[16] The Locomotives on Highways Bill was consigned to limbo along with other unfinished business. A general election ensued, at which a Conservative administration under Lord Salisbury was elected. In such a casual, unintentional manner, the issue of freedom for the motor car was thrown into the melting pot.

It was lost on no one that the Bill had been scratched rather than defeated: the paramount fact was that the party leaders on one side of the House, at least, had shown themselves in favour of giving the motor car the freedom of the roads. A government Bill, no less, had been presented, and had met no opposition, initially at any rate. This more than any other element gave the movement a whole new impetus. Another contributory factor was a step-up in reporting of foreign activity, particularly that of the sensational new sport of motor competitions. It gave the motor car a generous helping of publicity, and inspired the already converted.

The *Engineer*'s uncharacteristic flights of extravagance over the Shaw-Lefevre Bill appeared in the same issue as an unprecedentedly long, detailed and enthusiastic description of the Paris–Bordeaux race. The same spirit of excitement pervaded the leader and the race report. It was, indeed, a sensational event, which had been surrounded by drama since its conception. Following the success of the Paris–Rouen *concours*, the Comte de Dion had suggested a contest that would be openly a race, with more practical considerations taking second place – the reverse of Paris–Rouen. The contestants would drive from Paris to Bordeaux and back – a continuous run at maximum speed of no less than 732 miles, or nearly ten times further than the Paris–Rouen *concours*. No motor car had ever been subjected to such a test. Nor had public opinion, and *Le Petit Journal*'s proprietor refused to organise the event, for fear of the public censure that would follow what he regarded as the inevitable accidents. A committee of De Dion's friends therefore took over the running of the race. There were other sensations. Prizes to a value of 50,000 francs (over £2000) were offered – five times as much as in the Paris–Rouen *concours* – but they would be earned. No outside aid was allowed in the event of breakdowns, and only tools carried on the cars could be used.

Out of 46 entries, there were 22 starters on race day, 11 June – 13 petrol cars, two petrol motor bicycles, six steamers, and one electric. The last-named, naturally, had to have depots of batteries set up *en route*. The pace was killing, particularly to the heavier, more complex and fragile steamers. Only half the starters reached Bordeaux, and all but one of them were petrol cars. The exception was one of Amédée Bollée's big steamers, 15 years old. The motor cycles and the electric had fallen by the way too. The survivors still had to get back to Paris within a total time allowance of 100 hours, and nine succeeded. The earliest arrival was Levassor's two-seater Panhard, which had been 49 hours on the road, but it took second place to a Peugeot (the fourth to come in and the fastest on elapsed time) because the rules reserved first place for a four-seater car. Peugeots were also third and fourth. The Bollée steamer needed 50 hours for the whole distance, and finished last, at an average speed of 6 m.p.h. As for the rest, a Serpollet broke its crankshaft, and a De Dion, faster than anything else, lost time in coaling and then broke an axle. A combination of engine vibration, stretches of bad *pavé*, and in some cases iron tyres did the petrol vehicles no good either; and a Panhard's wheel was smashed in a collision with a dog. But eight out of nine finishers were petrol cars, which took all the prizes; only one steamer out of six completed the course. The superiority of petrol was now "beyond all question".[17]

Watching the race was a considerable contingent from the National Traction Engine Owners' and Users' Association. Collectively the party can have learned little that was useful to them, but Walter Arnold – whom one suspects of inspiring the expedition – no doubt enjoyed himself, and if another participant, the Kent county surveyor, took home a favourable impression of the motor car, the outing justified itself. The *Engineer* was quite carried away. The motor bicycle was a "monstrosity", but "so much has been done in the past few years in perfecting vehicles driven by steam, petroleum and electricity in France, that the time does not seem to be far distant when mechanical power will supersede animal traction upon the road for many purposes".

On this occasion, the *Engineer* was not alone in predicting the apotheosis of the motor car; though as yet only the technical press took notice of it. *Engineering*, normally unenthusiastic about the new machine, published a long report of the race. The winning Panhard had put up a "splendid performance", and in spite of smell and vibration, "it seems not at all unlikely that it is in the direction of the petroleum motor car that we must look for the solution of the problem of passenger locomotion on common roads." The *Implement and Machinery Review* also reported the race at length, and referred to an "enormous new field" for industry, with "golden possibilities . . . really magnificent to contemplate". It, too, saw the role of the horse contracting severely.

In August news came of another motor contest, this time in the United States. H.H. Kohlsaat, proprietor of the Chicago *Times-Herald* newspaper, had had motor cars drawn to his attention at the Chicago World's Fair two years earlier, and saw in the success of the French contests an opportunity of publicity not to be missed.[18] In July he announced what was described as a "horseless carriage race",[19] to be run on 2 November. Prizes and expenses totalling $5000 (about £1000) were offered. The event was not, in fact, a race alone; though that feature, naturally, was the one seized upon by the media. Cost, utility, economy, appearance and quality were all to count in the results. The *Engineer* reported and illustrated the preparations copiously, as well it might. The contest was the first of its kind in the United States, with the significance there of Paris–Rouen and Paris–Bordeaux combined. But while noting how entries flooded in, the *Engineer's* correspondent sounded a note of warning – on the other side of the Atlantic, roads that were passable in winter were the exception; and in the north-eastern states winter was on the way by November.

Eventually, the number of entries rose to 89. They deserve some attention, since some of the vehicles represented would soon be seen in Britain. None of the native entrants was as yet manufacturing cars for sale, though in 1894 Charles Duryea had founded the Duryea Motor Waggon Company with that end in view. The brothers entered their second experimental vehicle, which had been running "for some months".[20] Its horizontal engine now had two cylinders and electric ignition. There were three forward speeds, and final drive was through gears.[21] Top speed was 16 m.p.h. on a good road.

There were no foreign entrants properly so called. Typical of the entries of foreign origin – which was not the same thing – was Hieronymous Mueller's car, which was a Benz modified in respect of cooling arrangements, Mueller's own carburettor and spark plug, and three forward speeds and reverse. This car had been much used, too. No other entries could claim such experience, though they did not lack ingenuity – the De La Vergne company's trap, for example, with its Hornsby-Akroyd compression-ignition engine, surely the world's first "diesel" motor car?

In some entries, inventiveness was misdirected. Two victorias and two motor cycles were entered by Thomas Kane & Company, petrol engine and furniture manufacturers of Racine, Wisconsin. These machines, called Kane-Penningtons, were built to the design of Edward Joel Pennington, a type of person not seen in self-propelled vehicle circles since the heyday of Francis Maceroni. He was a highly plausible company promoter first and a constructor second; a man of limited mechanical talent given to making exaggerated claims for his wares, but a man, also, of considerable vision, total self-confidence in his abilities, and disarmingly genuine enthusiasm. Added to these qualities were a commanding presence and a mastery of theatrical effect.

Pennington's first creation, dating possibly from 1894, was a motor bicycle for which he claimed a speed of 57 m.p.h. and the ability to leap 45-foot ravines. He then made a quadricycle by joining together two motor bicycles with a tubular frame containing the mechanism. Pennington's designs combined originality with crudeness. In general, the machinery was unsprung and exposed to the elements, and lubrication was primitive. Other "trademarks" were large-section "unpuncturable" pneumatic tyres, a fuel metering valve (a form of fuel injection), and – in the early vehicles – air cooling. The absence of a carburettor and of a water cooling system made his engines simpler, lighter and cheaper to build than other types, claimed Pennington. He made much of his ignition system – a heated spiral of wire inside the cylinder which was supposed first to vaporise the mixture and then to ignite it. Pennington insisted that his engines ran much cooler with this "long-mingling spark" ignition, so (he said) allowing water cooling to be dispensed with, but it seems never actually to have been fitted to a vehicle. Probably for this reason, Pennington's machines worked, up to a point. In any case, the age was one that was wide open to experiment. Other "systems" that worked a lot better had been tried and tested, but they were patented. It is not surprising that Pennington succeeded in persuading Thomas Kane and a bicycle manufacturer to finance him, and in selling his engines to other constructors.

So many entrants had purely experimental, untried vehicles that more than a third of them asked for a postponement – a situation reminiscent of Paris–Rouen. The event was split, those cars that were ready running on the original date, 2 November, for a special prize of $500. Only two – the Duryea and the Mueller – took part. The course was from Chicago to Waukegan and back, a distance of 92 miles, which had to be covered in 15 hours at most. The Duryea was damaged in an accident, leaving the Mueller to win in $9\frac{1}{2}$ hours, including stops.

The main event took place on Thanksgiving Day, 28 November; a 54-mile run from Chicago to Evanston and back. The road was level, but was macadamised only in the city streets; outside them were five miles of unsurfaced road, including patches of sand and clay "almost impassable" in wet weather.[22] On the day, the road was invisible beneath 6 inches of snow. Six cars turned up at the bitterly cold start in Jackson Park. Four were petrol-driven – the Duryea and three Benz derivatives. These were the Mueller, a Benz substituted by the De la Vergne company for their original entry, and a Roger-Benz phaeton owned by the R.H. Macy company of New York. The other two starters were electrics: a Morrison-Sturges that had been built for the 1893 World's Fair, and had been running ever since; and a Morris & Salom Electrobat, the best-known American town car of its day. The only finishers, again, were the Mueller and the Duryea; but this time in reverse order. The winning Duryea did well, in deep snow, frozen ruts and ice, to cover the course in $10\frac{1}{2}$ hours. It used up $3\frac{1}{2}$ gallons of fuel, and (in spite of the cold) 19 gallons of water. Neither electric car had the power to cope with the snow.

The Paris–Bordeaux and Chicago *Times-Herald* events made motoring a source of public (as opposed to engineering) interest for the first time. As a rule, however, the public reacts, it does not initiate; this is left to special interest groups. It was significant that no detectable campaigning by interested parties other than the *Engineer* had preceded the "conversion" of the Liberal government. How much more might be accomplished by organised pressure, skilfully applied? In the summer and autumn of 1895, this pressure arose from half a dozen different directions. It came from old names and new. Some of it was amateur, some trade; some was gentlemanly and conventional, and some the very reverse.

Naturally enough, it was the *Engineer* that responded first to the new encouragement. Its coverage of the Paris–Bordeaux race and of Shaw-Lefevre's abortive Bill provoked a correspondence bigger, even, than had been aroused by subjects such as the Thomson engines in the 1870s. Editorially, it kept the pot boiling with comment and references, and with historical retrospectives to the days of Gurney and Hancock. Historical accounts of self-propelled vehicles, which had begun to appear in the 1880s in a spirit of valediction, became a popular way of filling columns, and not only in the *Engineer*.

Most important, on 5 July, the *Engineer* announced a "Thousand-guinea road carriage competition", to encourage the evolution of the most practical type of vehicle. The announcement itself was a statement of confidence, signifying an assumption that the motor car would soon be free of its restrictions. Detailed regulations were published in November. The event would take the form of a road trial of not less than 200 miles, to be held in October 1896 – by which time the law should have been changed to permit it. The prize fund was to be divided between the winners of classes for passenger and goods vehicles of different capacity and weight.

Other rules showed that the *Engineer* was out of touch with the direction and spirit of the motor car movement. Entries would be accepted of vehicles driven by any means of propulsion save petroleum spirit. The organisers made this exception on safety grounds. They favoured kerosene among the liquid fuels, as being less dangerous and more readily available; an attitude shared by other authorities. No average speed over 10 m.p.h. would be recognised. This at least showed consistency, for no petrol cars of the latest type could have demonstrated their full potential within such a limit.

No single firm or individual was allowed more than one entry. This would no doubt discourage commercial exploitation of the contest; but if manufacturers and importers stayed away, the most successful and developed machines would be absent too. The field would be dominated by the tentative creations of under-financed private experimenters, which is perhaps what the *Engineer*, in its dedication to pure scientific enquiry, wanted. In April 1896 the *Engineer* relented insofar as any means of propulsion became permissible; 100 guineas extra prize money was added for the best petrol vehicle. But by this time its conservatism and lack of vision had long since forfeited the initiative to more empirical and practical campaigners.

Nevertheless, back in July 1895, the announcement of the competition had brought welcome publicity to the cause; and it was quickly followed by more energetic and direct action. Declaring that the demand for change must be brought to the notice of the new government, the *Engineer* in August drafted a memorial to the Conservative President of the Local Government Board, explaining the need for a Bill "with the least possible delay". On request, copies of the document would be sent to "engineers, manufacturers, and employers of labour" nationwide for signature and return, thus transforming it into a petition.

The President of the Local Government Board was now Henry Chaplin, later first Viscount Chaplin, a figure even more formidable than Shaw-Lefevre. The Member for Mid-Lincolnshire, he came from the same ancient East Anglian landowning stock as his brother Edward. He was called "Squire" Chaplin, for his paramount interest in agriculture, and acted as its spokesman in the Commons for half a century. He had been President of the Board of Agriculture from 1889 to 1892,[23] and had sat on the Royal Commission on agriculture with Shaw-Lefevre. At heart, he was not a politician – he was only really at home in his hunting and racing stables, and farming his 23,000 acres. This very wealthy man wielded influence far beyond his own land and offices. He was the son-in-law of the third Duke of Sutherland, and a personal friend of the Prince of Wales and other members of the royal family. If such a man became its ally, the motor car would indeed have a promising future.

The *Engineer* described the response to its memorial as "gratifying". Best of all, in the Commons John Cumming Macdona had asked his front bench what action it proposed to take as a result. Macdona was a Conservative of liberal principles and a social reformer, typical in this of the progressive wing of his party. Chaplin replied that although he was making no commitment, he intended to "consider carefully" the whole subject of the horseless carriage, and the Bill brought in by his predecessor. Probably at this time, Chaplin asked Macdona to obtain more information about motor cars, and the Member for Southwark became the latest in a long line of distinguished British observers of the Paris motoring scene. He reported back that cars were safe and quiet, and were now being made in nine factories. The signs were favourable in a general sense, too, for this government was resolved to distinguish itself by policies of social reform, and its progressive zeal might rub off on the motor car. It was also more likely to be able to carry out its policies than the late Liberal administration, in that although it was formed of a coalition of Conservatives and Liberal Unionists, the Conservatives by themselves had an absolute majority over the opposition.

Meanwhile the Daimler Motor Syndicate – in other words Frederick Simms and Evelyn Ellis – had also read the auspices, and began preparing the ground for the commercial exploitation of motor cars. An *Engineer* correspondent reported that a French car had been brought over by an Englishman, and had run many miles in southern England "without protest from anyone". The Englishman was Evelyn Ellis. Following the demise of Shaw-Lefevre's Bill, Ellis determined to

keep the issue of freedom for the motor car alive by ostentatiously
defying the law, much as Henry Hewetson did. On 3 July he brought
his Panhard over to Southampton, with the intention of driving it
without a man in front and in excess of the speed limit. He hoped to
attract a summons, and consequent public attention. In his case, of
course, the effect would be to publicise both the cause, and the cars for
which his syndicate held the patents. The liberation of the one should
lead to profit from the other.

On 6 July the *Saturday Review* published details of the Syndicate's
cars. Running costs, it said, were three to one in favour of cars and
against horse vehicles: up to $\frac{3}{4}$d a mile, compared with 2d a mile. The
article suggested that the red flag was enshrined in law, and said of
such restrictions that "these ridiculous conditions must be altered".
That done, "in a short time there may be no horses except those that
are ridden".

The *Saturday Review* had been well primed: its article appeared
the day after a spectacular, if ill-rewarded, challenge to the law on the
part of Ellis and Simms. At a little before 9.30 a.m. on 5 July, they had
left Micheldever in Hampshire to motor to Ellis's home at Datchet.
Rain overnight had laid the dust, and by 11 a.m. the Panhard was at
Basingstoke. There was a half-hour stop for water and refreshments at
Mapledurwellhatch, and another nearly as long at Blackwater. At
Virginia Water the motorists took a late lunch – very late, it being
nearly 3.30 – and attended to the lubrication. They stopped again for
almost half an hour at Englefield Green, finally reaching Datchet at
5.40. The 56-mile journey had taken just over $5\frac{1}{2}$ hours running time,
an average speed of a little under 10 m.p.h. Simms's published account
glossed over the prolonged halts – he was, after all, on a selling trip – so
their causes can only be guessed at. The cruising speed had been
between 8 and 12 m.p.h.; two or three times the legal maximum.

The response of the police to this open provocation was
disappointing – when Ellis produced his ordinary carriage licence, as
required by the 1888 Act, they were usually satisfied that all was in
order. In other words, the nature of the vehicle, rather than what it
was doing, was of interest.

Simms related how on the way to Datchet, the new met the old and
the not-so-old: "The departure of coaches was delayed to enable their
passengers to have a look at our horseless vehicle, while cyclists would
stop to gaze enviously at us." Ellis added, (with, one suspects, some
dramatic licence): "One old stone-breaker threw down his hammer
and threw up his arms in amazement, as he saw the carriage
approaching him, and said, 'Well, I'm blessed if Mother Shipton's
prophecy ain't come true! Here come a carriage without a horse!'"

The horses, with whose reactions the motorists were particularly concerned, were much more *blasé*. Of 133 counted on the road between Micheldever and Datchet, said Simms, only two shied at the car.

The *Windsor and Eton Express* naturally mentioned the exploit of a distinguished local citizen. Ellis encouraged them to do so by giving their reporter a ride to Windsor and back: "The sensation of being whirled rapidly along is decidedly pleasing." The *Saturday Review* printed two long letters from Simms describing the trip and the car's specification and performance; but *The Times*, while also quoting Simms' figures, was more circumspect – the vehicle was "said to be" free of smoke, heat, smell and vibration.

This was the first commercial promotion of a motor car in Britain, and the first continuous long-distance motor car journey to be made in that country. Ellis capped it immediately by driving on to West Malvern via Abingdon, Cirencester and Tewkesbury, covering one stretch of 26 miles in 2 hours. It was said that the total cost of fuel, oil, and "other little necessaries" for this 120-mile expedition was 10s, or 1d a mile.

The Syndicate's effort bore modest fruit immediately. In May T.R.B. Elliot of Clifton Park, Kelso, had been in Paris, where he was much taken with the Panhard car. He had been put off buying one by fear of prosecution, but Ellis's freedom from molestation encouraged him to contact Simms, who ordered a car for him. The British motor trade had made its first sale; though Simms's Syndicate itself would play no part in its future development.

In the autumn of 1895 Sir David Salomons emerged as the most dedicated, powerful and professional propagandist that the motor car had among private owners. By October he had bought a Peugeot victoria in Paris and imported it. Early that month, Britain's first motor exhibition was announced. Organised and paid for by Salomons, it would be held on the 15th at the South Eastern Counties Agricultural Show ground at Tunbridge Wells. This was private land, where cars could be exercised without fear of the law. Salomons saw his role as a provider of information as well as a lobbyist,[24] and he approached this task, as all others, in a spirit of energetic, high-minded purposefulness. Not for him the direct action, the search for martyrdom of Ellis or Hewetson – when he took his Peugeot out, it was at 7 a.m., and he relied on his status as Mayor, and later ex-Mayor, of Tunbridge Wells to save him from prosecution.

A long, didactic article addressed to all intending visitors to the exhibition appeared in the *Kent and Sussex Courier*, was much quoted elsewhere, and was subsequently expanded as a pamphlet entitled

The Horseless Carriage. The article was mostly concerned with the law on self-propelled vehicles, an exposition of their advantages and capabilities, and a description of current types. Running costs, said Salomons, were 1d a mile.[25]

All this was standard; not so his contention that a motor car owner who took out a carriage licence, in accordance with the Customs and Inland Revenue Act of 1888, had to be allowed to exercise the rights of a carriage user. According to Salomons, by taxing motor cars as carriages the law recognised them as such, and therefore as different from traction engines. This was disingenuous. While some police forces might be content to regard self-propelled vehicles such as that of Ellis as carriages, it was in the strict sense better law to classify them as traction engines. The argument was tried by most motorists when they were first challenged,[26] though as we shall see, it did nothing to save them from conviction.

Single-mindedness in Salomons tended to affect his judgement in other ways, too; betraying him, for example, into ungenerosity of spirit and self-righteousness. He was inclined to claim all the credit for the progress of the motor car movement in Britain, and to regard competitors for this credit as either rogues or fools.

Probably the most important feature of Salomons' article was the airing it gave to a new and very pertinent argument in favour of the motor vehicle. In a letter to the *Engineer* in September, Walter Arnold had drawn attention to its potential usefulness for transporting farm produce. He was saying, in effect, that here – in a time of depression – was another means of carriage worth consideration in the battle against high transport costs. Salomons picked the argument up in his article, and it was subsequently echoed on all sides. Arnold may have originally raised it simply because it was obvious to him as a haulage contractor; Salomons the publicist probably had one eye fixed firmly on the leading preoccupation of the new President of the Local Government Board, and the other on the strongest interest group in Parliament.

The reaction was gratifying. "The motorcar is the key which will solve the problem of agricultural depression . . . motorcars can collect farm and cottage produce, bring it to centres for distribution, working districts which cannot be reached [*i.e.* by rail], and thereby greatly increase railway revenue . . . the best friend of the farmer will be the motorcar."[27] Some saw the new machine's potential as an agricultural feeder as its most important function, while *The Times* and others pointed out its advantages over light railways – it could travel "door to door", direct from producer to market, and it would be able to use, free of charge, an existing and all-pervading road system. The *Morning*

Post agreed, as did other authoritative voices.

The aim of the Tunbridge Wells exhibition, wrote Salomons, was to provide the public with practical information on a subject of immense potential benefit to the nation. He emphasised that the display would be completely free of trade links; by which he meant that the organisation would be private and independent. The seriousness of the occasion was reflected in the arrangements for spectators: admission was originally to be by invitation only; though in the end all were admitted, at 1s a head. Prizes would be awarded to participating private, trade and agricultural vehicles.

The exhibition was a popular success on a scale Salomons cannot have anticipated, but which delighted him. It was achieved by wide and well-placed publicity; but the public must by now have been in a receptive mood to respond in such numbers. For the first time, the motor car had become a focus of popular interest in Britain, and it is difficult to imagine this happening without the stimulus of events since June. A "snowball" effect was beginning to gain momentum. An estimated 5000 spectators turned up for the one-day event, some by special train. They included newspapermen, Members of Parliament, county councillors, engineers, a delegation from the Royal Agricultural Society, and numerous foreign visitors, mostly French but also German and American. This was a national – even an international – event, not a local one. Probably the most significant figures among the spectators were G.J. Shaw-Lefevre, whom we have already met, and Harry John Lawson, who was about to give the motor car movement an entirely new character and impetus.

The spectacle was on a modest scale compared with those in France, but was full of incident. Out of the five self-propelled vehicles billed to appear, four did so. These were Salomons' Peugeot, Ellis's Panhard, a De Dion tricycle ridden by Georges Bouton, and a De Dion steam tractor accompanied by its noble constructor and hauling a barouche with front wheels removed. The carriage belonged to Salomons. He and De Dion knew one another, probably through their membership of the Automobile Club de France.[28] The proceedings were lively. "Two velocipede bath chairs" (possibly Sherrin electrics) gatecrashed, entering the ground ahead of Salomons. For this *lèse-majesté*, Salomons caused the police to expel them. A traction engine intruded, too, so as to remind spectators that the legal disabilities affected more than motor cars. During two hours of evolutions, all the vehicles performed satisfactorily in spite of the resistance offered by the sloping grassy surface of the ground; though the De Dion steamer made a bad impression with its noise, smell, cinders and clouds of steam. Ellis's man-hauled fire engine with its Daimler pump gave a demonstration.

Finally, Salomons, riding in the De Dion steamer, led the cars out on to the Tunbridge Wells road and nearly into the town – without, it was noted, any alarm being caused to horses.

Press comment on the event was widespread and generally friendly. *The Times* called the De Dion steamer "quite unfitted for use on the highway", but bestowed moderate praise on the petrol vehicles, which were "fairly noiseless", with "not much smell" from the exhaust. Their worst feature was vibration – "the carriage quivers and shakes like a living thing", said the *Daily Chronicle* of Salomons' Peugeot – and their best, their ease of steering and stopping as compared with horse vehicles. This paper described the regulations as "grotesquely absurd", and foresaw – with an enthusiasm that sounded misplaced even at the time – an age when "Hyde Park in the season will simmer with benzine". In a long article the *Daily Telegraph*, too, spoke out against the legal restrictions, and predicted their demise.

Good publicist though Salomons was – the more so for being an amateur – he was about to be put in the shade. Promoters of public companies who were neither engineers nor manufacturers had been familiar figures in the days of Gurney and Hancock, speculating in patents and generally doing the image of the self-propelled vehicle no good. Now, with signs of bipartisan support for the motor car appearing in Parliament, a new generation of promoters saw potential profits in the road vehicle.

In Britain in 1895, company promotion itself had almost become an industry. Technological discoveries of the 1870s and 1880s that had caught the public imagination offered a rich field for the promoters (they were already notorious for their attentions to the infant electrical industry), as did the opening-up of huge new areas for investment in the world's wild places. In southern Africa and Australia in particular, gold, diamonds and other riches were being dug up in fabulous quantities, and in conveniently remote locations. The particular target of the promoters was a new and growing investing public – a rising class of prosperous small men such as shopkeepers and tradesmen with spare money but little education or knowledge of the world, no experience of finance, and no relevant technical knowledge. They were impressed by grandiose projects, easily dazzled by scientific advances, and since money was the short cut to improved social status, they were willing to gamble for quick, large profits. They were thus easy prey for the promoters, for whom this was a golden age.

Quite the most spectacular of the promoters was Ernest Terah Hooley, originally a Nottingham stockbroker. His technique, and that of his fellows, was to buy control of businesses he regarded as promising but under-capitalised, then refloat them as public limited companies with glowing but vague prospectuses that solicited the public's money on an enormous scale. Apart from whatever sums Hooley cared to set aside for the operating costs of the new company, the difference between what he paid for the original company's shares and what he and his partners received after a successful flotation was pure profit. The public were left with wildly over-valued shares, the price of which bore no relation to the actual assets and performance of the company concerned, and on which it was unrealistic to expect dividends to be paid. Hooley's particular "trademark" was the exploitation of "front" directors – peers who, for a consideration, would allow their names to be used to attract investors. It was an old idea, but Hooley systematised it, with a fixed scale of emoluments related to the status of the persons concerned. His grander acquisitions included the Duke of Somerset and the seventh Earl de la Warr.[29]

Hooley's flotations included Bovril and Schweppes; but he was particularly attracted by the potential of the cycle industry. The first promotion in this field in which Hooley was involved was Humber & Company, from which in 1895 he netted £365,000. The public stampede for cycle company shares was on. In 1896 followed the Raleigh Cycle Company, which Hooley floated for £250,000, the Singer Cycle Company (£600,000) and the Swift Cycle Company (£375,000). The biggest coup in which he was concerned, which came in the same year, was the purchase of the Dunlop patents for £3 million and the subsequent flotation of the Dunlop Pneumatic Tyre Company for £5 million.[30]

In all, Hooley took part in the flotation of 26 public companies with a total capital of over £18.6 million. He was said to have made at least £3 million profit for himself and his partners; other figures varied up to £15 million. At his apogee, this flamboyant and by now hugely wealthy man owned 40,000 acres and derived an income of £80,000 a year from his investments.[31] He went far towards achieving respectability, as well. He became Sheriff of Cambridgeshire and Huntingdonshire, a deputy lieutenant and a magistrate, and Conservative candidate for Ilkeston. He openly canvassed for a baronetcy in the Diamond Jubilee Honours List of 1897; but by 1898 he was bankrupt and fallen. His grossly over-capitalised companies had over-produced, and failed to meet their commitments. There was panic selling of shares, and companies went into liquidation. The end of the cycle boom spread ruin all around, except in the case of Hooley, who was left with personal assets of £200,000, which he had transferred to his wife's name.

Hooley was only the most prominent of the promoters, and was not the first in the chosen field. Harvey du Cros, son of the founder of the original Dunlop company, had acquired the Triumph Cycle Company in 1895 for £10,000 and refloated it for £35,000. In 1896 he and his father Arthur were left as the largest shareholders in the new Dunlop company, and in the same year he took part with Hooley in the acquisition of the Swift company.

Participating with Hooley and du Cros in the Dunlop and Swift promotions, and with Hooley in the Humber flotation, was Henry John Lawson, known as Harry, who had been a company promoter for longer than either. Like Pennington in America, he had a certain mechanical talent and a genuine interest in mechanical propulsion, even if this took second place to its money-making possibilities. There were other parallels, too – as well as possessing all the company promoter's brassy business expertise and relentlessly extrovert self-confidence, Lawson was quick-witted, energetic, tenacious, imaginative and generous. As with so many far-sighted and talented young men – and enthusiastic racing cyclists – he at first chose the up-and-coming cycle industry as a career. At the age of 24, with experience of the cycle trade in Brighton behind him, Lawson in 1876 patented a "low" as opposed to the conventional "high" bicycle, with lever drive and wheels of small, more nearly equal size. A few examples were made. When the safety bicycle boomed after 1885, Lawson claimed to have invented it; an assertion which – like so many of his – had a colouring of truth in it to help carry conviction. In fact Lawson's designs in this field were imperfect and were never developed.

Lawson moved to Coventry, the heart of the cycle industry, where in 1879 he patented another small bicycle. This had chain drive to a rear wheel slightly smaller than that at the front. It was christened the "Bicyclette", and was built in small numbers. In the following year Lawson patented a light self-propelled tricycle. The patent foresaw an engine working on compressed gas, with two speeds and gear drive. If the drive was disengaged, the vehicle could be pedalled. The patent was provisional and sketchy, and Lawson built no such machine, but – this time with no justification at all – he later claimed to have invented the internal-combustion-engined road vehicle as well.

Thereafter, less and less was heard of Lawson the engineer; though he continued to take out patents. He had found his true *métier* in company promotion. In 1887, as a'prentice effort, he got control of the Haynes and Jefferies syndicate, for which he had worked in Coventry, and refloated it as the Rudge Cycle Company. In the same year he acquired Humber & Company for £125,000, but the business was prospering, and he did not at this time float a new company. Between 1888 and early 1896 Lawson promoted at least 22 companies, diversifying immediately into whatever promising fields presented themselves. In 1890–1 alone, he launched nine high-sounding companies with solid insurance and banking connotations – for example, the Issue Bank of England and Wales, capitalised at nearly £296,000; the Discount Banking Company of England and Wales (£250,000); the London and Scottish Trustee & Investment Company (£351,000); and the Assurance Trust Corporation (£1 million). The fourth Marquess of Exeter, an obscure peer, figured as a shareholder in four of the promotions.

Lawson then seems to have transferred his attentions back to the field of which he had most knowledge – the cycle industry. The Beeston Pneumatic Tyre Company, a flotation of 1893, was liquidated two years later, then refloated. In November 1895 Lawson was involved with Hooley in the promotion of Humber & Company for £500,000, with three offshoot Humber companies capitalised at another £450,000 between them. When one uses vague phrases such as "involved with", "played a part in" and "associated with", one is echoing the vagueness of contemporaries; promoters did not advertise the internal workings of their enterprises. What is almost certainly meant is that, in such cases, a number of partners put up the money for a purchase between them. In Lawson's case, his early participation in cycle and other promotions was sometimes backed financially by Hooley.[32]

Once Parliament had shown that it was open to reconsideration of the restrictions on motor cars, it was natural for Lawson, by experience and temperament already part of the cycle world, to interest himself in the new machine. He believed that the public could be persuaded that the motor car was as good an investment as the bicycle, or better, and would rush for shares with even more enthusiasm. In the City, his business skills were held in low esteem. Not one of the 22 promotions mentioned succeeded in raising all the capital solicited.[33] This did not mean that Lawson lost money, but it did mean that he had a record of failure as a company promoter. None of this, however, was known to the general public. In the case of the motor car he would be taking a bigger risk, since almost nothing was known of it; but he took measures to cover himself. His initial personal stake might be nominal;[34] and he tried to make sure that if success came, he would reap most of the rewards.

Lawson's guiding principle, which worked well enough with Dunlop, was to acquire what appeared to be the most valuable patents in his chosen field – or, in the case of foreign patents, the British licences under those patents. This would ensure that no one could manufacture goods made according to the patents concerned without paying Lawson for the privilege, or import them other than through

Lawson, in which case they would have to pay him a royalty. By buying all of what seemed to be the most important motor car patents, Lawson planned to gain control over the whole of a new industry before it came into existence, then milk it dry. This was audacity characteristic of the man. The process would be self-financing, after an initial investment to buy patents. A public limited company would then be floated. Its successful flotation would return the cost of the original patents bought, yield profits for the promoters, and provide a surplus to buy further patents. Other company flotations would raise capital for private profit and for the acquisition of still more patents.

Among the advertised intentions of some of the new companies was the manufacture or operation of vehicles under the rights concerned. Only the prospect of manufacture would tempt investors, for there lay the hope of profit. But Lawson was a promoter and a speculator, not a constructor: his "manufacturing" companies produced nothing until mere promises to do so lost their effectiveness, and credibility demanded the building of a token number of vehicles actually in the metal. Appearances were kept up, meanwhile, by the acquisition of disused but impressive-looking factory buildings as putative premises, and by letting it be known that some manufacture would be undertaken by companies bearing famous and respected names (which might also be Lawson promotions).[35] To maintain the facade, "dividends" were declared, but were either paid out of working capital, or took the form of shares in other Lawson companies.

Lawson was in fact interested only in the sale – at maximum profit – of licences under the patents he had acquired. No one with manufacture seriously in mind – that is, no one outside the Lawson circle – would buy them while the restrictions on motor vehicles were in force. When these were relaxed, Lawson and his associates would make their killing. Meanwhile, a great deal of money could still be made from the licences without actually parting with them. The real object of Lawson's "manufacturing" companies was no more than the purchase, for their own shares or for cash, of licences already belonging to other Lawson promotions. This trading took place in property, too: factory premises bought from their original owner by one Lawson concern were sold or rented to another.[36] In these ways much of the money raised from the public, ostensibly for the operating costs of the companies, found its way into the pockets of Lawson and his partners.[37] These people controlled both the buying and the selling concerns, but they played out the charade poker-faced. The monumental impudence of Lawson's design invested it with a certain awful grandeur of its own.

Some of the licences Lawson bought were non-exclusive, either because they were cheaper that way, or because the patent holders doubted Lawson's willingness to exploit them. Lawson naturally refrained from mentioning this weakness.

In October 1895 the only significant British licences that had already been sold were those of Roger-Benz and Daimler. The first had been acquired some time before June by a French-born Birmingham perambulator manufacturer, Léon l'Hollier, but he had so far done nothing with it. As for the Daimler patents, since Panhards and Peugeots used Daimler-based engines, the Daimler Motor Syndicate had rights in these as well. Having neither made nor imported cars in the four years between their acquisition of the Daimler licence and the summer of 1895, Simms and Ellis had recently been showing signs of greater activity. The publicity given to their run from Micheldever to Datchet had drawn enquiries and (as we have seen) at least one order. By October they were actively offering to supply their cars to British would-be motorists.[38] It was even said at the Tunbridge Wells exhibition – where Lawson was on hand – that they were about to begin manufacture. For all these reasons, Lawson set his sights on the Daimler Motor Syndicate first. In the same month of October he made an offer of £35,000 for the business, which was accepted. In November a new company, the British Motor Syndicate, was floated for £150,000. Its purpose, as set forth in the articles of association, was nothing if not comprehensive – to buy further patents, and to "manufacture, sell, let on hire or otherwise deal in motors . . . cycles . . . carts, wagons, vehicles, ships, boats . . . flying machines and carriages of all kinds". In fact, the first was almost the Syndicate's sole activity and virtually its only reason for existence. The only other one of significance was to "procure all Parliamentary powers to enable . . . the carrying of these objects into effect".

Lawson had "arrived" on the motor car scene. A number of other characters who would become familiar, forming a sort of Lawson entourage, had already begun to gather about him. Apart from Lawson, there were among the major shareholders in the British Motor Syndicate[39] three shadowy figures whose names recur repeatedly in promoters' prospectuses of the period. One was Martin Diederich Rucker, racing cyclist, "Hooley man", managing director of the Humber company and a main shareholder also in the Dunlop Pneumatic Tyre Company. The second was Bertram van Praagh, who figured as solicitor to the companies; and the third was Thomas Robinson, Lawson's brother-in-law. Hooley was the company's stockbroker and a principal shareholder, but he sold out before April 1896. As we have seen, Lawson continued to be involved with him in cycle and tyre company promotions, but Hooley does not seem to have participated in any more motor company flotations. Another name that recurred as a director of Lawson motor vehicle promotions was that of J.H. Mace. Charles Osborn, who had been secretary of two of Lawson's insurance and banking flotations, performed the same function in his latest promotions.

Other names were more detached from the rough-and-tumble of company promotion itself. Frederick Simms was now managing director of the British Motor Syndicate, and became consulting engineer of that and every other major Lawson company. He was also a major shareholder in one of them.[40] Evelyn Ellis, too, became concerned in Lawson's affairs. After selling out to the Daimler Motor Syndicate, he had acquired shares in its successor; he then joined the boards of three Lawson motor "manufacturing" flotations.[41] Neither Simms nor Ellis was at home in the raw, strident world of the promoters, but both were destined to become ever more deeply involved with Lawson. Like Simms and Ellis, Walter Bersey willingly gave up his independence, becoming a director or an officer of two Lawson promotions.[42] The Garrard & Blumfield patents, too, were acquired and the licence disposed of to a Lawson company.[43]

In fact, in 1895–6, most of the major names in the infant motoring world became associated with Lawson in one way or another, so near did he seem to achieving his ambition of controlling the unborn industry. The fact that many of these men had been racing cyclists, like Lawson, may have helped. H.O. Duncan, who had been connected with Rudge and Humber (and so had another reason for knowing Lawson) became the commercial manager of the British Motor Syndicate. Selwyn Francis Edge, a friend of Duncan, was at different times general manager of Rudge & Company and London manager of the Dunlop Pneumatic Tyre Company. Charles Jarrott, like the others a racing cyclist, joined the British Motor Syndicate in 1896, and found himself working with Edge. Later he became secretary of the Syndicate.[44]

The only important figures to remain outside the Lawson net were Salomons, and three men associated with the Benz, the patents of which never fell under Lawson's control – Henry Hewetson, Walter Arnold and Léon l'Hollier. L'Hollier imported a Roger-Benz dogcart from Paris in November 1895, and – initially left in peace by the police – began to run it about Birmingham. He embarked on an ener getic selling campaign. Advertisements for "Roger's Patent Horse less Carriage" appeared in the same month, and l'Hollier's car was exhibited at the Stanley Cycle Show at the end of November. There it was praised for its simplicity and good looks: "The absence of the usual shafts and horse are the only strange features."[45] Evelyn Ellis's

Panhard was shown too, as were a Gladiator and a De Dion tricycle; but it was Léon l'Hollier's vehicle that was significant, for its presence marked the beginning of a continuous motor trade in Britain. Also in November, Walter Arnold imported a Benz, which with Hewetson's machine meant three of the breed in Britain. For them as for l'Hollier, the Benz system was destined to stand for business as well as pleasure.

The last of the new sources of pressure to appear was the *Autocar* – "A journal published in the interests of the mechanically-propelled road carriage". The first issue, dated 2 November 1895, was in one sense a gambler's opening stake on a gaming table – a specialist journal for a market that did not yet exist, based on a presumption that Parliament was about to call one into being. In another sense the *Autocar* in its first year was an instrument of propaganda pure and simple. It existed in order to inform and persuade; to obtain support for the lifting of the restrictions on the motor car. On a commercial level, if it was to succeed as a gamble, it had to do its best to create its own market.

The men behind the *Autocar* had the right background for a piece of speculative specialist publishing. John James Henry Sturmey was an enthusiastic cyclist who had a highly successful book on the subject[46] published for him by William Isaac Iliffe. In 1879 Iliffe, a pioneer of popular magazine publishing,[47] appointed the 22-year-old Sturmey editor of the *Cyclist*, which became the most authoritative of the many cycling journals. With Iliffe, in the firm of Iliffe & Sturmey, Sturmey became co-proprietor of the *Cyclist*, and also of the magazine *Photography*. He filled the same dual role yet again in November 1895 when Iliffe & Sturmey published the first issue of the *Autocar*, an even riskier venture.

Sturmey always claimed that the *Autocar* was an independent organ, and so it was, in terms of financial control. But from the beginning, it was biased strongly in favour of Lawson and his pro-motions. On three occasions it published leading articles recommend-ing Lawson projects to its readers without reservation; also, editorial matter in the same vein from other journals was freely quoted. Criticism of Lawson was mentioned only in order to assail it.

Given Lawson's dominating position in the nascent motoring world, it was to be expected that journal assiduously recorded his words and reported his activities. There were, however, other factors involved, which would normally render objectivity incompatible with survival. On the one hand the *Autocar* was a commercial enterprise, and a specialised journal depended on specialised advertising; on the other hand, a motor trade and industry as a source of that advertising scarcely existed. There was virtually only Lawson, so the overwhelming quantity of advertising from his concerns in the *Autocar* should cause no surprise. He was not a subtle man, and it is likely that the *quid pro quo* of friendly editorial comment was demanded rather than simply expected.

Any journalist in Sturmey's position would have been subjected to these pressures; but it is clear that he had deeper involvements with Lawson than publishing expediency dictated. At least one dated back to pre-*Autocar*, pre-motor car days. Along with Martin Rucker and others, the firm of Iliffe & Sturmey were signatories to a testimonial presented to Lawson in July 1895 by the Rudge Cycle Company, in which he was congratulated on having "invented" the safety bicycle. In November 1895 Sturmey and Lawson became joint patentees of a system of unitary body-chassis construction for vehicles, using steel tubes and light panels;[48] later, the British Motor Syndicate bought Sturmey's interest in the patent. More to the point, Sturmey held nearly £14,000 worth of shares in, and was a director of, one Lawson "manufacturing" promotion,[49] and was a director of another.[50] It is possible that he and Lawson were initially drawn together by instinct and common circumstance – both had belonged to the slightly raffish brotherhood of racing cyclists; both were committed to highly speculative ventures in the same field; and both were prolific inventors of devices connected with road vehicles.

In view of all this, the *Autocar* might have shown itself a lot less independent in its first year than in fact it did. The activities, statements and achievements of motoring notabilities unconnected with Lawson – even those of Salomons, his sworn enemy – received full and more or less fair coverage; and the paper's Birmingham correspondent was allowed to report doubts concerning the claims of Edward Joel Pennington, even though by that time Pennington's patents were Lawson's property. Sturmey and Iliffe, professional journalists both, must have realised that their paper would lose all credibility if it became nothing but the instrument of a company promoter's schemes. Even such modified independence cannot have pleased Lawson. He was the kind of man to value false objectivity as a business ruse, and to regard true objectivity as another word for faint-heartedness. To him, the *Autocar* would have been important insofar as it helped him to a fortune. There is evidence, as we shall see, that he was dissatisfied with the service he was getting for his money.

By November 1895, then, all the new driving forces behind the motor car were present, with very different men pushing with equally various styles and motives and with almost total lack of co-ordination, but together constituting an ever louder and more insistent voice in favour of freedom. To sum up, there were broadly four camps – the earnest, technically oriented *Engineer*, with its competition and its petition; Sir David Salomons, with his patrician approach and policy of educating and persuading those in the seats of power; and two others whose thrusting, extrovert, speculative ways were in tune. These were the *Autocar*, and the raucous company promoters as personified by Lawson – confidence men who were beginning to make the motor car a familiar concept to the man in the street without actually producing any for him to see, and while spiriting the money from his pockets. Simms and Ellis had been absorbed into the Lawson world, though it was an uneasy relationship for Simms, as we shall see.

There were other ways in which the "climate" for the motor car was improving. One came in the form of what was, on the face of it, a wholly unexpected bonus – an almost total absence of organised, and therefore effective, hostility from the powerful horse-oriented interests. In the case of the latest generation of private passenger vehicles this neutrality, or lack of interest, assumed major importance. When they had appeared on previous occasions, the question of competition did not arise. No one had seriously imagined that the typical steam carriage of the 1860s constituted a rival to the horse carriage: it had too many built-in drawbacks, and had never achieved commercial production. The petrol motor car, on the other hand, had fewer obvious disadvantages; and a small but growing industry was already flourishing across the Channel. The motor car had won acceptance in France; legal restrictions alone seemed to stand in the way of its acceptance in Britain – restrictions that were under unprecedentedly strong attack, and showing signs of losing favour. Luckily for the motor car interests, the horse-related interests did not see the new vehicle in the light shed by hindsight.

On 20 August 1895 John Philipson of Atkinson & Philipson of Newcastle, coachbuilders, delivered his presidential address to the Institute of Carriage Manufacturers at Tunbridge Wells. Philipson, who later also became Master of the Coach and Coach Harness Makers' Company, was a highly respected figure in the carriage industry, known for his progressive opinions on technical education. Philipson's views as expressed in his address matched very closely some of those voiced later by Sir David Salomons from nearby Broomhill. It is not surprising that Salomons was of like mind, for the two men shared similar interests. Shaw-Lefevre's Bill, said Philipson, had concerned the coachbuilding trade as much as anyone. The restrictive Acts in force were inapplicable to "light horseless carriages", and should be repealed. Britain must follow the French lead in establishing a motor industry. The carriage industry would not suffer; it was possible to create a new industry without wrecking an old one.

Philipson had no doubt that the motor car would boom. Rather than fear the new trend, the trade should take advantage of it, making sure that they built every part of every motor car except its mechanism. Philipson believed in steam for long-distance motoring, and in electricity for town use. He practised what he preached. During 1895 his own firm advertised themselves as "motor carriage builders and repairers",[51] and Philipson became a director of the Britannia Motor Carriage Company, makers of electric cars. A successor of Philipson as President of the Institute, G.J. Jacobs, endorsed his views: "We have nothing to fear from, but for many reasons we shall welcome, the newcomer."

Such a degree of acceptance in such exalted quarters was highly significant, but far from unique. George Hooper was happy to leave the interests of the carriage industry in the hands of Sir David Salomons. George Smith of Geo. & J. Smith's Carriage Works, Tunbridge Wells, regarded motive power, together with rubber tyres, as mere "luxuries and adjuncts ... the concomitant of the future carriage", but he added: "Coachbuilders, to keep pace with the times, must shape their ideas and be prepared to construct carriages in harmony and agreement with the requirements of the age. These propellers, or so-called motor cars, are steadily gaining popular favour, and the trade must bestir themselves and be ready to build 'turn-outs' to meet the demand." John T. Clark, a coachbuilder of Aberdeen, became a keen Daimler owner in 1896.

But Clark's fellow body-builders were interested most in the potential of electric vehicles. An elegant body sat best on a town carriage of unobtrusive and refined habits; it was less suited to what *The Financial Times* felicitously described as "runaway coffee stalls". We have already seen how Thrupp & Maberly had built a car body as early as 1888, and in 1896 this famous house went on to make five complete electric carriages with Immisch-type motors, one of them a victoria for the Queen of Spain. George Thrupp himself rode on the Thrupp & Maberly-bodied Volk electric of 1888, and on a Duryea on the Brighton run of 1896.[52] Mulliner was another name of renown in coachbuilding to take an active interest in the new vehicle. Herbert Hall Mulliner[53] became a director of the British Motor Syndicate and of the Great Horseless Carriage Company; also Chairman of the London Electrical Cab Company, of which Henry Jervis Mulliner was a director too. In 1896 Mulliner bodies were appearing on petrol as well as electric vehicles. In that year, the house of Offord & Sons made their Electrocar, an Offord dogcart with electric propulsion. In October 1896 the Coach Makers' Company announced a competition, with valuable money prizes and medals, for "Designs of a self-propelled light motor carriage": recognition could hardly go further.

One reason for the coachbuilders' confidence when faced with the motor car appears in their own words – they saw motor cars as no more than self-propelled carriages, and believed, therefore, that anyone making bodies for the one could make them for the other – a view that was borne out in practice. They believed, anyway, that the motor car would never be a serious rival to the horse carriage. Even the owner of a motor car at this time kept one or more horse carriages as well, or hired them. The machine offered the exploration of new possibilities, and a highly sporting mode of transport – there was no thought of relying on it for every day-to-day need. To the motor car owner of the mid-1890s, as to his father's generation in the 1860s, his carriage was part of the natural order of things, which there was no thought of replacing.

G.J. Jacobs expressed a prevalent attitude when he said that motor cars, with their exposed machinery, were too unsightly ever to replace carriages for pleasure purposes. Salomons saw the petrol motor car as too lacking in mechanical refinement for such use. Both men agreed with a general view that it had a future as a working vehicle. In the workaday world, its potential for making short-distance or stop-and-start journeys all day long economically and without effort,[54] and its readiness for immediate use at all times, as compared with horses, were telling advantages. With a car or a motor van, a doctor, service engineer, commercial traveller, delivery man or tradesman would be able to make more calls in a day than when driving horses. Said the *Lancet*: "We believe that the motor carriage in some of its forms will prove to be admirably suited for the requirements of medical men, and will not be long in coming into extensive use." The *British Medical Journal* agreed. A doctor with a one-horse vehicle who had to travel 40 or 50 miles a day on his calls needed to keep four horses in relays – a single motor car would replace them all, thanks to what *The Times* called "the tirelessness of the propelling agency". For the country house owner, a motor car would be ideal for station work, for carrying estate supplies, for transporting guests and servants on sporting occasions, and for country visiting further afield than had been possible with horse carriages. None of these possibilities was seen as a threat to carriage builders.

It was not surprising that the coachbuilders should feel so bullish, for they had never been so prosperous. As the industrial and commercial wealth of the nation grew, so the class of "carriage folk" expanded. To the socially and financially rising middle classes, a carriage, whether owned or hired, was the clearest symbol of status. It became necessary as a railway feeder, particularly in the country. The bicycle, horse bus and tram were patently for those who could afford nothing better. In 1814 there had been 23,000 private four-wheeled carriages licensed in Britain. The number grew to 49,000 in 1834 and 125,000 in 1874. The total for all carriages in the latter year was 432,000. Soon after, 40,000 new carriages were being built annually. By about this time there were 14 private carriages per 1000 of population; a figure exceeded by motor cars only in 1926. Thereafter, the rising cost of fodder and the difficulty of finding space to keep a horse in town caused the number of larger carriages to remain static until the beginning of the new century, when it began to decline; but smaller carriages continued to multiply. With the growth of towns and railways, coachbuilders who made public service vehicles prospered equally. Between 1830 and 1900 the number of cabs in Britain increased tenfold, and there were four times as many horse buses in 1900 as in 1850.

Still more important for the motor car's future was the absence of effective hostility among the vastly more powerful interests directly concerned with the horse, or entirely dependent on it. In particular, virtually no organised opposition arose in quarters where it would matter politically – among the farmers and landowners who took their pleasure in horses, and whose interests might include breeding them and growing their feed. Indeed, their leaders were active on the other side – Salomons with his large stable; Henry Chaplin, a master of fox hounds and owner of Derby winners; and, as will be seen, Frederick Arthur Stanley, sixteenth Earl of Derby, an eminent race-horse owner. Lord Rosebery, another famous owner and Derby winner, had led the Liberal government that had introduced Shaw-Lefevre's Bill.

As with the carriage, so with the horse – those who held political power, even those among them who drove cars, found it impossible to conceive of a world in which the motor car was more than a rich man's diversion. Again, the confidence was entirely justifiable, for never had the trades connected with the horse been so prosperous. The factors that boosted the coachbuilding industry favoured the horse as well. Demand for horses, and therefore for harness and for fodder, boomed with the railways and with the economy in general. More and more horses were needed to draw the vans and wagons that fed the railways with freight; railway and independent carrying fleets grew fast. For example, the home establishment of the Great Western Railway alone expanded by 80 per cent, to nearly 1700 animals, between 1884 and 1890. In 1911 the Bishopsgate goods station of the Great Eastern Railway employed 1100 horses, 850 vehicles and nearly 800 men. The investment involved was considerable, and rising. In 1907 Bishopsgate vehicles were valued at £272,000 and its harness at £32,000. Railway horses that cost £45, on average, in 1869 were fetching £55 to £65 eight years later.

Intensive "high" farming had called for more horsepower, and the depression in arable farming had not led to any permanent decline. In 1821, before agriculture had adopted horse-driven machines to any great extent, there had been about 768,000 horses on the land. Numbers fluctuated, but the trend was clear – 1.27 million horses in agriculture in 1870, 1.55 million in 1896. The number of riding horses rose more slowly, but by the end of the century growing wealth was reflected in this area, too. Jobmasters flourished as the practice of hiring carriages and horses increased.[55] By 1902, the peak year for the horse in Britain, there were 3.5 million animals of all types, as compared with 1.4 million in about 1830.

The British breeder had less reason than anyone else in the horse world to fear the coming of the motor vehicle, or so it seemed. Most informed opinion saw it replacing only the tradesman's van and the private carriage used intensively for utilitarian purposes; both of them vehicles that were hauled by light draught horses. In this field the domestic breeder was undersold, and foreign animals already held sway. Horse imports rose from just under 13,000 in 1884 to nearly 41,000 a dozen years later. The riding horse and the heavy draught animal, which were the British breeder's bread and butter, were not seen as threatened. It was not imagined that motor cars could give pleasure in the same way as riding horses.[56]

The immensely influential farming establishment maintained a benevolent neutrality – it was willing to wait and see. Was the motor vehicle indeed a panacea for agricultural depression? Let it prove itself in front of practical farmers. In October 1895 David Salomons had had great difficulty in persuading the committee of the South-Eastern Counties Agricultural Show to allow him the use of their Tunbridge Wells ground, but thereafter his propaganda was largely effective. Cars reappeared at Tunbridge Wells on the occasion of the show held in July the following year. At the end of 1895 the Royal Agricultural Society *Journal* carried an article outlining the recent progress of the motor vehicle, and recommending it to farmers on the grounds of economy and speed. In the New Year there was news that the Royal Highland and Agricultural Society would hold a competition with prizes at its Perth show in July 1896. The West Midlands Agricultural Society offered prizes, too, at its Bridgnorth show to be held in the same month. In May came the greatest accolade – the Royal Agricultural Society announced a competition for heavy oil or steam vehicles with prizes for heavy and light vehicle classes, to be held at its 1897 meeting at Trafford Park, Manchester. It was assumed that the new machine would be liberated in the interim.

It might be supposed that the railway interest would come out against a form of private passenger transport that made uncomplicated, door-to-door, long-distance road travel a possibility. But no self-interested hostility from this quarter can be detected. Such opposition, if concerted, could have been lethal to the motor car lobby's hopes, for in the 1896 Parliament there were still 75 railway directors in the Commons and 54 in the Lords, six of them government ministers. As it was, we find that Sir David Salomons, the leader of the responsible motor car campaigners, was himself a director of the South Eastern Railway, and that his board favoured motor vehicles as potential railway feeders. By July 1896 Salomons had ordered one for the South Eastern as an experimental goods feeder. Colonel John James Miller (Conservative, Radcliffe), a cotton manufacturer who sat on the South Eastern board with Salomons, was in full agreement with him. John William Maclure, another railway director, was also an active Salomons supporter. As we have seen, others with railway interests before Salomons – engineers and shareholders alike – had seen no inconsistency in building, running and "boosting" self-propelled road vehicles. Only one railway-director M.P. is on record as opposing greater freedom for motor cars, and he did not suggest that they would harm railway receipts.[57]

The fact was that the railways had as little reason to feel threatened as the horse interests, and were just as self-confident in their wealth. It needed an engineer with foresight to appreciate the potential of the new arrival. The motor car might be capable of covering 100 miles in a day without effort, if nothing serious went wrong and the driver was sufficiently tough, but except for French racing drivers and a handful of other eccentric Continentals, no one actually tried to make it do so. In Britain in 1895–6, even 50 or 60 miles in a day was a rare achievement – partly because it was effectively illegal and invited fines, and partly because motor cars had to become more reliable, more comfortable and a great deal faster before they could compete with the passenger train. Not until the 1920s did railway companies start to worry about passenger-carrying motor vehicles, and these were the first scheduled long-distance coaches, with their cut-price fares, not private cars.

Even if the railway companies had felt a threat, the motor car's partisans and other less biased commentators would have dispelled it. As we have seen, it was regarded as being peculiarly suited to short journeys, whatever might be the theoretical possibilities of continuous runs of 50 or 100 miles. As late as 1902, the door-to-door holiday by car, cutting out the necessity for transhipment of people and luggage between short-haul horse vehicles and long-haul trains, was treated as a prospect rather than a reality.

While it was true that organised opinion was on the side of the motor car, and that concerted opposition was generally lacking where it might most have been expected, one must not infer from this a sudden consolidation of public opinion on the subject. Loud though its voice was, the motor car lobby came down to a handful of beady-eyed promoters concerned with money-making, not with motor cars, and an even smaller number of dedicated enthusiasts, amateurs and businessmen with faith in the future. They – particularly the promoters – might have little or no experience of motor cars, and as for the rest of the population, few at the end of 1895 knew enough about it to express a valid opinion. The great majority probably had no views at all. This general ignorance was one cause of the preponderance of arguments for the motor car's potential rather than for its performance – the coming wealth of an industry as yet unborn, the promised salvation of agriculture, and untried claims of superiority over horse transport.

Perhaps to divert attention from the lack of a solid base for their arguments, partisans of the new vehicle stressed the quantity rather than the quality of the public support for it. Salomons made much of his collection of over 300 press references to the Tunbridge Wells exhibition. Ninety per cent were in favour of motor cars, he said; eight per cent were doubtful, and only two per cent hostile. Salomons claimed that he subsequently converted every one of the "doubtfuls" and "antis". Week after week in its first year of life, the *Autocar* quoted national, local and specialist journals that had spoken approvingly of the new machine, or had at least decided to accept it – over 50 of them in all. It diligently recorded the favourable resolutions of trade associations and chambers of commerce, and the numbers of signatories to petitions against restrictions.

Given organised lobbying on the one side and almost none on the other, the proportion of "pros" to "antis" in Salomons' figures is probably an accurate reflection of formed public opinion in October 1895, but it means very little – "formed" is the relevant word. Support drummed up by theoretical argument was by nature highly artificial, and consequently volatile. A convert gained by one such argument could as easily be lost by another, while experience when it came could either confirm or upset a prejudice.

Given information in the form of experience, the public could make their decisions. Information – on the performance of motor cars, if not yet on their potential – began to be available as soon as motor cars manifested themselves. Most of the vehicles imported into Britain in 1894–5 have already been mentioned – the Benzes of Hewetson and

Arnold, l'Hollier's Roger-Benz, Ellis's Panhard, Salomons' Peugeot and De Dion, and the two motor tricycles at the Stanley Show. Edward Joel Pennington imported a victoria and a motor cycle in mid-December 1895, either as aids to negotiating the sale of the licence, or having sold it, to promote his design. Neither machine seems to have been run on the road at the time. As we shall see, Lawson imported a Daimler in the same month. Two other cars were brought in by people uninvolved in motor car "politics", who therefore – if named at all – have so far been mentioned only in passing.

When travelling in Germany early in 1895, John Adolphus Koosen of Southsea saw an advertisement for the Lutzmann car, liked the look of it, and ordered one. It was November before he took delivery, and his initial experiences were unfortunate. He wrote: "I had been told in a letter from the maker that to start the engine you had to turn the flywheel towards you, which I did until darkness overtook me. The only result was a pair of worn-out gloves." Koosen spent four more days trying to make the car go without petrol; then he put in some benzoline, and as Mrs Koosen's diary noted: "Motor *went* . . . awfully pleased." In December, as will be seen, Koosen came off worst in an encounter with the Fareham magistrates; but by January 1896 he was happy with his machine, and reported that he had been running it daily in his own town of Southsea without a man in front, and without trouble from the police. His problems were now of the humdrum kind to which every motorist had to become accustomed – a detached tyre, dirty fuel, slipping belts, backfiring, and flat batteries (which stopped a car with battery and coil ignition).

Koosen sold his car to a Southsea cycle manufacturer called Rose. No money had yet changed hands when Rose entered the Lutzmann in a local carnival. There the car stopped: its battery had run down again. Rose returned the car to Koosen and refused to pay him, upon which Koosen had to go to court to get his money. However, the worst of his luck had been no fault of the car, so we find him afterwards acquiring another Lutzmann, and by December 1896 he was the make's sole agent in Britain.

In December 1895 T.R.B. Elliot of Kelso received the Panhard phaeton he had ordered five months before from the Daimler Motor Syndicate. The Roxburghshire police let him know that they would not prosecute him for breaches of the law so long as no complaints were laid against him. In effect, he had the qualified freedom of his own county. Elliot drove the Panhard about 1250 miles before the legal restrictions on motor cars were lifted; though, as we shall see, he met a different reception outside Roxburghshire.[58]

During 1895 cars designed and built in Britain continued to be irrelevant to the main stream of progress. The number of constructors grew with the improving "climate" for self-propelled vehicles, but with no home market as an inducement to build cars for sale, none achieved commercial production; and with few exceptions, they directed their inventiveness into unfruitful channels. As noted, Atkinson & Philipson offered steamers, if they did not yet build them. In 1892 James Sumner had inherited an agricultural engineering business in Leyland, Lancashire. The engine of his first road steamer was adapted to drive a steam lawnmower, and Sumner's Leyland Steam Motor Company subsequently did very well with these highly specialised machines; but in 1894–5 Sumner made and sold two steam tricars, one of them for Theodore Carr,[59] the Carlisle biscuit maker. Three concerns kept their money on electricity. Offord & Sons built their Electrocar; while Walter Bersey progressed beyond pure experiment to a more commercial approach. Made by the Universal Electrical Carriage Syndicate, his latest vehicles had two forward speeds and chain final drive; bodies were by Mulliners of Northampton, and speed was about 9 m.p.h. A wide variety of types became available to order – taxicabs, victorias, landaus and phaetons – even bath-chairs. In 1895–6 at least one victoria and one landau were completed. The Britannia Electric Carriage Syndicate of Colchester (later the Britannia Motor Carriage Company) took over Sherrin's electric bath-chair design, and went on to offer formal landaus and barouches.[60]

Encouraged by some of the most respected engineering opinion in Britain, constructors who favoured internal combustion adhered to kerosene as often as to petrol, in spite of its inferiority as a producer of power. It could also, of course, be used legally. Although James D. Roots did not, it seems, actually make any cars in 1895, it is worth noting here that in that year he became the first constructor to advertise British-built internal-combustion-engined cars for sale. By November he was offering his "Roots Petrocar or Petroleum Carriage", obtainable from Roots & Venables[61] of Westminster Bridge Road, London, for £180. Engines could be had separately for £82. Claimed to be "neat, efficient, noiseless and odourless", it weighed $8\frac{1}{2}$ hundredweight empty, would reach 12–13 m.p.h. with two people on board, and cost only $\frac{1}{6}$d a mile to run, owing to the low price of kerosene.

Other constructors did put cars on the road. A prototype kerosene-engined vehicle was designed by Percival W. Petter and built by his firm, James B. Petter & Sons, foundrymen of Yeovil. It was a four-wheeled dogcart with a body by Hill & Boll, a local coachbuilder, and a 1-h.p. engine at the rear. Its single water-cooled horizontal cylinder had an automatic inlet valve and hot-tube ignition. Drive was by chain to either rear wheel, each of which provided a different ratio. Four m.p.h. was available on one, and 10 m.p.h. on the other, Later, a more powerful, two-cylinder engine was substituted, but it would still only turn at 250 r.p.m. Three Petters were built in 1895–6, but while they performed well enough on the streets of Yeovil, making little noise and alarming nobody, they lacked power and failed on hills.

For John Henry Knight, the transition from making stationary oil engines to building a motor car around one was natural. The machine was complete by April 1895, at which time it was powered by kerosene. The little three-wheeler was propelled by a rear-mounted engine with a single horizontal cylinder, automatic inlet valve, and coil and battery ignition. Primary drive was by belt, providing two forward speeds via separate pulleys, and final drive was by chain to one rear wheel. Suspension was by coil springs. By July Knight had substituted a petrol engine with surface carburettor, but this developed less than 1 h.p. at 500 r.p.m., and even with a weight of only 575 pounds, top speed was no more than 8–9 m.p.h. Even so, Knight found the car unstable, and in 1896 converted it into a four-wheeler. The front wheels were both independently sprung, each in its own cycle-type fork in the fashion pioneered by Amédée Bollée *père*. Originally, Knight's aim in building the car was "chiefly to bring to public notice the restrictions which have hitherto prevented the use of motor carriages in England", but within a year, thanks no doubt to the motor car's improving prospects, he was writing: "I . . . am now looking for someone to take up manufacture."

Three other experimenters of 1895 used petrol engines from the beginning, but two of them completely ignored prevalent trends in design. Colonel H.C.L. Holden began experimenting with a motor bicycle powered by a four-cylinder engine, driving direct to the rear wheel like the Hildebrand & Wolfmuller. Frederick Lanchester was a brilliant and versatile engineer who had studied in France and Germany, and experimented in optics, colour photography and aeronautics. He worked for a Birmingham firm of Otto-type gas engine manufacturers, and in 1893 made a petrol-engined punt.

Lanchester, however, is best known for the remarkable experimental motor car that he began to build, and probably finished, in 1895. It was a unique concept that owed nothing to Daimler and Benz with their stationary gas engine and horse carriage or bicycle background. Its most extraordinary feature was its engine. This had only a single horizontal cylinder, located transversely and air-cooled, but thanks to a complex and highly original disposition of cranks and connecting rods, it ran with unprecedented smoothness. The inlet valve was mechanically operated, and there was a wick carburettor of particularly efficient design. The engine drove through two-speed epicyclic gears to chain final drive. Another highly original aspect of this first Lanchester was its integral chassis and body frame in tubular steel, which provided a very stiff structure. Further improvements on standard practice were self-centring steering, by side lever; and pneumatic tyres. By February 1896 the car was complete and running in the streets.

George Johnston was little less adventurous. This Glasgow engineer designed a steam tramcar for the city council in 1895, and later experimented with an electric car; but in November 1895 he began to drive about the city in a petrol-driven 3 h.p. dogcart.[62] The machine probably had a radiator or other condensing device, for it was said by its constructor to use hardly any water at all. No fuller technical description that is strictly contemporary has survived, but if the vehicle resembled Johnston's later Arrol-Johnston cars in essentials, which is probable, its engine was an advanced design. Mounted transversely, this had two horizontally-opposed pistons for smoothness of running, and ignition by low-tension magneto. Both primary and final drive was by chain. Johnston motored at night, so as to have streets clear of traffic. He may also have been concerned to observe bye-laws restricting hours of operation; and, perhaps, to avoid drawing attention to himself, since he reached a speed of 12 m.p.h. On one occasion he covered nearly 20 miles of Glasgow streets in three hours. At all events, the police did not at first interfere.[63]

Thus it was that, around the end of 1895, there were perhaps a couple of dozen self-propelled passenger road vehicles in being in Britain, including machines that had been in evidence since the previous year; six months before there may have been no more than half a dozen. The encouraging effect of the pressures described earlier is obvious. At the first date there was just one imported petrol motor car; by the second date the number had grown to at least 11, or nearly half the total. Two things were by then clear: that the petrol motor car was the coming machine; and that it was being introduced into Britain by means of foreign products, since only these offered a practical combination of virtues, and were actually available.

The public acquired experience of these pioneer motor cars in two ways. They might be driven about on the roads and streets, either clandestinely to avoid prosecution, or openly to invite it and at the same time to advertise. But the public did not learn very much from a single vehicle out on a run, for if a car was running properly it was soon gone from sight. Furthermore – from the point of view of the motorist – road runs could make a bad impression as easily as a good one. The public might well catch a car when it was broken down or unable to climb a hill; horses and people might take alarm; and many people disapproved of law-breaking on principle, regardless of the justification. In any case, not all motorists were so dedicated to the cause that they sought out prosecution on its behalf. They were put off by the prospect rather than otherwise.[64]

The success of the Tunbridge Wells event had demonstrated that the public exhibition was a far more effective "showcase" for the motor car. It was therefore popular both with enthusiastic amateurs such as Salomons, and with the calculating company promoter whose interest lay in persuading the investing public that the motor car was the coming thing. A closed piece of private ground, of course, restricted vehicles to short, undemanding runs; and if a car did misbehave, there was none of the concealment afforded by an empty highway. But even these, the only disadvantages, had an obverse for all concerned. In controlled conditions, mechanical embarrassments were easier to guard against, other traffic was unlikely to be a problem, and surfaces and gradients could be made nearly ideal. Furthermore, in a confined space a vehicle's starting, manoeuvring and stopping abilities were at a premium, and could be shown off. The public had a chance to check one of the main claims made for the motor car – that it handled easily and safely.

The principal advantage of an exhibition over road runs by individual vehicles was, however, that thousands of people at a time could be familiarised with the motor car, and – if all went well – persuaded that it was a practical, useful machine with a future. Brief, rare, chance encounters on the road could never achieve this. Moreover, the public would usually see not just one vehicle, but several brought together for the occasion. They made a spectacle, so the public would come, and the press would respond. As spectacle, they would be most effective if held in or near the major centres of population, where they were most accessible to the most people. It was no accident that the biggest and most important of the forthcoming exhibitions were held in London rather than in places such as Tunbridge Wells. An organised event could be properly publicised. It allowed organisers to keep journalists on the spot fully briefed (or coached), and the prospect of wide coverage was good. Exhibitions were, too, a form of publicity that could be controlled, in the sense that they could be laid on when most needed. In our period they coincided with the passage through Parliament of a new Bill to free the motor car, with the drafting of additional regulations on the subject, and with the appearance of opposition.

As we shall see, there were variants and combinations of these means of spreading the word. Some promoters and motorists engineered, or at least took advantage of, invitations to unrelated trade, industrial or agricultural shows, where their vehicles constituted an added attraction. Some drove their cars to the show grounds. Some exhibitions were for the press only, not for the public. The intensity of the campaign to "educate" lay opinion rose to a peak in July 1896 – up to that point, major issues regarding the motor car had still to be decided, and opinion on them was still to be swayed. By that time the number of people who had driven or even ridden in a motor car was still minute, but one way or another, a great many more – opinion-makers, wielders of different sorts of power, and the public at large – in London, the south-east, the industrial Midlands, the north and Scotland were familiar with the machine in the sense of having seen it perform.

But in November 1895 all this was still in the future. Sir David Salomons, for the moment the undisputed leader of the motor car movement, saw the need for its different elements to work together through a single coordinating organisation in order to wield the maximum influence. Whether united or not, the movement's first objective was to persuade the Conservative government to introduce a new Bill in favour of the motor vehicle.

Salomons had already said, in a letter to the *Daily Telegraph*, that the time had come to organise. At first the interested parties, some of whom had met at Tunbridge Wells, came together informally at public lectures on the motor vehicle. These later multiplied, but never had more than a comparatively limited effect as propaganda. Their importance was at the beginning, as a catalyst. The Camera Club (which incorporated the Amateur Mechanics' Society) met on 21 November to listen to an address by J.H. Knight.[65] Salomons presided. Also there were Henry Sturmey; A.H. Bateman, builder of the Parkyns tricycle that had passed to Salomons; Colonel H.C.L. Holden; and Henry Hardinge Cunynghame, an assistant under secretary at the Home Office, which was making a study of the new vehicle. Salomons urged a deputation to Henry Chaplin at the Local Government Board, to ask for a new Bill.

On the 27th, an altogether more high-powered company met at the Society of Arts to hear Cunynghame of the Home Office deliver a paper on the current state of the motor vehicle. The fact of Home Office interest in the new machine was significant enough; far more so was the calibre of the audience. Some of the names were familiar – Salomons, Shaw-Lefevre, the Comte de Dion. All of these spoke in the discussion that was begun after the lecture, and which resumed a fortnight later. But other public figures, too, were now showing active interest in the motor vehicle. They were a mixed, if eminent, bag, and included several celebrities.

Sir Frederick Bramwell, respected veteran of steam on the road and a judge of the forthcoming *Engineer* competition, was in the chair. John Wolfe Wolfe-Barry was there – Britain's most eminent civil engineer. The designer of the country's most modern docks and one of the architects of Tower Bridge, his main interest was in town traffic. He persuaded London's Underground railway companies to experiment with electric traction, and was a convert to the motor vehicle. With him, and speaking in favour of the new machine, was Sir Hiram Maxim, electrical engineer, inventor of the revolutionary machine-gun bearing his name, conductor of skilfully publicised experiments with an aeroplane, and advocate of lightweight petrol engines. Other "names" present were Professor Vernon Boys, already famous as an experimental physicist and inventor of scientific instruments, and Alexander Siemens, a member of the light railways committee of 1895. After referring to the restrictions on motor cars as "perfectly monstrous", Shaw-Lefevre followed Salomons' example in suggesting a deputation to Henry Chaplin.[66]

These gatherings had Salomons as the most significant common factor, and it was he who announced a public meeting with the object of founding a body in which motor-car interests would be united. It would be held at the Cannon Street Hotel in London on 10 December. This turned out to be a still more impressive occasion than its predecessors. It drew between 300 and 400 people, for the first time representing all the major pressure groups as well as car owners, politicians and engineers. Salomons reiterated his standard arguments, emphasising the vast potential of a motor vehicle industry once the law was changed. Harry Lawson agreed, on this first and last occasion on which he and Salomons shared a platform. Salomons also introduced a new argument – that of public hygiene. Horses shed manure in colossal quantities[67] – the motor car would mean cleaner streets, and a bonus in the shape of lower rates. John Philipson and Walter Arnold both pressed the advantages of motor vehicles to farmers.

The stated objects of the Self-Propelled Traffic Association, as it was christened, were the changing of the law, the popularisation of all kinds of self-propelled vehicle, and their technical improvement; in that order. Membership was solicited from people with business interests in such vehicles, and from private owners and supporters. There was discrimination only in the subscription payable – five times as much for the trade as for amateurs.

The officers and council of the S.P.T.A. as at first constituted reflected its ecumenical intent. In addition, not just those directly involved, but all interests whose support and influence would be in any way valuable, were recruited. Needless to say, Salomons was elected president. The vice presidents were John Philipson, Sir Frederick Bramwell, Alexander Siemens, and the twelfth Earl of Winchilsea, President of the National Agricultural Union.[68]

Among the council members were the M.P.s Sir Albert Rollit (Conservative, South Islington) and Salomons' colleague Colonel Miller. Rollit was a man of progressive views and very considerable influence. A wealthy Yorkshire shipowner, and prominent figure in Hull, he had married the third Duke of Sutherland's widow. He had sat on the light railways committee of 1895; he was for long a vice-president of the Stanley Cycle Club, and regularly opened the club's annual show. Others on the council included E.R. Shipton, Secretary of the Cyclists' Touring Club; Sir Henry Trueman Wood, Secretary of the Society of Arts; Professor Boys; the industrialists George Stephenson, William Cross and Richard Tangye (of *Cornubia* fame); the eminent physician Sir Benjamin Ward Richardson, President of the Society of Cyclists, who had ridden on Salomons' Peugeot at Tunbridge Wells; and another constructor in the person of J.H. Knight. Horse and coachbuilding interests were represented not only by Salomons and Philipson, but also by G.J. Jacobs and by the S.P.T.A.'s secretary, Andrew Barr, who was Secretary of the Institute of British Carriage Manufacturers and a liveryman of the Coach Makers' Company.

The next strongest interest represented on the council of the S.P.T.A. was that of the company promoters and their associates – Harry Lawson, Martin Rucker and Evelyn Ellis. Frederick Simms was a member of the association, but was not on its council. While insisting on his own amateur status, Salomons realised that motor traders and manufacturers were fully qualified members of the movement; but he had already made public his dislike of patent monopolies, and drew the line at associating with company promoters, who would do the industry no good. It was their aim, said Salomons, "to make the Association little more or less than a company promoting concern."

Nothing is known of the circumstances in which the Lawson men left the S.P.T.A. council, but they were certainly gone by January 1896. With them went Lord Winchilsea, to join the board of a Lawson promotion[69] and become his prime badge of respectability. In their places came a powerful influx of political "muscle" – Shaw-Lefevre, Cumming Macdona, J.W. Maclure the railway director, and the first Marquess of Abergavenny, whose seat at Eridge Castle near Tunbridge Wells was in "Salomons country". William Worby

Beaumont joined the council too, as did Walter Hancock, nephew of his famous namesake, and Alfred Richard Sennett, an engineer and skilful publicist of whom more will be heard.

The two least congenial elements in the mix of interests campaigning for the motor car – the high-minded Salomons and the sleazy, dynamic Lawson – had collided head-on and repelled each other. Henceforth they would both expend energy better directed elsewhere in attacking each other, as well as in going their separate ways towards a common goal. Salomons had the sort of organisation he wanted, suited to his policy of disarming political opponents and exercising influence privately in high places. The presence on its council of unscrupulous men dedicated to parting investors from their money would have destroyed its credibility. As for the promoters, it was all or nothing for them as well. They, too, saw the value of the S.P.T.A. as a propaganda instrument, but as Salomons knew, they would regard it only as a respectable "front". If they could not run it their way, there was no point in their staying. The S.P.T.A. lost something by the breach – it was never as good at winning public attention as the more professional, lively and uninhibited Lawson camp – but without the rupture, it could not have filled the role for which Salomons had cast it.

2

Prelude to Battle, 1895–6

As might be expected, during December 1895 the different camps continued to act independently as well as together. Salomons paid a week's visit to the Paris Salon du Cycle and to the city's motor manufacturers, reporting back to different journals as part of his campaign for spreading information. The Salon – the French equivalent of the Stanley Show – was mainly for cycles, but this year was also the "first serious attempt at organising a representative show"[1] of motor cars in France – the first static show, that is. The gathering pace of the movement in France since the Paris–Bordeaux race was noticeable. Among makes old and new on display, Panhard & Levassor showed 10 vehicles and Peugeot up to 18. De Dion exhibited five motor tricycles and only one steamer, a tractor.

Following the lead of Salomons, Lawson adopted exhibitions as a publicity tool. The private ground chosen for his first display – the paths of the Crystal Palace – were soft, but the demonstration was a success, even though the British Motor Syndicate could muster only a single Daimler of the old type for the occasion. It was a show for press and friends only, not a public display as at Tunbridge Wells. Those attending included William Worby Beaumont; the German engineer Otto Mayer, who had come from Canstatt to be chief engineer for the Daimler Motor Company; and about 20 journalists, including Henry Sturmey. The representative of *Engineering* filed what was for that journal an unusually enthusiastic report. The car was started within a quarter of a minute "from the striking of the match", and it appeared to be easily controlled. From a speed of 10–12 m.p.h., the machine could stop quicker than a horse carriage. The petrol motor car was at last to be taken seriously – "it is high time for the steam people to bestir themselves."

At about the same time in December, the British Motor Syndicate, through Frederick Simms, announced that the public works department of Colombo, Ceylon, had been authorised to buy "a few"

Daimlers for mail-carrying.[2] Simms notified the press at large, for this was a publicity exercise. It appeared to be one without any basis in fact. The pot was kept boiling by news of a firm order – for one van only – in the spring of 1896, but 18 months later it transpired that no van had ever been sent to Ceylon.

The *Engineer* memorial, or petition, was presented to Henry Chaplin with over 1700 signatures on it. It was said that most of the principal manufacturing engineers had appended their names, together with many engineering societies and – more to the point – numerous representatives of county and other local authorities. More important still, the *Engineer* reported that Chaplin had made up his mind about the motor vehicle. He was "so entirely in sympathy" with the petition that there had been no need for a deputation to accompany it and speak up for it. But Chaplin had better news still – a Bill to relieve the motor vehicle of its restrictions would be brought before Parliament during the coming session. The policy was now fully bi-partisan; the major parties would make no political capital out of it. Also, it was once more official government policy; the subject of a public Bill. The first objective of all the campaigners had been achieved; but William Worby Beaumont added a warning. Supporters of the Bill must not relax their efforts, for, he added ominously, the opposition had had no chance to show its strength. The fact that little hostility had so far manifested itself did not mean that it would not do so.

Beaumont need not have worried: the motor car's friends showed no signs of resting on their laurels. On 11 January the *Autocar* followed the lead of the *Engineer* in announcing a petition praying for a change in the law, addressed this time to the House of Commons. The breach between Salomons and Lawson had been made public at the end of the previous month, when Simms announced that he had originated the idea of a motoring organisation at the Tunbridge Wells exhibition – a claim which elicited an indignant repudiation from Salomons.

At the same time Simms announced the imminent formation of another body to represent motoring interests. The company promoters, scenting commercial advantage, had decided to create one of their own. The Motor Car Club, open to "inventors, manufacturers, buyers or users", was founded in January 1896 for, in its own words, "the protection, encouragement and development of the motor car industry". The prospectus had an altogether more earthy flavour than the pronouncements of the S.P.T.A. Behind the fine-sounding words was no altruism, but hard self-interest. Nothing made this clearer than the facilities offered to club members, which included "help to investors in perfecting and disposing of their inventions or rights relating thereto", and introductions to "buyers and capitalists" for manufacturers and inventors.

If these blandishments did not give the game away, certain other facts were inescapable. The names of the men who ran the M.C.C. were the names of directors of Lawson companies. Lawson himself was the club chairman. Frederick Simms was officially its founder, and a vice president too, as also were Evelyn Ellis, Martin Rucker, Bertram van Praagh and J.H. Mace. As with Lawson's companies, so with his club: a veneer of respectability was later provided by the addition of titled nonentities as further vice presidents. The symbol the club chose – an allegorical lady in flowing garments brandishing a sheaf of lightning-flashes in one hand and absent-mindedly steering a self-propelled chariot with the other – was identical to that of the British Motor Syndicate. So, too, was its office address at one time – 40 Holborn Viaduct, the home of all Lawson's major promotions.[3] The club's own secretary, Charles Harrington Moore, spelt it all out, describing how early in 1896, "Mr Lawson and Mr Simms were engaged in forming the Motor Car Club". It was freely said – though vigorously denied – that the club was supported financially by Lawson. Claude Goodman Johnson[4] was specific: the British Motor Syndicate subsidised the Motor Car Club to the tune of £6000.

Simms cannot have been pleased with these revelations. He always tried very hard to blur the M.C.C.'s association with the promoters, partly, no doubt, because a show of independence was good policy for the club, and partly, perhaps, out of an orthodox businessman's distaste for the Hooleys and Lawsons of the world, with whom he was now so deeply involved. He said: "It will be clearly understood that this club is not formed for any trade purposes whatever, for its main objects are to hold exhibitions, arrange competitions, give prizes, and generally protect, control and further the motor carriage movement." He was not believed. To contemporaries with eyes to see, the M.C.C. was simply "a proprietors' club",[5] or, in the words of a modern historian, a promotional organisation for Lawson's commercial undertakings. If further evidence were needed, it would be found, as we shall see, in the names of the men who organised the exhibition of which Simms spoke.[6]

At the same time, business interests unconnected with Lawson found it useful to belong to the M.C.C., probably because those who ran it turned out to be so skilful at drumming up publicity for everybody's motor cars. Simms was no doubt glad to have them, as they lent much-needed colour to the club's claims of independence without inhibiting its usefulness to Lawson. By November 1896 names that represented virtually the whole British motor business – l'Hollier

Gascoigne, Arnold, Lutzmann, Petter, Roots, Radcliffe Ward, Britannia, Thrupp & Maberly and Offord – were members of the M.C.C., and eligible to take part in its exhibitions.[7] Walter Arnold and one of his agents went out of their way to defend the club against its detractors.

In mid-January the Lawson camp issued the prospectus of the Daimler Motor Company, which had acquired the licence to make vehicles according to the patents held by the British Motor Syndicate. The directors included Lawson (as chairman), Ellis, Sturmey, Mace and Gottlieb Daimler; Simms was consulting engineer. The flotation was Lawson's first complete promotional success, in that all the £100,000-worth of ordinary £10 shares were taken up. Indeed, the issue was over-subscribed. Of 550 shareholders, only two held over £1000 worth of equity. Lawson's faith in the credulity of British small investors seemed to be justified.

The Daimler patents were the most valuable in existence, declared the prospectus; and production could be started in two months – note "could", not "would". "Perhaps never has such an immense and immediate future been presented to any new industry as that now opening for motor traffic of all kinds . . . this new industry is, in the opinion of the directors, likely to cause a revolution equal to that achieved by the most sensational inventions ever brought before the public, even including the steam engine." It is ironic that this rhetoric, intended to mislead, was in fact a true forecast of what was to come.

It is, perhaps, hardly surprising that the public flocked to buy Daimler Motor Company shares when the newspapers they read, frivolous and serious, local and national, spoke the same language as the prospectus. Irrespective of whether it looked with favour on the prospect, press comment tended towards the conviction that, as the *Sporting and Dramatic News* put it, "Autocars . . . have come to stay." The *Daily Telegraph* proclaimed: "We are now on the eve apparently of a great engineering departure similar to that which produced the vast cycle industry 30 years ago – only here the possibilities are far greater . . . the thing is becoming almost a craze." At about the same time, the *Southampton Echo* was saying that "The autocar . . . is destined to make a revolution in vehicular locomotion."

Along with these quotes, which the prospectus reproduced quite legitimately, was what it described as an "extract from the *Saturday Review*", which was in fact merely a letter from Frederick Simms that it had published in July 1895 after his pioneer drive with Ellis, praising the Daimler system. The *Saturday Review* publicly objected to this misattribution, as did Salomons to the use of his name (in bold type) in the prospectus to imply support for a company-promoting operation.

The rupture between Salomons on the one hand, and Simms and the Lawson camp on the other, was by now complete. It was being said that Salomons had a financial interest in the Daimler Motor Company, and he firmly believed that Simms and the Motor Car Club were behind what he regarded as a gross slander.

Lawson's claim for the Daimler patents was made also for the patents he acquired subsequently – between them they were "master patents", without which practical motor vehicles could not be built. The truth of the matter was that there was no such thing as a master patent. The nearest approximation to such a thing, Otto's British patent, had expired in 1891. No one could say that the important patents that remained in force could not be by-passed without violating them. Lawson had no excuse for not knowing this. He was not so good or so versatile an engineer as he made out, but he had an extensive technical background as a bicycle designer and engineer, and as a patentee of other innovations concerned with road vehicles. He knew nothing of motor vehicles, but he was ideally placed to acquire this expertise from others. Frederick Simms. H.O. Duncan and Charles McRobie Turrell, his secretary and a trained engineer, were all employees or close collaborators, and could supply the technical knowledge he lacked, and, indeed, were given the specialised job of seeking out the most promising patents to buy.

Sir David Salomons was well aware of the facts, and lost no opportunity of broadcasting them, but Lawson gambled – successfully – on ignorant investors being sufficiently impressed by his claims to part with their money. He could do so because, except for Salomons and the men concerned with the Benz patents, virtually all the few engineers in Britain who knew the truth, and were prominent enough to be listened to, were in one way or another dependent on him or on the success of his promotions, or were beholden to him in some fashion. The same went for the *Autocar*. Even William Worby Beaumont, never in the Lawson camp, sold him his patents.

These engineers, and everyone else with a stake in Lawson, had another reason for silence. In the short run – which in most cases was their sole concern – the value of the licences did not depend on their exclusivity, but on the fact that they presented their purchasers with ready-made engineering expertise. Anyone with access to them could, in theory anyway, undertake manufacture undelayed by the need for research and development, while would-be competitors spent time finding ways round them. At the same time, they were a legal defence against the importation of finished vehicles by others, which further hampered rivals. Lawson's claims were merely an added bait.

Meanwhile, beyond the fringes of the battle between the followers of Lawson and Salomons, others sought to profit from the public attention aroused by the din. By January 1896 the Acme Motor Carriage Company was taking orders for Mannheim-built Benz cars. Henry Hewetson had gone into the business of importing these machines, as Léon l'Hollier had with the Roger-Benz, and "Acme" was the name he chose for them. At the same time, it was announced that l'Hollier had entered into an agreement with Edmund Gascoigne, an engineer of Maidstone, and with a Frenchman, Daniel Courtois, to manufacture the Roger-Benz in Gascoigne's home town. L'Hollier's function would be to sell the cars that the others made. The announcement was premature, in the sense that the three men continued for the present as importers only, and cars were never actually built at Maidstone; but the move was symptomatic of the optimism of the times.

The great burgeoning of activity that is being described took place against a background of equally sudden and widespread retribution upon motorists in the magistrates' courts. The public martyrdom that some had sought for so long was finally visited upon almost all – for the police to show leniency became rare enough to merit special mention [8] – and like many martyrs they flourished on it. Prosecutions were advertisements of bad law; the more effective when (as happened) the court itself acknowledged the law's shortcomings. They did not ordinarily imply hostility to the motor car as such, but an impersonal determination to uphold the law because it was the law. In this sense it was nothing new.

From the coincidence of increased action with positive reaction, it does seem as though, in part at least, the one prompted the other. When Evelyn Ellis had flaunted his Panhard all over southern and western England, local authorities had been slow to respond, faced with a machine that was virtually unknown and unheard-of. Now it was neither, and they were ready for it. Another consideration was that Ellis was quickly come and gone, never to return, giving complainants and police in each neighbourhood little chance – in the days before number-plates – of identifying him. The latest victims were local men who drove their vehicles regularly within a short distance of their homes, and were therefore much more vulnerable. The experience of Hewetson should have warned them.

As befitted a pioneer motorist, John Henry Knight was the first of the latest martyrs to suffer. He was summoned before the Farnham magistrates on the last day of October 1895 for "permitting a locomotive to be at work" two weeks earlier without a licence from the county council. He was fined 2s 6d, with 12s 6d costs. An employee of

Plate 1 Competitors in the Paris–Bordeaux race of 1895 at Versailles. No. 12, in the foreground, is a Roger-Benz that finished fifth, at 11.3 m.p.h. For a relatively inefficient design such an average speed compared very well with that of Emile Levassor's Panhard, no. 5 – the car immediately behind. It was the fastest machine in the race, averaging 15 m.p.h. This race did more to publicise the motor car in Britain than any other before 1897.

Plate 2   The Daimler range of products, 1896. The new, Panhard-type cars are not yet on sale, but a wide variety of other products is, from

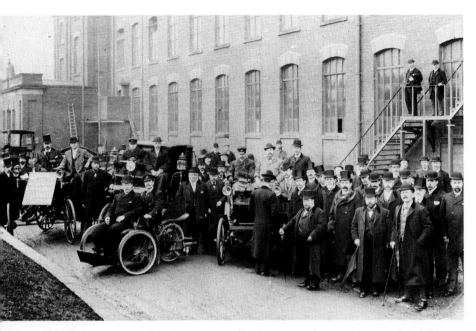

Plate 3 Harry Lawson's citadel: the Motor Mills, Coventry, about 1896–7, with employees, visitors and vehicles covering the Lawson company licences. Among them are a Léon Bollée tricar in the foreground; at least four old-type Daimlers behind it, including a landau and a roofed phaeton with windshield; and a new Panhard-type Daimler (or Panhard) at far left in the background. The placard on one Daimler advertising magazines and the large number of well-dressed men in outdoor attire, near the camera, suggest a special occasion: no doubt one of Lawson's many promotional exercises for the press.

Plate 4 A De Dion Bouton tricycle at a pedal cycle racing track, the venues of Britain's first motor races. The rider is the racing cyclist F. Bidlake. (Photograph by Argent Archer.)

Plate 5 In a London street on the way to the start of the London–Brighton run, November 1896. Vehicle no. 14 should be a Peugeot bus, according to the official list of starters; in fact the car carrying the number is the Panhard that had been fastest in the Paris–Marseilles race. At the tiller is Charles McRobie Turrell, Harry Lawson's private secretary, in Motor Car Club uniform. His unidentified passenger is in some way connected with Lawson's promotions (he appears in Plate 9, which is a promotional shot); he carries a red, white and blue flag that is a composite of the Union Jack and Tricolor, with a traction engine's "red flag" on the same pole.

Plate 6 The Offord Electro-car, 1896. Coachbuilders saw more future in electricity than in the petrol engine.

Plate 7 Public transport: one of the battery-electric buses of Radcliffe Ward, whose extensive and well-publicised experiments in London streets helped to accustom the public to all self-propelled road vehicles. This drawing appeared in 1896.

Plate 8 A Panhard-Levassor of pre-1895 type, with pneumatic front tyres, which date the scene probably to about 1896. Although the proud party is unidentified, the photograph is unusual and interesting for this early period in being not a stiff commercial publicity shot, but a glimpse into the still-tiny world of the private motorist.

Plate 9   Prince Ranjitsinhji, the famous Indian cricketer, sits in the nearside front seat of a Coventry-built Daimler, 1897. "Ranji" was a director of the refloated British Motor Syndicate. (Photograph by Argent Archer.)

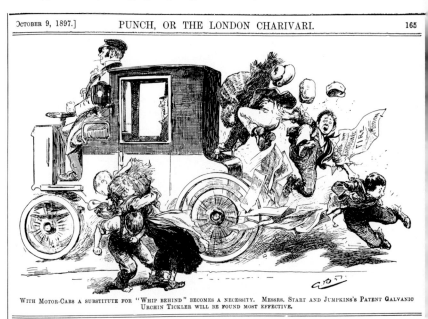

WITH MOTOR-CABS A SUBSTITUTE FOR "WHIP BEHIND" BECOMES A NECESSITY. MESSRS. START AND JUMPKINS'S PATENT GALVANIC URCHIN TICKLER WILL BE FOUND MOST EFFECTIVE.

Plate 10   The Bersey taxicab, new on London's streets in 1897. A favourite sport of urchins was to hang on to the backs of horsedrawn cabs until a passer-by shouted "Whip behind!" to the driver. The driver of an electric cab had no whip, but according to *Punch* would be able to secure the same effect with an electric charge.

Plate 11 Desperate measures: Harry Lawson's fast-foundering British Motor Syndicate tries to recapture vanishing public confidence in its shares and patents, 1897. Daimler, Léon Bollée, De Dion, Pennington and Bersey patents are illustrated.

Plate 12 A popular view: an episode in the fictitious "Story of an Auto-Motor Car" illustrated by W. Ralston, 1896, in which "Jones, Brown and Robinson hire a motor car". Soon, "the car bumped over a stone and shot Brown out on to his head". This was merely the first disaster of many.

Plate 13 An Arnold of 1896 with its owner, Alfred Cornell of Tonbridge, at the helm. Cornell was the make's enthusiastic local agent.

his, James Pullinger, who was at the wheel of the petrol-engined three-wheeler at the time, was convicted of operating the vehicle within prohibited hours, and penalised to the same amount. Knight did not contest the charges, stating that his only purpose in breaking the law was to draw attention to its defects. He even attended court in his car, to demonstrate its harmlessness. The case got much publicity, and provoked a wave of sympathy for Knight, but he henceforth restricted his motoring to private ground.

Thereafter, prosecutions became so common that such concern grew rare. John Adolphus Koosen was the next to be penalised; on 16 December 1895 he was fined 1s and 15s 7d costs at Fareham for not having a man in front, while travelling at up to 7 m.p.h. on the Gosport road. His defence – that he had been granted a carriage licence, and that the Lutzmann was thereby accepted as a carriage and not a locomotive – was rejected, though the court decided to impose only a nominal penalty. As we have seen, Koosen found a warmer reception in adjoining Southsea, where he lived, and was undiscouraged.

At the end of November the Glasgow magistrates had refused the permission sought by a local umbrella manufacturer to run a delivery van in the streets. This anonymous tradesman reacted with gusto: "Those in authority in our city", he declared, "might as well try to beat back the waves of the sea with a broom as try to stem the tide of horseless carriages that are looming in the distance." Such heroics were lost on the Glasgow bench. Less than a month later George Johnston, summonsed on a charge of driving within prohibited hours, was fined 2s 6d. He pleaded in vain that his car was licensed as a carriage, and was not a locomotive.

Léon l'Hollier offended by motoring on the Stratford road at Solihull without a man stationed 20 yards in front. On 4 February 1896, following Knight's example, he drove his car to court to help him plead his case that it was not a locomotive, but to equally little avail. He was fined 1s and costs, the court commenting that it would be "a very good thing if the law were altered".

The Berwick-on-Tweed bench that convicted T.R.B. Elliot on 19 March reacted in much the same way. On the last day of February he had undertaken a 30-mile night run from Kelso to Berwick – his first trip outside his native county – which was completed in a time of $4\frac{1}{2}$ hours, including stops. At Berwick he courted police attention, expressing to them his open doubts that he was acting within the law. His purpose was to induce a prosecution, and in this he was successful. In court, he freely admitted that he had been travelling at 14 m.p.h. within the magistrates' jurisdiction, but claimed that existing legislation did not apply to his vehicle, which was not a locomotive. Elliot's counsel rightly described him as "a most obliging defendant". He was convicted only of failure to have a man 20 yards in front, for which the bench fined him a derisory 6d, with 19s 7d costs, adding that they "very much regretted having to do so".

In each case so far noted, we see a court rightly convicting because the law had been broken, but imposing a nominal fine and otherwise expressing or implying a criticism of the law. Johnston, for instance, had been liable to a fine of up to £5; while l'Hollier could have been fined £10.

The same could not be said for the prosecution of Walter Arnold at Tonbridge on 28 January, for offences committed at Paddock Wood a week or so earlier. Charges and penalty all suggested that an example was being made. The self-propelled vehicle interests had been particularly strong in Kent since the earliest days of the traction engine, but the corollary was endemic hostility. Salomons had avoided prosecution by exercising a combination of prudence and influence, as he cheerfully admitted; but local businessmen such as Hewetson and Arnold, though prominent figures, were lesser fry, and operated with less discretion. A Kent county councillor brought the prosecution, making no fewer than four complaints – there was no man in front, there were insufficient people in charge, no name or address were displayed, and the speed was over 2 m.p.h. Again the defence was made that a carriage licence had been obtained, and that the car was therefore not a locomotive but a carriage; and again it failed. Arnold was found guilty on all four charges, and this time the fines and costs totalled a punitive £4 7s 0d, with the alternative of seven days' imprisonment on each charge.

The court's action had the effect of enlisting the outspoken sympathy of the *Kent and Sussex Courier* and the *Tunbridge Wells Gazette*, which were already friendly to Salomons. At most, Arnold had been guilty of "a technical breach of statute", which would actually be a good thing, as it would draw attention to bad law. The *Gazette* referred to a "vexatious" prosecution that pandered to "an absurd anomaly". The *Courier* appealed for a public subscription to pay Arnold's fine; this "Horseless Carriage Defence Fund" was over-subscribed. The contributions were accompanied by many friendly letters, which the *Courier* printed. When thanking subscribers, Arnold stipulated that the money should be turned over to the Tunbridge Wells hospital, in acknowledgement of the town's support for motor cars.

Much was made of these prosecutions by propagandists, and they recurred while motorists continued to defy the law, but no other instance of overt hostility to the motor car in a court of law was recorded at this time. In every other case, benches had clearly come to believe that the law had not long to run, and demanded only token respect. The *County Council Times* held that the policy of imposing nominal fines had initially been sound, as giving publicity to bad law, but it had then become ridiculous, and finally vexatious. This organ advised magistrates to decline to impose fines of any sort.

With the exception of Knight, none of the motorists concerned stopped driving on public roads because of prosecution.[9] There is no record of further prosecution of these people, so it is clear that they subsequently learned to avoid it, or else, like Koosen, found jurisdictions where toleration or liberal interpretation of the law ruled.

That there was no dismay at the prosecutions is obvious from the gathering momentum of the motor car movement. Each of the pressure groups involved pursued its way vigorously. Chaplin at the Local Government Board had already expressed his full sympathy with the case for amending the law, and had said that a Bill was on its way, but that did not save him from further, heavier pressure designed to harden and make explicit the government's commitment. This sort of tactic was Salomons' *forte*. On 12 February Chaplin received a deputation from the S.P.T.A. It was numerous and high-powered, and it represented a broad band of interests; Salomons was at its head. With him, among others, were Conservative and Liberal M.P.s and ex-M.P.s, emphasising the deputation's bipartisan character – Shaw-Lefevre, Cumming Macdona, J.W. Maclure and Arthur Griffith-Boscawen. Shaw-Lefevre promised his successor at the Local Government Board his full support. The Conservative member for South-West Kent, Griffith-Boscawen, was President of the National Traction Engine Owners' and Users' Association. He was a friend of Walter Arnold, and David Salomons was one of his constituents. He was in favour of any legislation to lift the "ridiculous restrictions . . . upon horseless carriages". Giving the company a truly ecumenical character were the Secretary of the Central Chamber of Agriculture – another of the many organisations that had sprung up to promote the welfare of farmers – and representatives of the London County Council, who told Chaplin that the L.C.C. Highways Committee favoured motor vehicles as a means of reducing traffic congestion. As early as 17 December the Highways Committee had passed a resolution inviting the government to reintroduce Shaw-Lefevre's Bill; a little later it recommended that restrictions preventing the use of motor vehicles in London should be abolished.

Chaplin repeated the assurances he had previously given. A Bill was now in an advanced state of preparation. He and his Parliamentary Private Secretary, T.W. Russell (Liberal Unionist, Tyrone South) would do their best for it, and hoped to carry it without significant opposition in the current session of Parliament.

This first major effort by the S.P.T.A. was promptly upstaged, in terms of publicity if not solid achievement, by the Motor Car Club – a pattern which soon became familiar. Three days afterwards, the club's first display of motor vehicles took place. The site was the Imperial Institute, London's most prestigious exhibition centre. There were four vehicles on show – the Simms Daimler, one of Hewetson's Acmes, the Garrard & Blumfield electric, and a newcomer to Britain, one of the Kane-Penningtons that their designer had brought over from America in December. The electric and the Kane-Pennington were shown in the 230-yard-long north gallery of the Institute, and the two others in the central quadrangle, where a ramp with a gradient of 1:10 had been constructed. Press opinion differed as to whether any cars climbed the slope. The *Engineer* claimed that only three were in working order, but singled out the running of the Daimler and the Acme for some qualified praise. Probably the Kane-Pennington was the backslider: the *Autocar* commented at the time that it was not a satisfactory vehicle.

Lawson could not have wished for a more distinguished company of visitors. As President of the Institute, the Prince of Wales attended on the day before the exhibition. He took his first ride in a petrol motor car – the Daimler, with Ellis and Simms in charge.[10] Among the 1600–1700 people estimated to be present were a minor elderly "Royal", Prince Edward of Saxe-Weimar, nephew by marriage of Queen Victoria; Cunynghame of the Home Office; Sir Hiram Maxim; and three Members of Parliament. The most influential of these was Sir William Harcourt, who had been a friend of Shaw-Lefevre's 1895 Bill. Dr James Rentoul was both a London county councillor and Conservative M.P. for County Down East. Another spectator whose views would be heeded was the eminent chemist Sir Frederick Abel, the inventor of the Abel petroleum flashpoint test and the explosive cordite, and a scientific adviser to the government.

Lawson followed up his success at the Imperial Institute with an announcement that the Daimler Motor Company had acquired the land and buildings of a large disused cotton mill at Foleshill, Coventry, for the purpose of starting manufacture. It offered 106,000 square feet of space on four floors, steam power to drive machinery, and access to railway sidings and a canal. Before these premises were chosen, Birmingham and Cheltenham had been considered. One wonders what the retired gentry of the Cotswold spa would have thought of the intrusion of Lawson's business ethics and a motor car factory. As for the city councillors of Coventry – who included many members of the cycle trade – they had taken the words of the propagandists to heart. They had recently voted in favour of sending a memorial to the Board of Trade requesting removal of the restrictions on motor vehicles; now they prepared to welcome a new industry.

For Lawson, the decisive consideration was the availability of ready-made factory space. This, he said, would enable manufacture to begin without the delay involved in building on an empty site. A building in being would also, of course, constitute instant reassurance to investors. It would impart an impression of solidity to an otherwise insubstantial enterprise, and it was an immediately realisable asset.

On 13 March the directors of the Daimler Motor Company, together with Frederick Simms, left for Paris and Canstatt ostensibly to study motor factory methods. On the following day the company boldly stated that it intended to enter a Mulliner-bodied car – by implication, though not in fact, a British-built machine – in the Paris–Marseilles race scheduled for July.

While Lawson steadily built up his position and his image, the *Autocar's* petition closed with a total of over 8000 signatures. They represented more than 50 town councils, as well as individuals in all walks of life – from landed proprietors, magistrates and doctors to policemen, cycle dealers and workmen in the cycle industry, to name those who had an interest of some kind in the fate of the motor vehicle.

Trade interests outside Lawson's orbit followed him and Salomons in mounting public demonstrations and exhibitions. On 2 February two Acme Motor Carriage Company engineers drove one of Hewetson's imports from Catford to Eltham – about six miles – over appalling roads. This was the car that was seen at the Imperial Institute two weeks later. On 3 March l'Hollier Gascoigne & Company showed one of their cars, a phaeton, at the Maidstone athletic ground, where it performed at speeds of up to 18 m.p.h. On the 28th they demonstrated a larger machine in Cannon Hill Park, Birmingham.

Although the traction engine interests had yielded the limelight to the motor car, the National Traction Engine Owners' and Users' Association was as determined as ever to press its case. The result was that the new session of Parliament brought notice not of one, but of two Bills to do with road vehicles; which helped to keep the whole subject in the public eye. The first was the Locomotives on Roads Bill, a private measure presented in the Commons by Arthur Griffith-Boscawen on 14 February, and concerned with relaxing the restrictions as they applied to traction engines. Summarised, the Bill proposed a single licence to permit locomotives to operate anywhere, uniformity of by-laws, and the amendment of the 1878 Act in the matter of speed and hours of operation.[11] If the motor car interests failed to get a Bill of their own, this one could be a consolation prize.

The aim of the engine operators in asking for this Bill was to put pressure on the government to take the initiative in reform. The Liberal President of the Local Government Board had promised them a Bill in 1895; now it was time for the Conservatives to follow suit, as they had done in the case of the motor car. That the Bill was a tactical device is clear from what happened: after its first, formal reading the government promptly appointed a Commons select committee on traction engines, and the Bill was dropped. Griffith-Boscawen was appointed to the committee, which sat between March and July 1896. The chairman was Henry Hobhouse (Liberal Unionist, Somerset East), a farmer, local government specialist, and member of the light railways committee of 1895. Among the other select committee members was H.C.F. Luttrell (Liberal, Tavistock), a member of a family of distinguished horsemen. These names recur in the debates on the coming motor car Bill. Furthermore, six members of the select committee on the traction engine Bill sat on another committee that was to judge the motor car Bill. [12] Griffith-Boscawen was one of these, so he had a finger in every pie.

Different though their objects and arguments were, it is impossible to dissociate the two Bills, partly because the content of the traction engines Bill made its fate of particular interest to motor-car partisans, and partly because men judging the one were considered competent to judge the other. So far, only the County Councils Association had perceived a clear distinction between the two types of vehicle; and some individual county councillors still failed to do so.

There was, however, no comparison between links of this nature and the wholly subordinate, even unrecognised, position occupied by private road vehicles when the traction engine had ruled the road. The motor car had come of age. On 23 March Lord Harris, on behalf of the Local Government Board, presented to his peers[13] the Locomotives on Highways Bill; a measure that set a seal on the motor car's independence. A year earlier, a single Bill to deal with both forms of transport had been intended. Since then the motor car had grown in stature so fast that it got a government Bill of its own from the start, while the traction engine was left with a private member's measure that had no immediate prospect of becoming law. Here was another sign that the motor car had "arrived" in Britain.

At this point, before we begin to follow the progress of the Locomotives on Highways Bill through Parliament, it is helpful to look again at the state of public opinion on the motor car, for doing so may explain the turn that the debates took. Comment in the lay press, which was reported *ad lib* in the technical journals, was a reliable indicator of movements of public opinion. Before the end of 1895 comment was infrequent, and with few exceptions favourable. The lay press was ignorant of the motor car, so either did not offer any opinions at all, or echoed those of the motor car's friends. It is significant that, as the latter increasingly publicised their machines through exhibitions and demonstrations, so the praise became diluted with criticism or downright hostility – for all the simultaneous increase in pro-motor-car propaganda. Until then, hostility had had no reason to exist – it had nothing on which to nourish itself. Now, however, people were equipped to make their decisions about the motor car, and the reality was seen to be less attractive than the promise. Furthermore, the visible spread of motor cars awakened prejudices that were as unanswerable as the theoretical arguments of the vehicle's supporters, and just as immune to the facts of the situation. Too much should not be made of the trend – opposition was fitful and diffuse, opinion was divided and fickle, and hostility was generally unorganised – but it was clear for legislators to see.

When talking of the motor car's characteristics, its friends naturally concentrated on its supposed advantages in relation to other, more familiar road vehicles. It was notable, said its partisans, for ease of steering and stopping, and generally for its combination of safety with speed. Everyone agreed that in other than skilled and experienced hands, the horse vehicle was tricky to manage, especially in traffic. The fact was, however, that some of the first motor cars were hard to control at any but modest speeds, and not always then. The design characteristics already noted united with rough, loose road surfaces and steep cambers to make fast, accident-free motoring dependent on skill, strength, endurance, and at least a fair share of luck. Even on an exhibition ground such as the Crystal Palace, some cars struck different observers as being hard to steer and poorly braked.[14]

Reporting of motor accidents, real and imaginary, did nothing to help the vehicle's image. In February 1896 the *Daily Graphic* carried the scare story of a motor car catching fire and burning until "there was nothing left but a black mass of cinders". In June an "explosion" in France was reported under the heading "A Danger from Horseless Carriages".[15] A genuine accident late that month to a De Dion steamer in Paris, in which a wagonette was overturned, was widely and sensationally reported. In fact caused by the horse drawing the wagonette, it was attributed to reckless driving by the motorist. Britain's first motor accident occurred on 17 August, when – as will appear – a Roger-Benz demonstrator taking part in an exhibition on private ground knocked down and killed an Irish labourer's wife.

These stories coincided with the appearance of attacks on the dangers of motor cars, and although only one related to Britain and was accurately reported, all probably contributed to the fears expressed. A columnist in the *Sporting Times* suggested that cars "might blow up". In an obvious attempt to curdle his readers' blood, he added: "Picture for an instant your son or daughter, or your servant, riding or driving a young or timid horse, and being brought suddenly face to face with an infernal machine." A car that was probably T.R.B. Elliot's Panhard produced alarm on the Borders on account of its speed, and its lack of a man in front to calm young horses. In March several Maidstone town councillors reacted to a demonstration in their streets by describing l'Hollier Gascoigne's cars as "dangerous to life". *Punch* picked up the mood in a cartoon that showed a car running away on a hill. Even the *Daily Graphic*, normally sympathetic towards motor cars, celebrated their liberation with a front page cartoon showing pedestrians, cyclists and horses fleeing before them. "The autocar is upon us", lamented the author of a letter to the press in October, demanding protection against the "slaughter" already taking place abroad, if not at home. Another commentator disagreed with such apocalyptic utterances, but his remarks were scarcely more complimentary. An Oldham citizen reported back from a London exhibition to the effect that motor cars reminded him of perambulators; that "they were of the humblest and meanest description, and no one need have any fear of them".

Other voices were raised to challenge the assumption that the motor car would do no harm to the horse and allied interests. Friends of the motor car had done much to encourage such fears: not all had learned to avoid antagonising powerful forces gratuitously. The Lawson camp was the most obtuse, displaying itself at its most insensitive during a public procession of cars at Eastbourne in May 1896. Behind the Daimler Motor Company's machine walked a horse with the letters "R.I.P." on its saddlecloth, attended by a groom carrying a heart-shaped funeral tribute "in loving memory". Even Salomons could tell a newspaper that "in a very short time, horses will have almost disappeared from . . . the chief cities of Europe. Horses will be kept probably only for fashion's sake, and for racing and hunting".

Such propaganda was all too successful – the lay press believed it. The Locomotives on Highways Act was "an Act for the abolition of horses in the public streets".[16] Some representatives of horse and farming interests accepted what they had come to regard as inevitable. "A country gentleman"[17] who remarked that "the purpose of mechanically-propelled vehicles is more or less to supersede the use of horses on common roads" regarded this as a reason not to attack them, but to encourage the most useful types of vehicle. Even the

Leicester Daily Post, which spoke for the heart of the shires, admitted that "the motor car is going to be the vehicle of the future". A long, intelligent and balanced leading article concluded that horses "will be very much disestablished for general purposes".

But not all those interested in horses and the land were so resigned. A reader of the *Field* could not see how agriculture would benefit from the motor vehicle, but could see, he said, how it would be injured: a reduction in the number of horses in use would cut demand for fodder. The *Sporting Times* agreed; and so did the Maidstone Farmers' Club. Unmoved by an address from Walter Arnold, it carried unanimously a motion declaring that the motor car Bill then before Parliament would be detrimental to agriculture.[18] Horse breeding and agriculture would both suffer. The President of the Kingston Shire Horse Society felt the same way about horse breeding. Individual farmers shared these fears; one noted in addition that if horses were superseded, manure for the land would be lost. On at least one occasion, resentment boiled over into violence. In July John Harlow, a drunken cab driver, tried to overtake one of Arnold's cars in Margate, cut in and rammed it. "The road belongs to us", he shouted, "and if you don't get out of the way, I shall smash you up." Properly objective, the local magistrate fined him £1 6s 0d.

Confusion over the true nature of motor cars reawakened one of the oldest fears of all. Despite plentiful reassurance that a horseless carriage caused less damage to roads than four or more pounding hooves, it was equated in some quarters, such as the Council of Central and Associated Chambers of Agriculture, with that notorious road-breaker, the traction engine.

Potentially much more dangerous to the motor car than drunken cab drivers was the appearance of organised opposition from horse-oriented interests. A.R. Sennett, interviewed by the *Saddlers', Harness Makers' and Carriage Builders' Gazette* in April 1896, remarked that the saddle and harness trade, as well as the coach-builders, was taking a deep interest in motor cars. He was right. The *Autocar* reported that "certain of the horse and harness interests are working hard with the view of obtaining the introduction of restrictive clauses [in the Locomotives on Highways Bill]". In the spring the chamber of commerce of Walsall, guided by the town's saddlery interest, had proposed restrictions on the motor car in the guise of promoting public safety. It sought cleverly to draw upon the anxiety already felt over motor cars, at the same time using this to cloak its more selfish interests. Measures much more restrictive than those in the Bill as it then stood were put forward. Drivers of motor vehicles should stop when meeting horses. There should be a speed limit of 8 m.p.h. in towns and 15 m.p.h. in country areas. Non-return speed indicators to catch offenders should be obligatory, as should lights at night and a bell or other audible warning of approach.

By June a Road Safety Association had been formed in the town, under the eminent presidency of Hugh Cecil Lowther, fifth Earl of Lonsdale. Its ostensible aim, as set forth in a letter to the Home Office in July, was to draw attention to the harm that would be done to horsedrawn vehicles and their occupants, and to pedestrians, unless the Bill before Parliament made "reasonable" provisions for their safety. These provisions were by now tougher and more comprehensive. The speed limit should be 6 m.p.h. and 12 m.p.h. in town and country respectively. Cars should give way to horses in narrow roads, and (the earliest mention of such a proposal) they should carry numbers for easy identification by the police. Another provision betrayed the true interests at stake – motor vehicles should not bear a lesser tax burden than horsedrawn vehicles.

Given the general willingness of Parliament and government to accommodate criticism of the Bill, it was fortunate for the motor car movement that the orchestration of hostility seems to have begun and ended in Walsall. The Road Safety Association, a lobby called into being by the Locomotives on Highways Bill, sank from sight when the issue was settled, and passions evaporated with it. The Earl of Lonsdale is next heard of in November, as chairman of a company supplying motor cars,[19] and eventually became President of the Automobile Association.

There had been a few half-hearted attempts to present the motor car as socially acceptable. The comparison here was with road steamers. But the claim was true only of electric vehicles. The petrol car was thoroughly objectionable – most people agreed that it was noisy, that it smelt, and that it vibrated abominably. The *Autocar* went so far as to devote an entire editorial to the vibration problem. It was disingenuous of the *Pall Mall Gazette* merely to emphasise absence in the petrol car of the steamer's smoke, steam and locomotive-type noises when it had a different, but equally nasty, set of habits. "A beastly nuisance" was how it was described;[20] the *St James' Gazette* feared that "buzzing and humming autocars" would ruin the peace and quiet of the countryside. To *The Times*, the motor car's biggest defect was the "stink" of unburned petrol from the exhausts of governed engines.

Beyond this, propagandists for the motor car clung to the arguments that could not yet be proved or disproved, passing over what the vehicle was, in favour of what it would be. There were good reasons for such selectivity. Ignorance, even on the part of the motor car's friends, was one. Another was that they simply did not have the means of delivering the millennium that the promoters promised. The petrol motor car of the middle 1890s was an improvement on what had gone before, but in its current stage of development it was still a mechanical nightmare, wretchedly incapable of filling its allotted role as an agent of social and economic revolution.

The reluctance of belts to transmit power from engine to wheels has already been noticed. Hot-tube ignition burners were liable to be extinguished by wind or rain; when they came into contact with petrol vapour, they caused conflagrations. If they did not keep the tubes sufficiently hot, late ignition and loss of power resulted. If they burned too hot, there was over-heating, pre-ignition and backfiring. The tubes themselves were liable to burst. Even so, this system was more reliable than contemporary battery-and-coil ignition, which was afflicted with faulty insulation, and with accumulators that suddenly lost their charge, or disintegrated.

Because inlet valves were not positively operated, they had to be very light, and therefore broke easily. The inlet valve springs needed to be light, for the same reason; and they, too, broke or lost their tension. The hammering to which valves were subjected spoiled their seating and led to loss of compression; or else they became gummed up and would not work satisfactorily. A regularly used car needed its valves ground in once a week – a job which took two or three hours. Another fruitful source of stoppages was the carburettor float that leaked, and therefore stopped petrol reaching the engine.

More serious was the distortion of cylinder heads, which in the earliest days of the motor car (as now) were cast separately from the block. It was difficult to keep a gas-tight joint between them. Loss of compression was one outcome; others were leakage of hot gases into the cooling water, causing overheating, and of water into the cylinders. The only effective remedy was a machining job, to restore a flush fit.

It is clear that finding adequate materials was a problem. The main lack was of steel alloys that combined lightness, strength and good powers of heat diffusion. Mild steel, a sensational advance when used for the boilers of steam carriages a generation earlier, was no longer equal to its tasks. Iron-reinforced wood frames, a legacy of horse carriage technology, were used for the heavier cars. They distorted easily under the stresses of weight, speed and driving forces. For lack of means of absorbing the resultant flexing in the transmission, gear bearings heated up and wore out in weeks, and the clutch shaft got out of line very quickly. The clutch would then either slip, or become very fierce. Before Panhard adopted an enclosed gearbox for their production cars in 1896, gears were always completely exposed to flying mud and road grit which ground them away remorselessly. Solid rubber tyres could not burst, but they regularly came off at high speed, and had to be wired back on.

Not even the petrol in the tank could be relied on. Leaving aside the care in handling that it needed, it was liable to be sold adulterated with water, or containing dirt, or too "heavy" – non-volatile – for its purpose. If left standing, even petrol that was of the correct specific gravity soon became heavy. In these conditions, the fuel would either never reach the carburettor, or would refuse to vaporise properly.

Petrol of any quality was usually hard to find. J.A. Koosen went first to chemists' shops, where petrol was dispensed as a dry cleaner in small bottles; then he was forced to buy in the only other way he knew – in a quantity of nearly 300 gallons, sold in wooden casks where it evaporated before he could use it. Petrol in practical quantities was obtainable only from refiners such as Carless, Capel & Leonard, or from engine and vehicle suppliers like the Daimler Motor Syndicate, who bought from Carless, Capel & Leonard. It was rather as if nowadays, every motorists in the south-east had to go either to a Thames estuary refinery or to Dagenham whenever he needed to fill his tank. The first motorists had much more excuse for running out of petrol than their modern counterparts.

Workmanship was as defective as materials. In 1896 the *Engineer* described that of a representative cross-section of cars as "about as good as that of a lawnmower". J.A. Koosen called his year-old Lutzmann "old and worn-out". In October 1896 – after restrictions on the motor car had been relaxed, and demand might have been expected to pick up – T.R.B. Elliot got £112 for the Panhard he had bought 10 months before for £250. Defective workmanship may in some cases have been due to simple lack of understanding of the stresses involved, and lack of the skills to deal with them. The same factors may have helped to explain the use of defective materials. One way and another, it is not surprising that Sir David Salomons advised the new owner of a motor car to "have it completely dismantled under his eyes" as a first priority.

Such were merely the most common causes of refusals to start, and of involuntary stops by the roadside. All were noted by motorists and engineers at the time, or very soon afterwards, and therefore accurately reflect contemporary opinion. They must be distinguished from criticisms of early cars made often by the same motorists reminiscing in later life, when they tended to judge the cars of the 1890s by the standards of the 1930s or later. The first petrol motor cars had grave faults, but the comparisons drawn were invidious. Notably unfair were gibes at the difficulty of starting the engine. This was a long and complex process, but the earliest motorists knew no other. Moreover, if all was in order and executed correctly, the engine might fire on the first pull-up of the handle or spin of the flywheel.

The very real problems of the pioneer motorists were exacerbated by punishment from rough roads, and from the hands of the motorist himself. With the exception of a few experimenters and works drivers, there was no such thing as an experienced motorist – all, of necessity, were novices. Ignorance spawned not only mishandling, but also high comedy. On embarking on his maiden drive, a beginner was sometimes defeated before he moved a yard. Without instruction, intelligent men who had never driven anything but horses might forget to put fuel in, or would fill their tanks with kerosene. If they were not told, they might not realise that a petrol tap had to be turned on. Another tyro put his car into gear, let in the clutch, and expected it to move off without his having first started the engine. Complex machinery was not yet a familiar feature of the everyday life of the average man. It would have been illogical to expect him to make the required mental jump that modern man, living with machines since childhood, usually makes automatically even if he is "unmechanical". Every breakdown or failure to start drew down equally uncomprehending ridicule, and sometimes converted a would-be motorist into an anti-motorist.

First cost was another factor to give the intending motorist pause. It is no accident that all the first pioneer private owner-drivers were, at the very least, comfortably off. Many "carriage folk" in Britain hired their turnouts, whether on contract from a jobmaster or for special occasions such as holidays – a carriage of one's own was a sign of real affluence. Cars were not yet available for hire, and the purchase price was higher than for most types of horse carriage. The most elementary form of four-wheeled motoring was provided by the Benz Velo, an example of which Hewetson bought in Germany for a little more than £80. The price of Koosen's Lutzmann was £150. The more sophisticated designs were dearer. Ellis's Panhard dogcart (a four-seater style) cost him about 4800 francs, or around £200. In 1894 prices in the Panhard range varied from £180 for a basic two-seater up to £225 for a four-seater. Peugeots were still more expensive. Salomons' victoria (in horse carriage terms, an open four-seater for town use) cost him £270, while a phaeton of 1894 was priced at the equivalent of £248. By 1895 the Panhard range was more complex. It now extended from a two-seater at £168, through the dogcart at £200 and a phaeton at £212, to a brougham (a closed town vehicle) at

£240. With each style it was possible to specify refinements such as rubber tyres.

T.R.B. Elliot paid a basic £235 for his iron-tyred Panhard; an outlay that went up to £250 with all extras. The *Engineer* and *The Economist* were among those who considered that such prices would severely limit demand for the new vehicles. Such suggestions did not deter those responsible. Addressing prospective shareholders, one manufacturing company prospectus made a virtue of the fact that selling prices were more than twice cost price.

By comparison, good-quality horse carriages of the same types ranged in price at about this period from around £60 for a two-wheeled dogcart (the cheapest variant) and £90 for a one-horse, two-seater phaeton to £145–£160 for a victoria. A good one- or two-horse wagonette – a utilitarian family vehicle seating at least four – cost about £100. To all these prices had to be added the cost of horses, at between £40 and £80 a head, and harness at £10 or more per horse.

As applied to horse carriages, all these terms related to informal, owner-driven vehicles. In motor-car terms, they bore an exactly similar connotation at this time, so like is being compared with like. The reservation that must be made is that there were variants within styles; for example, a phaeton was a good-class open vehicle with either two or four seats, and it is not usually clear which is meant when a car is mentioned. The landau and double brougham, among others, were larger, four-wheeled, four-passenger, two-horse styles driven by a coachman. They were less often copied by car builders, who catered in the early days for the sporting rather than the sedentary owner.

At this time, the only possible point of comparison was capital investment – no one in England could offer reliable or unbiased information on running costs. The only figures available were provided by commercially interested parties or by dedicated propagandists, and were testaments of faith rather than the products of objective scientific tests. Supporters of the motor car could be positive on one point alone; unlike the horse, "it only eats when it works".[21]

Otherwise the only certainty, to an Englishman contemplating the purchase of a car in 1894–6, was that if he chose a French dogcart or phaeton (the cheapest Paris styles), its initial cost would average around 50 per cent more than that of a horse carriage of equivalent type with its horses and harness. Only if one chose a Benz Velo, at the bottom end of the market, or a victoria or some other even more expensive model at the top end, would first costs coincide. When its regular commercial importation and distribution began, even the little Benz lost its edge. When imported by Walter Arnold in 1896, the cost of the Velo, or "Sociable", as he called it – £130 or more –

equalled that of a horsedrawn dogcart or phaeton outfit. Arnold's victoria – a bigger car – was £230. Another large-engined Benz derivative – Léon l'Hollier's imported Roger-Benz dogcart – was priced at £200 in 1895, while his victoria was £275 or more a few months later. The more elaborate Benzes were now as dear as any rivals. If a buyer wanted a car covered by one of Lawson's patents, he paid 10 per cent on top of the factory price by way of freight and royalty. It will be seen that for most buyers a car would involve an additional £70–£80 outlay (say £450 in terms of today's purchasing power) over that on a carriage. This was a prospect to make even the well-to-do look very hard at other considerations, such as smell, noise, vibration and reliability.

Another discouragement, perhaps, was long delay in delivery. Cars could not be bought "off the shelf" in Britain, and a second-hand market did not yet exist.[22] Until a native motor industry got under way, all cars had to be wrung from French or German factories that already had more orders than they could cope with. In October 1895 the Peugeot works announced a delay of four months in the execution of British orders. Henry Hewetson had to wait three months for his Benz, and T.R.B. Elliot five for his Panhard, while J.A. Koosen's Lutzmann took most of the year 1895 to arrive. By the autumn of 1896 Walter Arnold was promising delivery of one of his Benz derivatives within six weeks.

The intending purchaser of a horse carriage, on the other hand, could buy any vehicle of the more popular styles new from a coachbuilder's showroom, or else second-hand. If he wanted more individuality, he could find unpainted vehicles that could be finished in colours to his choice, and even then the waiting time bore no relation to that for a motor car. The very rich could have vehicles built to order, but the delay was then a matter of choice, not necessity.

It was even more difficult to see any good reason to buy a motor tricycle or bicycle, a vehicle that was in a class of its own in every respect. Unlike the motor car proper, it did not offer a serious alternative to an existing vehicle. It fell between two stools. It was in no sense competition for the horse carriage; and while the pedal cyclist may have fancied the idea of mechanical propulsion, the reality was elusive.

First of all, there was a much wider differential between the prices of a motor cycle and a bicycle than between those of a motor car and a horse carriage. Late in 1896 a De Dion tricycle cost £64, while the price of a Hildebrand & Wolfmüller motor bicycle in the spring of 1897 was £50; but a good-quality pedal bicycle could be had for little more than £20, and a cheap import for £12 or less. Moreover, the lure of effortless progress was a chimera. The motor bicycle of the mid-1890s – and later – was very heavy, it was inherently unstable, and it lacked a clutch, which meant that push-starts were the rule. It had no means of gear reduction, and pedal assistance was often needed on hills. For all these reasons, the motor bicycle was a machine only for the athletic and dedicated. The motor tricycle shared most of these disadvantages, and was even heavier.

Furthermore, motor cycles, whether with two wheels or three, suffered from a crudity of construction and a vulnerability to the elements exceptional even for the period. Their mechanism was entirely exposed to rain, mud and grit, and was very close to the road. The Paris–Mantes–Paris motor cycle race of 20 September 1896 highlighted their drawbacks cruelly. Significantly, there were only eight starters, and of these only one – a Duncan & Suberbie – was a motor bicycle, which failed to finish. Even the tricycles – De Dions and Léon Bollées – had a hard time. The weather was vile, and the roads very muddy as a result. Belts and chains quickly became clogged. The Duncan & Suberbie failed on the hills, and collided with a pedal cyclist. In the *Autocar's* view, the race confirmed that motor cycles of all types were unroadworthy, and useless in bad weather. In the opinion of another contemporary, "the attempt to attach motors to bicycles is a mistake."[23]

So the advantages of motor vehicles were revealed to be few and debatable, and their disadvantages manifold and obvious. It seemed to *Engineering* that a motorist had to be either "a very enthusiastic mechanical amateur, or a devoted seeker after notoriety". When the friends of the motor car began to supply information to the public, it cut both ways.

3

The Battle Joined, 1896

Chaplin's Locomotives on Highways Bill, as presented in the Upper House by Lord Harris on 23 March, was a more detailed but even more confusing and much less liberal measure than that of Shaw-Lefevre. Harris announced that the Bill would remove the disabilities that prevented the use, and therefore the manufacture, of motor cars; but it was a weird mixture of sensible forward thinking and built-in contradictions. The core was retained: existing legislation should not apply to vehicles of under 2 tons unladen weight that were not used for drawing another vehicle. For purposes of regulation, the exempted vehicles were to be called light locomotives;[1] and they should be regarded legally as carriages, so bringing them under the "umbrella" of existing regulations covering horse carriages, and confirming the status sought for them so determinedly by their users. Clearly none could be used while the Petroleum Acts were in force; provision was made for separate regulations to deal with the anomaly, notwithstanding the law. The penalty for contravening these regulations would be £2. The power of the Local Government Board to amend the measure, by making regulations governing the use of motor vehicles, was formally spelt out, with provision for a £10 fine if its enactments were disregarded.

But the Bill took away with one hand what it gave with the other. By the extension to motor vehicles of a clause in the 1878 Act covering horsedrawn vehicles and bicycles, county authorities and the City of London would effectively retain powers to make by-laws regulating or prohibiting motor traffic. Beside this invitation to anarchy, the drafters' other more or less inept and ignorant attempts to smooth the Bill's way through Parliament were insignificant. "Light locomotives" should emit no smoke or visible vapour (an impossible requirement); and negligent driving (already, in fact, covered by other legislation) should be punished with a penalty of £10.

The entire measure gave the impression of having been thrown together not only in ignorance but also in haste. The blame is hard to allocate. The Local Government Board was responsible for drawing up the Bill, but it was inexperienced at drafting legislation, and equally ignorant of motor cars. To mend the second deficiency it turned for advice to Sir David Salomons, the most eminent, respected and knowledgeable of the vehicle's partisans, and it was he who drafted the Bill for the Board.[2] As Salomons the diplomat said, "every prejudice had to be considered"; and as for the inconsistencies, they were left to be ironed out in debate.

Until now, Salomons had led and others had followed – in arranging exhibitions, in bringing together those interested in motoring. Now he began to exercise a talent for which he had no rival, and which was more valuable than any – the gift for influencing the wielders of power at the most critical point in the British motor movement's first days. The Bill as it first stood might have grave failings, but everyone was aware of them, and as we shall see, Salomons through the Self-Propelled Traffic Association did more than anyone else to rectify them. He was in a position to do so because he became accepted as an unofficial policy adviser on the issue, and the Local Government Board kept him informed of developments in the innermost circles of power.

The debate began on 23 April, when the Bill had its second reading and was considered by a committee of the whole House. Lord Harris tried to keep the temperature low, emphasising that the Bill was a Liberal legacy, that the motor car was "common" on the Continent and in America (a possibly unwise exaggeration), and that there was no question of doing away with horses. There was "an earnest desire" in the country for such a measure. Harris was well aware of the Bill's shortcomings. In effect, he apologised for it, emphasising that he would consider any amendments and submit them to Henry Chaplin. There was virtually no debate: the *Engineer* had no doubt that this was because motor cars had not yet got such a "pestilent Parliamentary reputation" as traction engines. Lord Clifden registered his support for the Bill, which he said would be of great benefit to farmers. Clifden added that he had himself once ridden to Parliament in a "light engine".[3]

The first positive reaction to the Bill came from London's electric bus interests, in the person of Major S. Flood-Page, one of the backers of Radcliffe Ward's machine.[4] The weight of the batteries would exclude it from the 2-ton limit, and thus from exemption from the law, so Flood-Page applied to Chaplin for a 4-ton limit. Salomons supported his case; so did M.P.s, Arthur Griffith-Boscawen among them, with agricultural interests at heart[5] and farmers themselves, for farm produce would call for heavy load-carriers.

On 19 May the Bill again came before the House of Lords in committee. This time the debate was livelier. Harris reported that Chaplin had agreed to substitute a 4-ton for a 2-ton upper limit on the weight of exempted vehicles. The fine for breaches of the as yet undrafted petrol regulations was increased fivefold to £10, and the redundant clause concerning negligent driving was dropped. Everyone had thus been given something, and Harris insisted that the Local Government Board would accept no further amendments to the Bill in the Lords. Nevertheless, the Board found itself compelled otherwise. As with the 2-ton rule, the provision excluding vehicles hauling trailers from the benefits of the Bill came under attack from both Salomons and from members of the agricultural interest.[6] Freight capacity was only one of the advantages put forward for trailers. Others were more *recherché*. The "country gentleman" already referred to favoured trailers because motor cars were expensive. The "average private individual" owning half a dozen different styles of carriage for different purposes could not be expected to replace them with the same number of cars. A single tractor unit with a choice of trailers was the answer.

On 9 June the amended Bill passed to the Lords Standing Committee on Law[7] for further consideration. There, three formidable Liberal peers went on to the offensive. The Earl of Morley, the Chairman of Committees, spoke on behalf of Lord Thring, a brilliant and abrasive legal reformer; both men were Bill draftsmen. In the teeth of opposition from Lord Harris on behalf of the Local Government Board, they succeeded in incorporating an additional amendment: one towed vehicle should be allowed, so long as the unladen weight of both vehicles together did not exceed the 4-ton limit. The Earl of Kimberley, a former Foreign Secretary and onetime Liberal Leader in the Lords, supported the amendment on the sensible grounds that passengers riding otherwise than in a trailer would find the vibration of the engine intolerable. On the 16th the Bill was read a third time; two days later it went to the Commons after an almost perfectly smooth passage through the Upper House.

With opposition in the country building up and their Bill pursuing an unpredictable course through Parliament, the friends of the motor car had meanwhile intensified propaganda aimed at convincing the powers that be and the public that it was both harmless and practical. Exhibitions were the major weapon – the most important of them large-scale displays lasting for most of the period when the Bill was before Parliament, and concluding only when its fate was decided. In the eyes of company promoters, of course, the principal purpose of exhibitions remained unchanged – to persuade the investing public to part with their money. It was no accident that the most spectacular of the displays mounted by the promoters coincided with new company flotations. To a lesser extent, they gratified the need for self-advertisement that motivated men such as Pennington and Lawson. At the same time, even such men as these recognised the public relations value of successful exhibitions. In this, if in nothing else, they saw eye-to-eye with David Salomons and his friends.

The two most elaborate, ambitious and well-publicised exhibitions opened between critical debates in the House of Lords. In February Salomons announced a Horse, Horseless Carriage and Road Locomotive Exhibition, to open at the Crystal Palace in May. It was Alfred Sennett's idea, and at first Salomons was said to be against it as liable to encourage company promotions. It sought to range horse interests on the motor car's side by embracing horsedrawn as well as self-propelled vehicles. It also took in cycles, so covering all forms of road transport; though the motor vehicles were expected to be the biggest draw. The organising committee was made up of S.P.T.A. members; assistance was given by the Institute of British Carriage Manufacturers and by the Coach Makers' Company, whose Master, the Lord Mayor of London, agreed to perform the opening ceremony.

This he duly did on 2 May; but there was widespread disappointment[8] – "the horseless carriage is more conspicuous by its absence than by its presence." The numbers on display varied. On opening day there were five: Salomons' Peugeot, Elliot's Panhard, a Benz imported by Walter Arnold, Knight's car, and an electric bus – presumably Ward's. Only two gave demonstration runs. In June the Salomons Peugeot, two of Arnold's Benz victorias, and two or three Delmer[9] victorias were usually on show. A Thornycroft steam van later put in an appearance,[10] as did a Delahaye. Rides were provided on two cars, Henry Hewetson charging 1s for two or three minutes on his Benz.[11]

Sir John H.A. Macdonald, the Lord Justice Clerk of Scotland, was a man whose good opinion was valuable, and who was predisposed to favour the new machine. He took a party to the Crystal Palace, but had difficulty in finding any cars at all. He ran them to earth in a shed, with "mechanics and machines looking equally melancholy and unbusinesslike". One car was eventually persuaded to run on the terrace, with much noise, smell and smoke. Macdonald remained confident in motor cars, for the moment. Not so his party, who were understandably unimpressed. Salomons, who gave rides to the most eminent visitors on his Peugeot, had a patchy reception too. Lady Salisbury, wife of the Prime Minister, was delighted with the experience, but nothing would induce her husband to follow suit;

while the Duchess of Albany, widow of Queen Victoria's fourth son and a German princess in her own right, made it clear that she regretted her adventure.

The main reason for the poverty of exhibits at the Crystal Palace was that Lawson had upstaged Salomons a second time. Late in January an International Horseless Carriage Exhibition was announced for the Imperial Institute. It would be opened on 15 May, the first day of the Institute's summer season, by the Prince of Wales. "With this mark of Royal approbation and the influence and backing of the Institute, the horseless carriage movement should be largely benefited." [12] On a far more ambitious scale than the February display on the same site, the exhibition was the responsibility of the Motor Car Club. On its organising committee were Lawson, Rucker, van Praagh, Mace and Simms. H.O. Duncan looked after the practical details. There can have been no doubt of the identity of the interests behind the project, nor of whom it was intended to advertise. The first announcement of the exhibition featured the name of the Queen as patron of the Imperial Institute and the Prince of Wales as president, in such a way as to suggest that they had the same connection with the Lawson enterprise. This device, too, bore Lawson's unmistakable "signature". At the Institute, Claude Johnson, the principal clerk, was put in charge of the exhibition under Sir Somers Vine, the secretary. Johnson had already made has name at the Institute as a genius for organisation. [13] Vine's enthusiasm could presumably be guaranteed, since by April he was a substantial shareholder in the British Motor Syndicate.

There would be medals and £1000 in prizes for the most meritorious exhibits, and daily demonstrations on a specially constructed test track in the gardens. As at the Crystal Palace, all forms of road transport would be shown, including horse carriages and bicycles, but as usual Lawson went one better in announcing that self-propelled agricultural implements, launches, yachts and even "aerial navigation" [14] would be represented.

London and its suburbs were "plastered with posters", [15] and the opening of the exhibition was the most spectacular occasion that the motoring movement in Britain had yet seen. To pre-empt publicity for the opening of Salomons' exhibition at the Crystal Palace on 2 May, Lawson organised two glossy functions at the Imperial Institute for the day before. On 1 May a preview and display of running on the test track was held for the press and members of the House of Lords. The Lords were at this moment between debates on the Locomotives on Highways Bill, so Lawson had a double motive. At least 20 peers turned up, among them Lord Harris and the seventh Earl of Dunmore, who had sponsored Thomson's steamers in the 1870s.

The major attraction was the largest number of motor vehicles yet assembled in Britain. They included a Benz imported by Walter Arnold and driven by Hewetson; Koosen's Lutzmann; Ellis' Panhard; a Peugeot bus; Simms's Daimler; a Kane-Pennington; a De Dion tricycle demonstrated by the Count himself; a Duncan & Suberbie motor bicycle; the first Léon Bollée tricar, driven by its makers; a Bersey electric with its designer at the wheel; and a Serpollet steamer. Among the other exhibits were working models of Lilienthal and Pilcher gliders – currently the most successful heavier-than-air flying machines – and of Hiram Maxim's aeroplane; Maxim's lightweight petrol engine; and a Daimler-powered tramcar.[16]

Koosen "drove different people about all day",[17] but press comment on the preview emphasised the gap between promise and performance. As always, the vibration of the petrol cars was criticised. The Bersey was smooth but slow; the Kane-Pennington was "disappointing", the Serpollet was disliked;[18] and the unfortunate Duncan & Suberbie motor cycle drew scorn and sarcasm. This is perhaps hardly surprising, since the *Engineer* said of the machine that "the return stroke of the piston ... is effected by powerful india-rubber bands stretched on the outgoing stroke".[19] Some of the vehicles shown were over-complicated, most lacked elegance, and the demonstrations were no proper test of their capabilities.

In another attempt to hog publicity, Lawson held the inaugural dinner of the Motor Car Club on the evening of the preview. Among the more distinguished visitors were the Comte de Dion, Sir Frederick Abel, Sir Hiram Maxim and – most significantly – two newspaper proprietors. Sir George Newnes had anticipated Harmsworth as a pioneer of mass-circulation journalism with his *Tit-Bits*, to which Harmsworth's *Answers* had been the challenge.[20] T.P. O'Connor was not only the proprietor of popular newspapers – the *Sun* and *Star* – but was also Irish Nationalist M.P. for Liverpool (Scotland) and a man with a wide circle of influential friends.

On 14 May the Prince of Wales, accompanied by a large suite, paid a private visit to the Imperial Institute in order to open the exhibition. With him were the Duke and Duchess of York, and Prince Edward of Saxe-Weimar. He was conducted round by Evelyn Ellis, and had a ride on the Bersey electric. The Prince of Wales and the Duke and Duchess would come to the exhibition again. Lawson never lacked royal patronage; a symptom of a new situation in which the very rich had become socially acceptable in the highest circles on the strength of their money alone.

On the following day the public were admitted for the first time. They were confronted with the same discrepancy between advertising and facts that the press and peers had encountered. Many of these visitors were eminent men – among them Lord Lathom, the Lord Chamberlain, and Sir John Macdonald, fresh from his disappointment at the Crystal Palace – but this tended only to ensure that the motor car's deficiencies were well advertised. When Macdonald visited the Imperial Institute, only Koosen's car was running. As at the Crystal Palace, there was "much clatter, much smell, much slowing down and expiring sigh".[21] This time, Macdonald had been wise enough to come alone, for it was a day for blind faith rather than for pride in achievement. By mid-June there were no rides at all available. In this sense, if in no other, the Crystal Palace scored over the Imperial Institute.

Several smaller-scale displays of motor vehicles were mounted by Lawson and others country-wide during the passage of the Bill through the Lords. As always, the Lawson interests were the most active. In this respect, the Léon Bollée shown at the Imperial Institute in May was not there long: it was sent off to Coventry, where the Mayor was treated to a highly illegal demonstration run. Simms, accompanied by Harrington Moore, drove his Daimler in the procession at the Eastbourne carnival in May. He made the most of the occasion: little girls bearing miniature red flags pretended to be drawing the car, while behind it came the symbolic – and tactless – horse already referred to. Walter Arnold also participated on one of his Mannheim imports.

The month of May also saw ambitious displays by Anthony George New[22] of a Hildebrand & Wolfmuller motor bicycle. In spite of the machine's crudity and appalling vibration, the intrepid New undertook an 81-mile ride from Woking to Devizes, and then circulated rapidly on the Catford cycle track, covering a mile at over 26 m.p.h.[23] In late May or early June the *Autocar* conducted trials of a Kane-Pennington victoria, motor bicycle and stationary engine at the Nunhead sports ground, Coventry. It was at Coventry, too, on 8 June, that 50 journalists and cycle trade representatives brought from London by special train visited Lawson's factory. H.O. Duncan treated them to a demonstration of a Duncan & Suberbie motor bicycle on the Kenilworth road, a De Dion tricycle was put through its paces, and Edward Joel Pennington showed off a "Humber" motor bicycle.[24] Also in June, a Daimler with a Mulliner body showed the flag at the Royal Agricultural Society's Leicester show. Towards the end of the month a Benz from the Crystal Palace exhibition, belonging to Francis Mulliner, was demonstrated in Blackpool.

Although it was not designed as commercial publicity, an ambitious Continental tour undertaken by Evelyn Ellis in February – the first by an Englishman – attracted considerable attention when reported four months later. The 660-mile route took Ellis through the Alpes Maritimes, where the Panhard successfully negotiated all the hills at which it was set. The total running time was nine days, and the average speed 9 m.p.h. Ellis, by now a sick man, was driven by his ex-coachman, who had been trained at the Panhard works in Paris for six weeks previously. This man may have been the first English chauffeur.

The success of the Imperial Institute exhibition, in terms of numbers of cars, status of visitors and amount of publicity, compared with that of the Crystal Palace, was due to the Lawson organisation's knack for gaining attention and exploiting glamorous promotional devices – a gift not only lacking but also unsought in Sydenham. This flair displayed itself far beyond the gardens and north gallery of the Imperial Institute. The exhibition was but one aspect of a larger design for self-aggrandisement, masked always in grandiose deception and highly coloured language, that had by now moved into high gear. On 17 April the key to the operation – the British Motor Syndicate, with its patent- and licence-buying function – declared a 10 per cent interim "dividend", which must have been paid in shares or out of capital, since the company had no significant outside earnings. By the following month the Lawson camp had bought licences or patents in nearly all the best-known vehicles, and – to be on the safe side – in many obscure but possibly valuable ones as well.

The Kane-Pennington rights came into Lawson's hands at a very early date – after the Daimler licence, possibly by November 1895. The price paid was £100,000. [25] In his role as consulting engineer to the British Motor Syndicate – and therefore as one of Lawson's sources of technical expertise – Frederick Simms visited the principal French manufacturers in the spring of 1896. Shortly after this "window-shopping" expedition, H.O. Duncan, another of Lawson's hired experts, entered into negotiations with two of the builders upon whom Simms had called – the Comte de Dion and Léon Bollée. He and Bollée brought one of the latter's machines over to England for Lawson's inspection early in May. After trying it out at the Imperial Institute, Lawson at once offered £20,000 for the British licence, and arranged to have the car built at the Humber works in Coventry. He paid the same sum for the De Dion tricycle licence.

Bollée and the Comte De Dion both distrusted Lawson. De Dion refused to accept British Motor Syndicate shares in part payment for the licence. For his part, Bollée got his solicitor to vet the documents relating to the sale of his licence. He tried to cash the cheque for £4000 down payment as soon as it was in his hands, but was frustrated because the banks were shut. The rest of his £20,000 was in promissory notes. After concluding the sale, he noticed that Lawson had not signed them, and was extremely agitated until he finally obtained Lawson's signature. Neither Frenchman made any secret of his contempt for Pennington, laughing openly at the claims being made in his advertising. These reflected to the full Pennington's taste for fairground showmanship. A new stunt was a 65-foot leap from a ramp on a motor bicycle. Nothing quite so outrageous was claimed for any other machines under the Lawson wing – when Lawson set out to deceive, he wisely avoided being too specific. *La France Automobile* bewailed the flood of patent rights into Britain, where the fruits of French expertise were being acquired so painlessly; but neither De Dion nor Bollée had any illusions concerning Lawson's real character and intentions.

By this time, too, Lawson had the Bersey and Garrard & Blumfield patents; and at some point he acquired those of William Worby Beaumont, Henry Sturmey and Henry Percy Holt, consulting engineer to Crossley Brothers, whom we last met building a sophisticated little steam carriage of his own. Holt had since patented a steam engine boiler, a method of reducing vibration in vertical-cylinder internal-combustion engines, and a drive in the form of a friction roller acting on a tyre.

Two new Lawson companies were promoted during the Imperial Institute exhibition, taking advantage of the publicity being generated for Lawson's projects and for motor cars in general. The first was the Great Horseless Carriage Company, floated in May for £750,000. The prospectus pulled out all the stops. The liberating Bill had already had its second reading in the Lords; a "Vehicle Revolution" was on the way; "the New Road Railways of the future" would create "a new industry". Accompanying the prospectus was an impressive engraving of "The Motor Mills", the Daimler Company's recently acquired Coventry factory. Part had been sold to the Great Horseless Carriage Company, and here vehicles would be built according to licences bought from the British Motor Syndicate.

The role of the Great Horseless Carriage Company is hard to define. Its publicity described it as a parent company; in other words a company that controlled other Lawson companies. Its advertised purpose was the exploitation of all the Lawson patents so far acquired – Daimler, Pennington, De Dion, Garrard & Blumfield, Bersey, Léon Bollée and the rest – but, as we shall see, neither the Kane-Pennington nor the De Dion licences were in the new company's name, and the Daimler company remained the owner of the Daimler licence and built Daimler cars. The Great Horseless Carriage Company seems, in fact, to have been primarily a provider of premises and plant rather than a manufacturing concern itself. Eventually, Daimlers, Kane-Penningtons and Léon Bollées were the only vehicles put together under the Motor Mills roof. The Daimler Company made its cars in its own part of the Motor Mills. Anyone wanting a Kane-Pennington in 1896 was told to apply direct to Pennington at the Motor Mills, not to the Great Horseless Carriage Company; while most Bollées were sold from another Coventry works by another Coventry Lawson company.[26]

The total cost of the patents to be exploited by the company was £500,000, or two-thirds of the capital.[27] The company's chairman was Lord Winchilsea; the other board members were Lawson, Mace, Ellis, Sturmey, H.H. Mulliner, Gottlieb Daimler, Edward Joel Pennington, the Comte De Dion and two directors of Humber & Company. Among the major shareholders, in addition, were Simms, Rucker and van Praagh. In all, about 3000 shareholders were persuaded to part with their money.

Also in May, it was announced that the Kane-Pennington licence had after all been sold to Humber & Company, a Lawson promotion that already existed. By early June, it was claimed, the first Kane-Pennington motor cycle made in Britain had been completed.[28] Later it transpired that Kane-Penningtons would also be built by T. Coulthard & Company of Preston, who had acquired a licence too.[29]

In mid-June the New Beeston Cycle Company was floated for £1 million. It would make bicycles, and also "self-working bicycles and tricycles", the tricycles being De Dions, manufacturing rights for which had just been acquired by the British Motor Syndicate. The Quinton Cycle Company, a Lawson acquisition, would make these machines as well. In the announcement of the new flotation, it was asserted that self-propelled cycles were "untouched by prohibitive legislation" – an impertinence, exceptional even for Lawson, that anyone from Sir Thomas Parkyns onwards could have contradicted. The prospectus itself was rather more circumspect – the company's products would be "cycles with auxiliary power" – but the attempt to mislead was still there. Lawson's stake in the new company was £5000; the other directors were the former racing cyclist Frank Shorland, sales manager of Humber & Company; Thomas Robinson; Lord Norreys, President of the Road and Path Cycling Association; and Harry Hewitt Griffin, editor of the *Wheelman and Motorcar Weekly*.

Initially, press comment on Lawson's empire-building was in general friendly. The *Financial News* was more than that: it positively slavered over the prospects awaiting investors. On the occasion of the opening of the Imperial Institute exhibition, it said: "It seems as if we were on the eve of the inauguration of a very great industry, which will not only be profitable in itself, but will augment the profits of innumerable other industries .... Just as the construction of railways opened a magnificent field for investment, this new industry may do the same." This journal's remarks on the Great Horseless Carriage Company promotion might have been written for the prospectus itself, and Pennington's extravagances were accepted at face value. Some of the Imperial Institute exhibits were "capable of covering a mile in less than a minute, and one, at least, able to fly through the air by the use of an inclined plane".

The *Star*, a gossipy, lightweight scandal sheet, crowned half a page of praise for Lawson with the prophecy that he would receive a knighthood. *To-day*, reporting the inaugural dinner of the Motor Car Club, was scarcely less enthusiastic. Lawson was "engaged in a national work that should bring him the national gratitude ... it is largely owing to him that Parliament has been moved to give [the motor vehicle] fair play".

Even so, by May 1896 Lawson evidently felt that he needed a press voice that was totally committed to his interests. On the 23rd there appeared the first issue of the *Wheelman and Motorcar Weekly*, incorporating *English Sports* and a cycling journal, the *Amateur Wheelman*. The motoring content – the *Motorcar Weekly* – took the form of a supplement at the end of a much longer cycling section, the *Amateur Wheelman*. Its editor, Harry Hewitt Griffin, had spoken at the launching of the S.P.T.A. in December 1895, and was now a director of the New Beeston Cycle Company. The proportion of Lawson-derived advertising in the *Motorcar Weekly* was overpowering; its editorial matter was largely given over to Lawsonian press releases and more or less illiterate stories of Lawson-inspired events, varied occasionally by spirited defences of speculative company promotion. Sir David Salomons contributed an article in the first issue, but no more.

Dissident voices were few, and, Salomons apart, were largely confined to specialist journals with limited circulation, known to be out of sympathy with Lawson's attitudes and methods. The *Engineer* said in June: "The time has come when we should speak out and warn the public asked to take shares in companies being formed to supply horseless carriages of all kinds, that no vehicle is yet on the market which is free from radical faults of construction." *Engineering*, already lukewarm towards motor vehicles in general, was virulent on the subject of Lawson: "The credulity of the investing public seems inexhaustible; no bait is too coarse, no lure too ill-concealed, to attract victims." Buyers of shares believed that "vulgar self-assertion and business shrewdness must always go hand in hand". It was no use trying to convince them otherwise – gambling was a basic human trait. There was argument over how successful the Great Horseless Carriage Company flotation had been. At the end of June the *Autocar* insisted that over half of the share issue had been subscribed – not, one would have thought, anything to be proud of, remembering the triumph of the Daimler promotion – but other estimates ranged as low as £9000 in the case of the *Sketch*.[30] Neither was the New Beeston Cycle Company issue fully subscribed: by October 1897 only £574,000 worth of shares had been taken up.

However, these clouds on Lawson's horizon were so inconspicuous that he could afford to ignore them. In practical terms, it mattered little if the share issue was not fully subscribed – the only major form of expenditure that involved money passing out of the hands of Lawson and his friends was the purchase of more patents, and most of those that they would buy were already in their hands. Aside from a minimum allocation for window-dressing, the rest of the money was destined for their own pockets.

Old rivals for the limelight were beginning to fade. After his exhibition at the Crystal Palace closed, Salomons organised no others. He was a behind-the-scenes political "fixer" first and foremost, and lacked Lawson's commercial incentive to mount exhibitions. Not one to shun publicity, he may also have become weary of being constantly upstaged by Lawson. As for the *Engineer*, it fell victim in June to its own perfectionist policy. It believed that no car should be run publicly, let alone put on sale, until it was fully developed. Also, although petrol cars had been admitted to the *Engineer* competition, that journal was still against them. The competition had been scheduled for October 1896. Alfred Sennett asked for a postponement. The aim of the contest was to encourage British constructors, he said, but their cars were not ready. The *Engineer* agreed. Announcing a postponement to 1897, a leader asserted that none of the vehicles so far shown to the British public was suitable for public use. Kerosene-powered vehicles were few, and the Petroleum Acts still made the rest illegal. All were noisy and smelly, and their vibration was "simply intolerable".[31] Furthermore, the Locomotives on Highways Bill might not become law in the current session of Parliament, particularly if more amendments were introduced. *Engineering* felt the same way about the offerings of constructors: "The motor carriages yet designed are extremely impractical."

With the Locomotives on Highways Bill off to a good start at Westminster, other entrepreneurs became increasingly confident of imminent profit from motor vehicles. Most of the names were familiar, but now they were formalising and expanding their operations. In February the first Roots & Venables kerosene car – still a three-wheeler, but more substantial than the tricycle of 1892 – was road-tested. Early in June a new car, a four-wheeled two-seater with rubber tyres, was seen near Horley in Sussex. In April 1896 Walter Arnold and Henry Hewetson had joined forces formally, to import and sell the Benz from Mannheim. Arnold was the senior partner – the business was called the Arnold Motor Carriage Company, with premises at East Peckham; the Acme car was renamed the Arnold; and Hewetson became sales manager.

By April also, two firms new to the field were interesting themselves in motor vehicles. New & Mayne, electrical and laundry engineers of Woking, Surrey, were importing the Hildebrand & Wolfmüller motor bicycle from Germany. They said that they would be ready to supply electric vehicles, too, by about the end of May. Bicycles and two- and four-seater "sociables" would be available.[32] By early September New & Mayne had "several" Hildebrand & Wolfmüller motor cycles in course of construction.[33] The other newcomer, Lister & Co. of Keighley, claimed to have delivered a car for export, but details of it are lacking.

Public companies were promoted independently of Lawson. In May the London Electric Omnibus Company solicited the public's money for the purpose of operating Radcliffe Ward's buses – £170,000 worth of shares were made available, out of a total capitalisation of £250,000. The company was floated by William Marshall, a mining and electrical engineer who had been financing Ward, and he became deputy chairman under Major S. Flood-Page. In June the Britannia Motor Carriage Company was floated for £100,000, to make electrics of the kind already mentioned. By July they were said to be "inundated with orders", but would not deliver any cars until the Bill had become law. Such honesty was foreign to most company promotions.[34]

While the oldest friends of the motor car were waiting for it to be perfected on the test bench, the more enterprising and realistic Lawson was at his peak: everything had been going his way. Parliament, even Salomons himself, were doing much of the promoters' work for them. A Commons Select Committee on Petroleum met for the first time late in March 1896. Its chairman was Anthony John Mundella, Liberal Member for Sheffield Brightside and a former President of the Board of Trade. He was a self-made Nottingham manufacturer of radical views on social and educational reform, and (as it turned out) a friend of the motor car.

Sir David Salomons memorialised the Home Office on the subject of petroleum, and contrived to have himself called as a witness before the committee. Its findings were bound to influence the new regulations allowed for in the Locomotives on Highways Bill, and Salomons intended that they should fit the needs of the motoring movement. On 24 June he underlined to the committee the need for sufficient national stocks of oil, and pleaded the case for petrol. He stressed in particular the usefulness of delivery vans such as those in use in Paris, and said that Whiteley's store in London had ordered one. Motor vehicles should be allowed to carry an adequate supply of petrol – up to 40 gallons, Salomons suggested. It was of significance for the future, though of no immediate relevance, that he also recommended a speed limit – 12 m.p.h. The most influential witness before the committee was Colonel Sir Vivian Majendie, H.M. Chief Inspector of Explosives since 1871 and the country's leading authority on petroleum. Salomons later described him as "a great stumbling block" – he seemed anxious to help the motor car, but would not be convinced that petrol could be stored safely otherwise than under the existing laws.

Salomons was having to work just as hard behind the scenes of the House of Commons itself. There, the Locomotives on Highways Bill still faced many vicissitudes. It had its first reading on 18 June – a formality, as usual; debate was reserved for the second reading. This was always more time-consuming. The Commons were very busy, and although the Lords had considered the Bill first, there was concern that it might not become law in the current session. According to the *Autocar*, it was among 35 Bills that "may or may not be dealt with". But a week later the prospects were brighter: another measure had been temporarily withdrawn. On the 24th Cumming Macdona wrote to Salomons with the gist of a conversation he had had with Chaplin. The President of the Local Government Board was "most anxious to expedite the passage of the Bill, and will do all in his power to carry it into law at once". Most important, "the matter has been discussed most keenly in the Cabinet, and all are unanimous to further its purposes."

This was just as well, for on the occasion of the measure's second reading in the Commons on 30 June, "the attitude of the members was unfriendly".[35] In anticipation of this, Chaplin's key speech in moving the second reading was deliberately cool in tone, while being positive. The aim of the Bill was "to afford the public a convenient and cheap mode of transport". There was an appeal to chauvinism, always likely to evoke sympathy at a time when Britain was politically isolated in the world. Britain was "greatly behind other countries", and the chief patents were "entirely in the hands of foreigners". The result was "a great reproach against ourselves". The Bill would develop "a very great trade ... and give a vast amount of employment". It would also be "a great advantage and boon to the agricultural interest", and would not depress railway passenger fares.[36] The Bill could not, therefore, be regarded as contentious, particularly since a similar measure had been introduced by the previous government.[37]

Chaplin needed all his powers of persuasion. Irish Nationalists opposed the Bill with arguments that may or may not have been sincerely meant, but even if their motives were as usual entirely ulterior, the violence of their reaction may well have encouraged members with genuine, if ill-formed fears to express them. Dr Charles Tanner (Mid-Cork) launched himself into a tirade full of irrelevance, ignorant prejudice and racist abuse, tinged with a hint of reason and an Irishman's concern for horse-flesh. Motor vehicles could not help agriculture; they were expensive and "bound to break down in a fortnight". Abroad, attempts were being made to put a stop to "this good old Semitic craze". Chaplin, supposedly a friend of the horse, had become "a tout for these non-sporting machines", which were "antagonistic to horse-flesh and therefore to genuine sport". Four-ton vehicles would harm the roads, and all would cause unemployment – Tanner had heard a cabman outside the Commons voice the hope that Chaplin would not "vote for those blessed autos". Tanner's comrade in arms, John Daly (Monaghan South), a county and district councillor, agreed that motor vehicles would do away with horse breeding, one of Ireland's staple industries.

Others were against the Bill as it stood. Among them was A.C. Humphreys-Owen (Liberal, Montgomery), a landowner and chairman of the Cambrian Railway, who – in common with John Daly – was under the impression that traction engines were under discussion, and lamented what appeared to be proposals for wholesale removal of restrictions on them. Henry Hobhouse supported the Bill on principle, but fearing road damage, objected to the 4-ton limit; 2 tons was better. C.B. Renshaw, the Conservative Member for Renfrew West and influential Chairman of the Scottish County Councils Association, felt in the same way. However, A.J. Mundella, who was currently chairing the petroleum committee, was unreservedly in favour of the Bill. He had "seen those autocars working with the greatest facility and freedom from incident in the south and west of France", and was convinced that there was "a vast industry in auto-motor cars" in the future. R.B. Martin, a banker and Liberal Unionist Member for Mid-Worcestershire, and the horse-loving H.C.F. Luttrell both agreed.

The Bill was given its second reading, but it was far from out of the wood yet, for on 10 July it went to the Commons Standing Committee on Law[38] for detailed consideration and amendment. Salomons had listened to the debates in the House, and anticipated the critical debate in the Standing Committee with a careful memorandum to the Local Government Board and Home Office which, in effect, laid down tactics for government supporters of the Bill. While warning against some clauses and suggesting amendments to them, he at the same time recommended concessions to the other side. He suggested that the words "except from an exceptional or temporary cause" be added to the total ban on visible steam and smoke, and also asked for provision in the Bill for appeal to the Local Government Board should local authorities use the powers given them in the Bill to deny roads and bridges to motor traffic. The most controversial among the various points raised was the maximum weight to qualify for exemption from the existing Acts.[39] As a *quid pro quo*, the weight limit should be reduced to 3 tons, provided that this did not include fuel, water or batteries. The proviso should be added whatever the weight limit adopted, since a vehicle's load could not logically include the means by which it moved itself. Henry Chaplin told Salomons non-committally that he would be happy to give the recommendations his careful attention.

Salomons' concern for the Bill foreshadowed all too accurately its fate at the hands of the Commons. In other respects the auguries looked good. Fifteen M.P.s who had shown a particular interest in the Bill were added to the Commons Standing Committee on Law for the occasion of the debate on the Bill, and two-thirds were known to be more or less friendly towards the measure. They included Chaplin, his Parliamentary Private Secretary T.W. Russell, Macdona, Griffith-Boscawen, Mundella, Renshaw, Martin and the confused Humphreys-Owen. Luttrell was already on the committee. The Bill's only known enemies on the committee were the Irish Nationalists Tanner and Daly, and their motives in opposing it would have been highly suspect.

But a simple head count would have been misleading. There were, after all, more than twice as many other M.P.s on the committee whose views were unknown. Furthermore, we now find even the friends of the Bill adding restrictive amendments wholesale, and attempts to liberalise the measure twice being defeated in divisions. This suggests not only ambivalence in the attitudes of supporters, but also the presence – confirmed by Salomons' memorandum – on the committee and in the House at large of a powerful body of hostile, if unorganised and so far silent, opinion.

Chaplin's "carrot" of a 3-ton instead of a 4-ton exemption limit, suggested by Salomons, was accepted by the committee. The voting was three to one in favour of the reduction. Accepted, too, was Chaplin's *quid pro quo* to the effect that the figure should not include fuel, water or batteries. Humphreys-Owen's recommendation that the weight should include any trailer was rejected. Griffith-Boscawen and Luttrell tried in different ways to ease the Bill's strict ban on smoke and vapour emission, but Luttrell's motion was convincingly defeated. The planned compromise, inspired by Salomons and put forward by Griffith-Boscawen, was accepted – there shall be no emissions other than from a "temporary or accidental cause".

But that was far from the end of it; in his memorandum, Salomons had not foreseen the full extent of the opposition to the Bill. The battle swung to and fro. Sidney Gedge (Conservative, Walsall) failed when he tried to introduce a speed limit of 12 m.p.h. in the country and 6 m.p.h. in towns. T.W. Russell won a major point of principle in securing the deletion of the proposal to give county councils blanket authority to regulate or prohibit motor traffic, and J. Parker-Smith (Liberal Unionist, Partick) failed to reverse this decision. But the Solicitor-General, Sir Robert Finlay (Liberal Unionist, Inverness Burghs) – one of the few original members of the committee to speak – obtained another provision that enabled the counties to make by-laws closing bridges. Finlay also asked for, and got, amendments giving the Local Government Board power to regulate the construction – as well as the use – of motor vehicles, and to apply its regulations locally as well as nationwide.

These amendments were duly incorporated in the Bill. The Standing Committee moved fast, reporting back to the Commons on the same day as it convened; 10 July. In the Commons on 30 July the committee's amendments were debated, with the Bill coming under still heavier fire. Chaplin was against any speed limit.[40] Luttrell proposed one of 14 m.p.h., but even this was too high for Members. When Thomas Lough (Liberal, Islington West) spoke in favour of 10 m.p.h., four other Members rose to support him in one degree or another – B.L. Cohen (Conservative, Islington East); John Wharton (Conservative, Ripon), the Chairman of Durham County Council; Sir John Dorington (Conservative, Tewkesbury), the Chairman of Gloucestershire County Council; and Henry Llewellyn (Conservative, Somerset North). The 14-m.p.h. figure was accepted only when Sir Robert Finlay suggested a rider to the effect that the Local Government Board regulations should be empowered to reduce it.

The spectacle of Conservative backbenchers defying their leaders was to be expected. Both Shaw-Lefevre and Chaplin had emphasised that the issue was bipartisan. To them, this signified that all good

Liberals and all good Conservatives ought to support the Bill; but the absence of a party whip also implied freedom to oppose it with impunity. One therefore finds M.P.s who might have kept silent, in an age of increasingly strict party discipline, voicing their inmost opinions – usefully for the historian, to whom the existence of such views is otherwise a matter of conjecture and deduction. It will be seen, too, that county councillors were now far from unanimous in favouring the motor car, notwithstanding the friendliness of their association a year earlier.

Luttrell asked for a clause making lights compulsory. In the standing committee a similar proposal from Chaplin had been rejected, but it was now agreed to, the Local Government Board being left to make detailed regulations. Luttrell wanted motor vehicles to carry a bell or some other means of warning; Chaplin did not, but Luttrell got his way. However, when the Member for Tavistock tried to reinstate the 4-ton maximum and to allow motor cars to emit visible vapour, he was defeated. Lough claimed that Luttrell was trying to "make these cars twice too heavy, to let them go too fast, and to encourage them to pump out steam". Commander G.R. Bethell (Conservative, Holderness) wanted county authorities to have full powers to control motor traffic on bridges, without the possibility of appeal to the Local Government Board. This amendment, too, was allowed. Chaplin himself proposed, and obtained, one further restriction: on application from a local authority, the Local Government Board would be able, if safety required it, to restrict the use of motor cars in the area concerned.

At the same time, Chaplin carried a crucial amendment that regained much of the ground lost to the opposition: regulations made by the Local Government Board should take effect notwithstanding by-laws made by local authorities. This meant that at the end of the day, the central authority of the Local Government Board would prevail over all expressions of regionalism, whether originally approved by the board or not.

Another amendment of Chaplin's imposed an excise duty on motor vehicles, at the rate of £2 2s 0d per vehicle of between 1 and 2 tons unladen, and £3 3s 0d above 2 tons. It did not affect most private motor cars, which generally weighed well under a ton; its object was to penalise heavier vehicles. The separate carriage duty, as first demanded by the Customs and Inland Revenue Act of 1888, would remain. This revenue went to the county councils; so would the proceeds of the new, discriminatory imposition. Lough, Luttrell and Bethell, who agreed on almost nothing else, joined forces in attacking it – "the men who were making this start were public benefactors" whose enterprise would be discouraged by any clause that made motor car ownership more expensive. A uniform fine of £10 was proposed for any breach of a Local Government Board regulation, local by-law or provision of the Bill. Finally, the measure would come into force within three months of receiving the royal assent. The purpose of this provision was to give the Local Government Board time to draw up its regulations supplementary to the Act.

The Local Government Act of 1888 had made lights and some form of audible warning of approach compulsory for cycles, so it was natural for these rules to find their way into the motor car Bill. At the same time, the correspondence between the Commons amendments and the demands of the Road Safety Association for lights, bells, a speed limit and a tax on motor vehicles is significant, particularly when one notes the activity on the standing committee of the Member for Walsall.[41] It is remarkable that one small, local pressure group should so influence Parliament. That it seems to have done so is, perhaps, a measure of the government's lack of confidence in dealing with a still-unfamiliar subject. This is comparable with its matching willingness to fall in with the recommendations of individual campaigners on the other side, such as Sir David Salomons.

J. Parker-Smith wanted all Local Government Board regulations on construction and use to be confirmed by Parliament. But Chaplin had had enough, alike from the Bill's enemies, from its faint-hearted friends, and from mavericks such as Luttrell. The end of the session was close at hand, he said, and the Bill had to have time to make its regulations. If these were subject to the delay involved in obtaining Parliament's approval, there was a danger that "the manufacturers of the new vehicles, who were looking forward with the greatest anxiety to the passing of this Bill", would find that there was no use for their vehicles before the next session of Parliament. Regulations might be shown to Parliament for its comment, but that was all. On 3 August the Bill had its third reading in the Commons, and on the following day went back to the Lords with its amendments.

But the Bill was "over the hump" by 30 July: from now on its course lay downhill. On 10 August Lord Harris moved acceptance of the Commons amendments. The little opposition that arose was in favour of more liberality towards the motor vehicle, not less. Lord Glenesk, the Conservative owner of the *Morning Post*, held that "a desire to check this new enterprise was manifested in the amendments". He particularly disliked the excise duty for its probable effect in this direction.[42] So did Lawson's man, Lord Winchilsea. There was no tax on wagons and horses used in agriculture – "an industry everyone is trying to relieve" – and such an imposition would inhibit the usefulness of motor vehicles in agriculture. Winchilsea also regarded the 14-m.p.h. limit as restrictive. But the Lords gave the government the Bill it wanted, and the royal assent followed on 14 August.

The Locomotives on Highways Bill bore little resemblance to the sketchy, dashed-off Bill from which it sprang. Even so, it is more easily summarised than the complicated Locomotive Acts of the past that had tried to cover every possible eventuality without benefit of devolution to such bodies as the Local Government Board and Home Office:

Existing legislation not to apply to vehicles of less than 3 tons weight unladen (or 4 tons if another vehicle was drawn). Unladen weight not to include fuel, water or batteries. Such vehicles to be called light locomotives.

Light locomotives to be so constructed that no smoke or vapour should be emitted other than from a temporary or accidental cause.

Light locomotives to be regarded in law as carriages.

A bell or some other audible warning of approach to be carried.

Lights to be carried: the Local Government Board to provide detailed regulations.

Maximum speed 14 m.p.h., or less as Local Government Board regulations stipulated.

The storage and use of petroleum on light locomotives to be governed by Home Office regulations to follow, the petroleum Acts notwithstanding.

The Local Government Board empowered to make regulations regarding construction and use, to be applicable either locally or nationally. Such regulations could be requested by local authorities for the prohibition or restriction of traffic in the interests of safety.

County councils to have power to regulate the use of light locomotives on their bridges.

Penalty for breach of any provision of the Act, or Local Government Board or Home Office regulation, to be £10.

Excise duties on light locomotives (in addition to carriage duty): £2 2s 0d for vehicles of between 1 and 2 tons; £3 3s 0d over 2 tons. (No excise duty on vehicles lighter than 1 ton.)

The Act to be applicable to Scotland and Ireland as well as England and Wales, with the Secretary for Scotland and the Irish Local Government Board exercising the powers of the Local Government Board for England and Wales.

The Act to come into force at the end of three months from the date of the royal assent.

The reaction among interested parties to the passing of the Bill into law was predictable. In a letter to the press, Sir David Salomons combined self-satisfaction with instruction in a manner that showed him in his worst light. He appropriated all the credit for the Act, reminding his readers how the government had accepted his recommendations; and he appealed for prudence and consideration from motorists, especially in relation to alarming horses, damaging roads, and handling petrol. There was a great deal of truth in his claims for himself, but his manner of asserting it was peculiarly unattractive.

Engineering, by contrast, was the opposite of complacent. The Act was characterised by an "absence of proper and necessary restrictions". The 14-m.p.h. speed limit was "licence run mad", and would "lead to disaster" – motor cars were unsafe at half that speed. However, the very failings of the Act gave the Local Government Board and local authorities the opportunity and the incentive to nullify it; and in any case, "the high-speed motor car is, for the present, a craze" – the real future lay with goods vehicles. The *Autocar* was agitated too, but for diametrically opposed reasons. It disliked any provision for a maximum speed, because different circumstances demanded varying speeds, and, anyway, no onlooker could estimate speed accurately. The excise duty was bad because it discriminated against motor vehicles. At the same time, like *Engineering* at the opposite pole, the *Autocar* suspended final judgement until the Local Government Board produced its regulations, for these could change the picture completely.

It is time now to retrace our steps to the campaigns being waged outside Parliament during the later stages of the struggle inside it. As the battle moved from the Lords to the Commons, the motor car interests kept up their publicity work. From time to time Lawson tried to maintain the momentum of his Imperial Institute exhibition with special occasions and demonstrations. On 10 June the Motor Car Club held a reception at the Institute in aid of Guy's Hospital. The Prince of Wales returned, and 4000 people are said to have attended. A display of running was mounted at the same time. The dozen or so participants – presumably all the exhibits that were in running order – included Ellis's Panhard, Koosen's indefatigable Lutzmann, and a newcomer in the shape of a Roots & Venables vehicle.

In the first week of July H.O. Duncan brought over another Léon Bollée from France. He drove it 24 miles from Victoria Station, London, to Harmondsworth, on the Bath road near Slough, then returned to show it off to Henry Sturmey and others in and around the Imperial Institute. From Kensington Duncan drove Lawson to his home in Hampstead. In spite of the din the Bollée made, it apparently avoided the attention of both horses and police. The car was then taken by rail to Coventry, and was driven about the Midlands in search of steep hills to test its capabilities.

On 8 August Lawson staged another demonstration run, this time to the Harrods furniture store at Barnes, where there was room to show the cars off. Taking part were two Daimler victorias, a Peugeot bus, Koosen's Lutzmann, the De Dion tricycle and the Duncan & Suberbie motor bicycle, all from the Imperial Institute.

Salomons, too, arranged an exercise, in connection with his Crystal Palace exhibition. He had issued invitations to leading members of the French and recently founded Belgian automobile clubs, and to Peugeot, Delahaye and Serpollet among motor manufacturers, to a reception and demonstration at the Hurlingham polo club ground on 15 July. The visitors would travel thence in cars from the Crystal Palace exhibition. As 2 m.p.h. was not a practicable speed, and Salomons did not believe in baiting the law, he sought and obtained special dispensation for the trip from the London County Council and the Metropolitan Police. Sir Edward Bradford, the Commissioner of Police, was "most considerate and broad-minded."[43] The Peugeot, the Serpollet, the Delahaye, an Arnold, a De Dion tricycle, and newcomers to the Crystal Palace in the shape of four of l'Hollier Gascoigne & Company's Roger-Benz derivatives made the journey. The display ground offered firm going and no gradients, allowing a successful two hours' evolutions. On the 16th and 17th, Salomons entertained his distinguished foreign visitors back at the Crystal Palace.

But again, the brash promoter promptly stole the high-minded idealist's thunder: it is really no wonder that Salomons felt persecuted. No sooner had Salomons finished entertaining his guests than Lawson and his Motor Car Club took them back to the Hurlingham polo ground on six cars from the Imperial Institute. According to Harrington-Moore the journey down crowded Kensington High Street and across Hammersmith Broadway was without incident. Horses took hardly any notice, and his Daimler was an "object of general admiration". The Koosens' Lutzmann, the Peugeot bus and Ellis's Panhard took part as well; though the Lutzmann disgraced itself on the return journey – "something went wrong with the works, so we took a hansom."[44] After the demonstration, Lawson in his turn entertained the foreign visitors at the Imperial Institute.

Both big exhibitions were over by mid-August, by which time, too, the Bill had run its course through Parliament; and both ended on a depressed note. It was announced that none of the awards offered at the Imperial Institute would be presented: the reason given was that the cars could not be properly judged off the public road. In the context of Motor Car Club ethics, this sounds more like an excuse for making economies. The Crystal Palace exhibition was dogged by misfortune to the end. On the 17th it had the melancholy distinction of being the scene of Britain's first fatal motor accident. There were signs in the Crystal Palace grounds warning visitors to "Beware of Horseless Carriages", but when a Roger-Benz came motoring down the terrace – one of three cars on it at the time – Bridget Driscoll, a Croydon labourer's wife, hesitated in its path. She was knocked down and fatally injured. Some witnesses claimed that the car was going too fast at the time, passing another car; for the driver, Arthur James Edsell, of l'Hollier Gascoigne & Company, it was said that he was doing 4 m.p.h. and sounding his warning bell. The verdict was accidental death.

While the Imperial Institute and Crystal Palace exhibitions fought to retain public interest, the struggle for the Bill was reaching its climax, and lesser displays multiplied. The slickest was not a Lawson inspiration, but that of l'Hollier Gascoigne & Company, who on 10 July demonstrated a Roger-Benz in Palace Yard, Westminster, before members of the Commons Standing Committee on Law who were meeting on the Bill that day. Although there were the usual complaints of vibration and smell, "scores" of distinguished Parliamentarians were said to have taken the opportunity of riding in the car.[45] Among them were Sir James Fergusson, chairman of the Committee; H.H. Asquith, a former Liberal Home Secretary and future Prime Minister; J.M. Maclean (Conservative, Cardiff District), a journalist and part-owner of the *Western Mail*; the Duke of Norfolk, England's premier duke; and the Marquess of Lorne, son-in-law of the Queen, a relation by marriage of the Dukes of Sutherland, and heir of the Duke of Argyll.

On the 11th the Daimler Motor Company bore its flag further afield than usual. The Daimler that had carried the Prince of Wales at the Imperial Institute in February was now in the hands of John T. Clark, an Aberdeen coachbuilder who had made bodies for the Queen. He had been appointed local agent for the Daimler Motor Company, and had fitted one of his bodies to his motor car. With Otto Mayer and distinguished local personages in tow, he drove up Deeside, giving rides to other local worthies on the way. Crowds gathered everywhere. The night was spent at Ballater, Clark's home. On the following day the party were invited to demonstrate their car at Balmoral before the royal household; an invitation carrying much prestige, even if it was only the housekeeper who took a ride in the grounds. Including the return to Aberdeen, 125 miles were covered in two days, and between 5 and $5\frac{1}{2}$ gallons of fuel were used. There were apparently no breakdowns. Speeds of over 20 m.p.h. were claimed, though without repercussions. The Daimler was exhibited in Aberdeen, on one occasion ferrying the Lord Provost from his home to the town hall; and Clark gave a lecture to the local engineering society. The Daimler was on display again at the Royal Highland and Agricultural Society's show at Perth at the end of July, where it won a silver medal.

The Lawson interests were busy displaying their wares further south, too. At the beginning of August Clark's Daimler appeared at the Scarborough Sports, Games and Industrial Exhibition. In mid-July the Léon Bollée that had been exercising around the Imperial Institute was back in the Midlands, being seen in Warwick and Stratford on the occasion of the Humber company works outing. But on the 17th it was totally destroyed when the Humber works burned down. Also lost were an English-built tricar in course of construction, and all the drawings. Duncan was sent post-haste back to Le Mans for a replacement vehicle. After delays while the nervous Léon Bollée waited for Lawson's cheques to be cleared, Duncan returned with a new car. It was necessary for Lawson to be seen to be still in business; it was announced, furthermore, that manufacture of the Léon Bollée would be transferred to the Motor Mills.

Other owners and entrepreneurs were busy as well. The Provost of Perth had asked T.R.B. Elliot to demonstrate his Panhard at the Royal Highland and Agricultural Society's show. So keen was the Provost that he used his influence with 14 separate police authorities to enable Elliot to drive the 125 miles from Kelso to Perth. Elliot was glad of any help he could get, for the going was hilly and the journey slow. It took $1\frac{1}{2}$ days, the 50 miles to Edinburgh alone occupying nine hours. Once it had arrived, both the Lord Provost and the president of the show, the Marquess of Breadalbane, took rides in the car.[46] Around the middle of July a French Millet motor bicycle, the British licence for which had been acquired by A.R. Greville, was being shown off at Towcester.

For his part, Walter Arnold was active in Kent. Alfred Cornell, a jeweller of Tonbridge, became his local agent.[47] In the second half of July Cornell demonstrated his Arnold on the front at Margate, having first sought permission of the local magistrates. Cornell's care for the susceptibilities of the bench may have helped him after his misadventure with the Margate cab-driver. Cornell advertised his car widely, in runs to Canterbury, Brighton, and as far afield as Southampton. Late in July two of Arnold's cars circulated during the South-Eastern Counties Agricultural Show at Tunbridge Wells, on the ground which had seen Salomons' pioneer exhibition nearly a year earlier. The Marquis of Abergavenny was a passenger, and one of the cars found a buyer.

After the amendments of the Commons Standing Committee on Law were made known, the motor car's supporters could be fairly sure that they had a Bill that would allow them on the roads, watered-down though it was. The House would be unwilling to debate additional amendments, partly because it was the function of the committee to take over such work on the Bill, and partly because the Local Government Board would in any case be dealing with the more controversial issues by means of regulation. And so it turned out, with Chaplin on the government's behalf resolutely – and successfully – refusing further amendments before the full House on 30 July.

One is therefore not surprised to find Lawson as confident as ever of the gullibility of the public, asking them for more money well before the Bill received the royal assent. At an extraordinary general meeting of the British Motor Syndicate, called in the third week of July, Lawson announced that its capital would be increased from £150,000 to £1 million, for the purchase of further patents. He stressed how profitable, if speculative, they would be. As if to prove the point, he announced a second interim dividend, this time of no less than 30 per cent, payable at the end of the month. In fact all of this was window-dressing. The Syndicate – now renamed the British Motor Company – had already made its major acquisitions, income was so far virtually non-existent, and the dividend was paid in shares in the Great Horseless Carriage Company. The general effect was enhanced, however, by a classified advertisement in the issue of the *Autocar* that reported the meeting, looking for a buyer for 250 Syndicate shares at £2 15s 0d each – a healthy mark-up on the issue price of £1.

At the same time, the Lawson interests poured forth a smokescreen of misleading and confusing statements to conceal the fact that they were nowhere near ready for commercial manufacture, and that such vehicles as they had on the road were prototypes – if of British construction – or else imported. An added inducement, no doubt, was that Great Horseless Carriage Company shareholders were reported to be worrying about their investments, and in need of reassurance.

It was said early in July that the Daimler Motor Company's machinery had been started up, although it would be "some little time" – five or six weeks – before the first car would leave the Motor Mills.[48] The first English-made Daimler was alleged to be on the road by late August, but the company's own works manager, J.S. Critchley, gave the lie to this. He afterwards said that he completed his first car in October 1896. From his sketchy description, it seems that this was one of the old-type Daimlers that Canstatt were still making alongside their modern, Panhard-based cars.[49] The Daimlers that had been so prominent in British demonstrations were Canstatt-built, even if their bodies were in some cases British.

In the middle of July a Kane-Pennington advertisement said that victorias were "now being built" at the Coventry works. This was a prototype, not the first of a production batch. Two months later the Kane-Pennington was admitted to be in a still-experimental state, and early in October Pennington himself was saying that orders would be accepted only after the new Act was in force – that is, in November.

At the beginning of August the *Autocar* stated that the New Beeston Cycle Company was in production with the De Dion tricycle; that all the Coventry firms, indeed, were "engaged in the manufacture" of vehicles. "With five or six firms at least, orders may now be placed for delivery within a few weeks." Not all the manufacturing concerns referred to were Lawson's, but the statement was true of none of them. The first New Beeston tricycle – as the English De Dion was named – was to have emerged from the Quinton works in mid-August. But as far as the tricycles for sale were concerned, Lawson was still only making promises a fortnight afterwards, though speaking in the same breath of an "enormous flow of orders" for them.[50] Alas for the hopes he raised; a month later, there was talk of motor cycles to be on sale in Coventry in "a few weeks".[51] It finally transpired, as late as early December, that no New Beeston tricycles of any description had yet been completed.

The emergence of the first "English" Léon Bollée was more shrouded in mystery than that of any Lawson-built vehicle. Early in September, Charles Crowden, works manager at the Motor Mills, was saying that one would be on the road that very week; then, according to a speaker at the ordinary general meeting of the Great Horseless Carriage Company in mid-month, it was to appear that very *day*. Two weeks later, the machine was said to be on test.

Notwithstanding their unfortunate experiences with the Léon Bollée, in October Humber & Company were given another and much less promising "baby" to nurture – the French Pingault electric tandem bicycle, built at the Gladiator works for pacing cyclists. By October a Humber-built Pingault was circulating in London, on the Wood Green and Crystal Palace cycle tracks.

On the day before the new Act came into force, the *Autocar* offered its readers, without comment, a collection of the latest obfuscations of the Lawson "manufacturing" enterprises. The potential weekly capacity of the Daimler Motor Company was announced as seven cars – four-seaters, to cost about £250 each – and 200 employees were already working overtime; but the equipment of the works was not yet complete. Pennington was still preparing to satisfy the market awaiting his vehicles – 500 would be needed, a modest enough figure in Pennington terms. Meanwhile he had ordered, from T. Coulthard of Preston, 24 buses with his engines for local and London services, for delivery in the spring of 1897 – "actual building will be commenced shortly." The works of the New Beeston Cycle Company, which was working on the New Beeston tricycle, would be completed "in a few months" to meet the demand for an estimated 10,000 machines. As for the Humber company, it was "continuing experiments" with the Léon Bollée.[52]

The state of readiness of the Motor Mills, where nearly all these vehicles were supposed to be built, was just as uncertain, so it is not surprising that the machines themselves failed to materialise on cue. Early in September the Great Horseless Carriage Company had only just got around to ordering its machine tools, but a report by Lord Winchilsea on the condition of the factory a month later gave an impression of great activity. Three of the four floors were in use. On the ground floor Humber & Company were at work on the English Léon Bollée, while on the second floor Edward Joel Pennington was busy on his odd creations, also the subject of Humber-owned patents. Other Lawson manufacturing businesses listed as having premises in the building were the Daimler Motor Company (the original purchasers) and the Beeston Pneumatic Tyre Company.

Just how misleading this account was transpired only in mid-November, when a Great Horseless Carriage Company advertisement let the cat out of the bag. They had "nearly completed the organisation and equipment of their immense new works at Coventry". In smaller type, they said that orders could now be taken for "some" of the following makes – Daimler, Kane-Pennington, Léon Bollée and Bersey.[53]

Altered though it was in the process, the Bill's successful negotiation of its many vicissitudes encouraged more and more businesses to expand existing activities or start from scratch. As we have seen, by July the British licence for the Millet motor bicycle had found a buyer. In September Walter Arnold extended his activities to the north of England. James Edward Tuke of Bradford, Yorkshire, rode in an Arnold demonstrator from East Peckham to Maidstone. By the following month he was the agent for the Arnold car on his home ground. An advertisement for the Arnold in October claimed that they "have been sold and delivered in all parts of England". In October, too, another Coventry cycle manufacturer, the Riley Cycle Company, was experimenting with a motor bicycle. By November Julius Harvey & Company of London was offering to supply Lutzmann vehicles; a month later, as we have seen, J.A. Koosen was sole agent. By November, also, W.H. Dunkley of Birmingham had built a gas-engined carriage capable of 15 m.p.h., and had accepted an order for a bus similarly powered. In the same month Radcliffe Ward was running a private car – an electric dogcart with pneumatic tyres – on the London streets, as well as his bus.

At the end of September came a new company promotion with a Lawson taint. There were already links between New & Mayne and the Lawson empire: A.G. New and Edward Joel Pennington had been joint owners of patents bought by the Great Horseless Carriage Company, and Lawson company vehicles had featured in New & Mayne exhibition displays. Now New & Mayne Ltd was floated. It asked £150,000 from the public, and Arthur James Mayne and M.D. Rucker were its directors. Some time before November the Britannia Motor Carriage Company also passed into the Lawson net. It sold its patents to the British Motor Syndicate for £16,000. The company received a licence from the Syndicate, free of charge, to continue building its vehicles, and contracted with the Syndicate to supply it with carriages to the value of £10,000 a year – an undertaking never realised.

Company promotions outside the Lawson net multiplied. Around July the Roots Oil Motor & Horseless Carriage Company was floated. By this time the Roots & Venables car was available to order. The major non-Lawson promotion was, however, that of the Anglo-French Motor Carriage Company, floated in the second week of August for £300,000, with the Earl of Lonsdale as chairman. According to its prospectus, this ambitious enterprise was established to absorb l'Hollier Gascoigne & Company and to acquire Emile Roger & Cie of Paris, with all their patent rights. The French works would be extended, and manufacture would take place in Birmingham as well as Maidstone. L'Hollier Gascoigne appears to have been retained as the name of the sales organisation,[54] with Edmund Gascoigne as manager of the British side of the operation. At the end of September, the new company was not yet making cars, but was forecasting production at the rate of 10 or 20 vehicles per week within three months. So the English child took over the French parent. In the first week of November, the Yeovil Motor Carriage & Cycle Company was floated, to make the Petter car. During 1896 there were other company promotions, too, but unlike those mentioned, none was backed by a motor vehicle actually working on the road. They were based on nothing more than vague promises and unproven "systems", and none had sufficient substance to deserve note here.

The friends of the motor car faced two more hurdles before they could be sure of just how much freedom they had been given. The Home Office regulations on petroleum had not yet been released; and the Local Government Board had still to show how it would use the discretion granted to it by Parliament – whether it would tighten the curbs, or loosen them. Sir David Salomons had done his best when testifying before the petroleum committee; now he set out to perform what could be his last major service for the cause.

For lack of experience of motor vehicles, Henry Chaplin relied on Salomons for help in composing the Local Government Board regulations. He did not, however, depend on Salomons to produce the first draft, as he had done in the case of the Bill; nor did he rely on Salomons alone at any stage. From the end of August Salomons maintained close liaison with Major Tulloch, Chief Engineering Inspector of the Local Government Board, whose job it was to collect the information that would enable the board to reach its decisions. Tulloch knew how to get the best out of Salomons, adopting an effusive, almost obsequious tone throughout their connection. On 31 August he wrote: "I shall take it as a great favour if you could possibly [illegible] me an hour of your valuable time to discuss with you the subject of the regulations which this Board have to draw up for the traffic of these new vehicles." As another means of obtaining guidance, Tulloch proposed to visit Paris, where motor traffic was most common, and where it had been the subject of police regulation since 1893. These regulations, and the way they had worked in practice, could provide useful lessons. Tulloch asked Salomons for the addresses of Paris motor manufacturers, so that he could contact them, and got hold of a copy of the Paris regulations.

By early September Tulloch had drawn up a first draft, on which he asked Salomons to comment. Salomons offered to accompany him to Paris: "It would indeed be a treat for me to be in Paris with you, and I thank you so much for your offer to show me everything", enthused his *protégé* in reply. Tulloch was hospitably received in France. He was dined by the Automobile Club de France, and watched the Paris–Marseilles race. This 10-day event, the start of which had been postponed to 24 September, set another distance record, for it was 1080 miles long. There were many English spectators, in addition to Tulloch – it was said that over 40 members of the Motor Car Club alone were due to attend. Among those who followed the race in their own vehicles were Evelyn Ellis, Charles Harrington Moore, and – aboard the Panhard that had arrived first in the Paris–Bordeaux race – Harry Lawson, H.O. Duncan and Charles McRobie Turrell. Lawson had bought the car for the inflated sum of £1200, for publicity purposes.

There was plenty of excitement, for on the second day the weather was nightmarish. Gale-force winds extinguished burners, blew one car down a hill to destruction, and felled trees across the road. Levassor in his Panhard hit one such tree at 25 m.p.h. when trying to avoid a dog, sustaining injuries from which he eventually died. Out of 32 starters, only 15 reached the halfway mark at Marseilles. The winner was the amateur Mayade, on a new four-cylinder Panhard. Merckel's two-cylinder Panhard was second. Only two steamers started, and neither finished. In the end there were 14 finishers, the rigours of the outward journey having weeded out the rest. The *Engineer* was disappointed: the sole criterion had been speed, which was undesirable; steam (with which the future lay) was represented only by De Dion tractors, which were hardly motor cars; and the retirement of over half the field proved that petrol motor car design was backward.

More to the point of his visit, Tulloch conducted his investigation of Paris traffic conditions. He was said to be pleased with the motor car's safety and ease of control, and its ability to manoeuvre and stop. By 5 October he had returned to London and was writing to Salomons to thank him for his help – "I owe you a debt which I shall never be able to repay."

On 20 October the Local Government Board distributed to local authorities a circular setting forth the draft regulations, for their comment. It is clear from the main points of these that a spirit of conservatism and a keen sensitivity to the feelings of the motor car's opponents had dominated the board's thinking. Some of the regulations were in principle sensible. A reverse gear would be compulsory on all but lightweight vehicles; there must be two independent brakes; and lights must be carried front and rear. In others, archaic modes of thought were reflected. Vehicles of between 15 hundredweight and 1 ton in weight must have tyres at least $2\frac{1}{2}$ inches wide; up to 2 tons the figure was 3 inches, and above that, 4 inches. No vehicle must be more than $7\frac{1}{2}$ feet wide. Neither enactment was unreasonable in the short view, given loose-surfaced, narrow roads, high speeds and iron tyres; but they perpetuated the ancient principle that vehicles must adapt themselves to roads, rather than the other way about. Still other regulations were vexatious, impractical or both. All vehicles must carry their owners' name and address, like any tradesman's van. They must stop at the bidding of a policeman or anyone in charge of a restive horse, and the driver's name and address must be given to anyone on request. No vehicle might be left unattended, in any circumstances: vague fears of petrol explosion lay behind this ruling.

To be fair, neither the progressive nor the retrograde features of these regulations should be attributed exclusively to pressures at work in Britain. The requirements concerning lights and independent brakes were reflected in the Paris regulations, as was the principle of controlling vehicle weight and width.

On 11 November, when the county councils had had their say, the finalised regulations were published in the form of the Light Locomotives on Highways Order. They would come into force three days later, at the same time as the Act which they supplemented. One regulation was so woolly as to be meaningless. All vehicles must be in the charge of a competent driver; they must be constructed so as to be controllable, and to cause no interference with other traffic; and they must be in a safe condition. At the same time, there was no provision for testing drivers or vehicles. The only excuse for the presence of such a requirement was that the Paris police regulations contained similar enactments; but in their case, means of checking that the law was obeyed were provided.

In other respects, publication of the regulations revealed that however cautious and retrograde the Local Government Board draft may have been, the county councils had thought it excessively libertarian. The rest of the changes cut deep into the principles and intentions of the Act, without going so far as to nullify them. The Local Government Board draft had left the 14 m.p.h. limit alone; now no greater speed than was "reasonable and proper" was permitted, and in any case it must not exceed 12 m.p.h. Vehicles weighing between $1\frac{1}{2}$ tons and 2 tons unladen were restricted to 8 m.p.h., and those over 2 tons to 5 m.p.h.

This regulation appeared to leave the way open to local authorities to fix lower (but not higher) speed limits in their jurisdictions; though, in fact, the Act had reserved ultimate powers of amendment to the board. The Act had contained positive encouragements to regional variations; this regulation invited still more. It is not hard to see where the board found the figure of 12 m.p.h. It was an anglicised version of the Paris limit; and it had been one of the demands of the Road Safety Association. It may even have owed its adoption in part to Salomons, who saw motor vehicles being used primarily for goods delivery in towns, where high speeds would be neither necessary nor desirable, and who had himself recommended a 12 m.p.h. limit. The same growing feeling that had called for a speed limit now demanded a reduction in the proposed figure. If the board thought that public opinion needed another sop, here was an obvious one. Finally, 12 m.p.h. was accepted as a normal speed for cyclists, and it would have been natural, if not logical, to think that what was good for one modern road machine was good for another. The same association of ideas suggested lights and bells for motor cars because they were required for cycles.

The maximum permissible width was cut to $6\frac{1}{2}$ feet. There were just two minor concessions to the motor car interests. Private cars would not be required to carry the owner's name and address, and the stipulation that standing vehicles must not be left unattended was dropped. This was regarded as important, given that doctors, commercial travellers and deliverymen were generally thought to have the most use for the new machines.

Though the Local Government Board regulations led a chequered career, their final shape is soon summarised. Those modifying existing provisions of the Act, as allowed for in the Act, were as follows:

A white light to be shown forward, and a red light to the rear.
    Maximum speed 12 m.p.h., but no maximum to exceed that which was safe, reasonable and proper. Limit for vehicles weighing $1\frac{1}{2}$–2 tons: 8 m.p.h. Limit for vehicles weighing over 2 tons: 5 m.p.h.

There were, in addition, several regulations that introduced new principles:

On vehicles weighing over 5 hundredweight, a means of reversing to be fitted.
    Minimum tyre widths: on vehicles weighing 15 hundredweight–1 ton, $2\frac{1}{2}$ inches; 1–2 tons, 3 inches; over 2 tons, 4 inches.
    Maximum width of vehicle $6\frac{1}{2}$ feet.
    Two independent brakes to be fitted.
    Every vehicle to be in the charge of a competent driver; and to be built so as to be roadworthy, under full control, and no hindrance to other traffic.
    Goods vehicles to carry the name and address of the owner.
    All vehicles to stop if so requested by a policeman or anyone in charge of a restive horse.
    Name and address of driver to be given to anyone on request.

The Home Office rules on petroleum had been published on 3 November, and they, too, acquired the force of law under the Act. The existing Acts would still apply, except for three new provisions. The maximum permitted quantity of petroleum spirit in any one container was now 20 gallons, with a 40-gallon limit per vehicle; it must be kept, used and conveyed in clearly labelled, strong metal containers proof against leakage; and all forms of artificial light must be kept away from it. The beneficent influence of Salomons was discernible in the all-important, and generous, fuel capacity limit.

The partisans of the motor car were left with a victory barely won. According to his own account, Salomons secured the deletion of two Local Government Board proposals – that cars should be numbered, and that drivers should be licensed. Taken for granted today, to contemporaries these propositions suggested the police state and the paid, trade driver. No gentleman-motorist would tolerate the one, or be associated with the other, in theory anyway. That the board should consider such measures is perfectly plausible, even so – the Road Safety Association had called for numbering, and drivers' licences were compulsory in Paris.

But Salomons had also favoured the application of two general principles to the regulations – that they should treat the motor car as a carriage rather than as a traction engine, so as to be consistent with the Act; and that they should be applicable nationwide, without local variations. No such broad-minded spirit was present in the final enactments. Reasonable though many of the construction and use regulations were, all exuded as air of having originated among people who know only traction engines; and the principle of country-wide uniformity, already diluted in the Act, was now further compromised. It is no wonder that Tulloch felt bound to apologise to Salomons for the extent to which his views had been rejected: "I am very sorry for it", he wrote.

It is sobering to realise that, restrictive though the Act and its embodied regulations were, many people still regarded them as being too generous to the motor vehicle. Judging by the reaction to it, the 12-m.p.h. maximum speed had been a compromise rather than a surrender. The Council of Central and Associated Chambers of Agriculture – representing an interest that had been inclined to be friendly towards the new machine – resolved to urge the Local Government Board to reduce the limit to 10 m.p.h. for 12 months.

Several county councils took immediate advantage of the freedom of action they saw in the regulations. The West Riding of Yorkshire decided on an 8-m.p.h. limit for 12 months. The North Riding chose 10 m.p.h., and Lancashire voted to halve the statutory limit to 6 m.p.h. Warwickshire's action was more significant, since so much of the infant motor industry was located within its borders, and would suffer directly. Motor cars were described at a council meeting as "diabolical machines", and Lord Willoughby de Broke, a prominent racehorse owner, opposed their presence in agricultural districts.[55] There was a special reason for Warwickshire's hostility: motor cars from Lawson's factories were frequently encountered out on test, and their works drivers drove noisily and without consideration for other road users or for the law. The result was a resolution in favour of a speed limit of 10 m.p.h. in the county. The London County Council's Highways Committee – a keen supporter of the motor car less than a year before – applied to the Local Government Board for an 8-m.p.h. limit in its jurisdiction. The other councils concerned were under the impression, understandably enough, that the Act and its regulations permitted them to make by-laws freely. Such decisions as these were so widespread that if they had not, in fact, required the ratification of the Local Government Board, the intentions of the Act would have been completely frustrated. As it was, when in the New Year the Warwickshire County Council asked Henry Chaplin if amendments could be made to the regulations – in particular, that vehicles should be numbered for easy identification – he refused, on the grounds that they had not had time to prove themselves. In Scotland, the board's writ did not run. T.R.B. Elliot had feared the consequences of the traditional separation of powers; with reason, as it turned out. When the Secretary for Scotland, Lord Balfour of Burleigh,[56] issued his regulations, they imposed a maximum speed limit of 10 m.p.h., or 6 m.p.h. if another vehicle were towed. Against this there was no appeal.

The Local Government Board had had to cope with difficult circumstances – an amorphous but perceptibly growing dislike of motor cars; two tiny, vociferous pressure groups clamouring for contrary concessions; and its own lack of experience and consequent inability to judge the merits of either case fairly. We cannot be surprised that the board chose to play safe – to incline towards preservation of the *status quo* rather than towards the uncertainties of change, without totally inhibiting that change. The motor car was granted the conditions in which it could work on the road; but only just. If one sets side by side the demands of the solidly anti-motoring Road Safety Association of Walsall and the provisions of the Act, with its attendent regulations, the comparison is instructive. Of the association's more important demands, all but one were now part of statute, the only exception being that for the numbering of vehicles.

The reaction of the specialist press to the regulations was not entirely as one might have expected. Predictably, *Engineering* applauded the lower speed limit; but the *Autocar*'s mood was one of resignation: the motor vehicle had won the best deal possible in the circumstances. The *Engineer* said in a leading article that fixing a maximum speed was a mistake, it being impossible to gauge speeds accurately.

If the number of trade displays organised during the Local Government Board's deliberations was any indication, the motor vehicle lobby regarded the regulations as every bit as important as the

Act itself. "Educating" the board was as necessary as educating Parliament. Exhibition organisers were now as keen to include motor cars in their displays, for their novelty value, as motorists were to take part – so much so that there was a shortage of vehicles for the purpose. If the board acted out of ignorance of the new machine, it was not the motorist's fault.

As usual, the Lawson interests set the pace, in more senses than one. With J.S. Critchley in charge, a party of Daimler Motor Company engineers on one of their cars made a demonstration run from Coventry to Banbury and back on 23 August. No motor car had previously been seen in either Banbury or Dunchurch. The average speed claimed for the Daimler was an alarming 15 m.p.h. A few days later Critchley was again in the news, moving house with the help of a Daimler parcels van.

More important was an exhibition laid on at Wembley Park by the British Motor Syndicate and the Motor Car Club, in connection with a fête and carnival held there on 29 August. Ten cars and three motor cycles took part, including a Panhard wagonette, a Daimler, three Britannia electrics and a De Dion tricycle. The organisers asked the police to allow the participating vehicles to be driven to the ground by day, but permission was refused – they must make the journey by night, as laid down in the local by-laws. This prospect cannot have appealed to Lawson, for whom there would be little publicity value in a run made in darkness. Once at Wembley, the vehicles ran about freely on the paths in the park, offering rides to anyone willing to pay for them.

From 24 August to 5 September Islington's Agricultural Hall was the scene of the entertaining named Horseless Carriage, Sanitary and Engineering Exhibition. Cycles, too, were on show. The catholicity of the exhibits was explained by the fact that its organiser, Charles Cordingley,[57] had been editor of the *Tricycling Journal*, was owner of *Laundry News* and *Industry and Iron*, and had promoted laundry and general engineering exhibitions at the Agricultural Hall in earlier years. The exhibition's motoring section, a novelty in 1896, was run by New & Mayne, the laundry and electrical engineers who had taken up self-propelled vehicles. They had constructed a track on which two Lawson electrics – a Bersey and the Garrard & Blumfield – were shown running, and two Hildebrand & Wolfmüller motor bicycles formed a static display. Later in the year New & Mayne took a stand at the Craftsmen's and Industrial Exhibition at the Westminster Aquarium, where a Hildebrand & Wolfmüller was again shown. Garrard, meanwhile, had moved on to the Gladiator motor cycle, and early in September drove a tricycle of that make around the track at the Birmingham Charity Sports at Edgbaston.

The Health Exhibition at Olympia, Newcastle-on-Tyne, late in the month was chosen by the Anglo-French Motor Carriage Company as the venue for a demonstration of one of their Roger-Benzes to local dignitaries. Rides in the grounds were offered. Around the middle of October there was further excitement in the north when James Tuke, "autocar agent of Harrogate and Bradford",[58] drove his Arnold in appalling weather from the first of these places to the second. It was the first car ever seen in Bradford, and Tuke gave private and public displays. Late in the month the Daimler Motor Company ran two of its vehicles in the Coventry Lifeboat Demonstration, to illustrate "Coventry's New Industry".

At the end of October a Kane-Pennington three-wheeler was tested on the Coventry bicycle racing track. The going was muddy, but 15–20 m.p.h. was apparently achieved. The machine was also tried out on the Warwick road. The same tricar engaged in a typical Pennington "stunt" early in November – a tug-of-war at Coventry between it and H.O. Duncan's Léon Bollée. It is hard to see why this was allowed, since one "Lawson" vehicle was bound to lose. Surprisingly, it was the Bollée that did so. The victor was the only type of Kane-Pennington to achieve production status. It was called a "torpedo". Its horizontal two-cylinder engine had automatic inlet valves; there were two forward speeds, and final drive was by chain. The tubular frame was made by Humber & Company. The driver sat on a saddle at the rear, but either he or a passenger sitting in front could steer. Four additional passengers could be accommodated on other saddles athwart the frame. Pennington's pneumatic tyres were fitted.

Around the time of the contest, a Daimler was used to take Conservative voters to the polling stations during the Coventry municipal elections. Tuke's Arnold was performing the same service in Bradford for the Liberal party, and running the candidate about.

A much more ambitious display than any of these was planned, in order to influence the Local Government Board's decisions, but never actually happened.[59] As for those that did, it is impossible to say for certain what effect, if any, they had on the board's thinking, or for that matter, what influence earlier demonstrations had had on the progress of the Bill through Parliament – whether increasing familiarity bred friendliness, toleration, dislike or merely contempt. Probably it produced all of these to some extent. But if we correlate the fact of slowly growing familiarity throughout 1896 with the fact of slowly growing hostility, the motorist's policy of showing the flag at every opportunity appears counter-productive. It is, indeed, hard to account for the hostility otherwise, and one is forced to conclude that there was no coincidence.

Although neither he nor any other individual could fairly claim to have acted as midwife to the motor car single-handed, Sir David Salomons, by virtue of his political influence, had made the greatest personal contribution of anyone. It could be said that if he had not organised the country's first motor exhibition, someone else would have done so soon; but he still deserves the credit for it. No company promoter of Lawson's stripe could have created a lobbying organisation with the weight of the Self-Propelled Traffic Association. One cannot see the Petroleum Committee calling Lawson to give evidence, let alone endorsing his views; neither would the Local Government Board have listened to the views of such a man so attentively when the Bill was being drafted, or when it was being manoeuvred through Parliament. The impression Salomons made on the draft of the Board's regulations was less, but that was not his fault.

Now Salomons had almost shot his bolt. We have seen how his influence on events had declined throughout the summer and autumn. In his sympathies, too, he was becoming more and more alienated from the main stream of the motoring movement. In particular, he lost faith in the future of the private petrol-driven car. As early as January 1896 he was speaking out against the single-speed, rough-running, "unscientific" petrol engine, and in favour of steam if its basic drawbacks could be overcome. The occasion of his conversion was his discovery of the Serpollet, a car previously unknown to him. Steam, said Salomons, would become more prominent than any other motive power. By May he was practising what he preached. Although he still had his Peugeot, and had ordered a De Dion tricycle and a Delmer, a Serpollet was being built for him.

By October Salomons had found a way of gratifying at one and the same time his new enthusiasm for the Serpollet system and his old dislike of commercialism. Private individuals wanting to import a Serpollet could not do so independently of the British licensee without infringing his rights; but Salomons obtained the concession to buy 50 cars direct from the factory for resale in Britain without reference to the licence holder. Salomons himself would handle all matters of royalty due to Serpollet, to save his customers the embarrassment. He planned to make no profit. We are not told the licencee's identity, nor his reaction to this apparently arbitrary redistribution of his assets.[60] "There is no doubt that the steam carriage, as solved by M. Serpollet, is the coming one", wrote Salomons at the end of October. Alfred Sennett, his close colleague and supporter, agreed at every point – steam was the power source of the future; petrol vehicles were unsuited to Britain, except as freight carriers; high speed and company promoters were equally undesirable.

Salomons had only two more contributions to make to the motoring scene, neither of any great significance in the present context. One was the monthly *Automotor and Horseless Vehicle Journal*, which he launched in October 1896. This publication had two objects. One was to provide the motor car movement with an independent voice; the other was to give Salomons' own Self-Propelled Traffic Association a means of communication with its members – a sort of club magazine. To Salomons the two aims were not incompatible, for "independence" meant independence of company promoters. The tone of the new magazine was self-consciously didactic and serious. Although it was a vehicle for Salomons' views, it strove to be objective; when it considered that vehicles performed well, it said so, even if they were Lawson's.[61] The pursuit of advertising revenue rather than editorial balance sometimes had the same effect. Although editorial comment could be merciless to Lawson's business methods, the November issue contained a prospectus for Lawson's latest promotion, the London Electrical Cab Company.

Since the *Automotor and Horseless Vehicle Journal* was a reflection of its proprietor's opinions, it had little relevance to the mainstream motoring scene at the end of 1896. The same could be said for the branch of the Self-Propelled Traffic Association founded in Liverpool in October. What was wanted by the city's businessmen was "a good and cheap means of carrying goods from Liverpool to Manchester".[62] Because the railways had a monopoly of local transport, they could charge what rates they pleased, making the cost of distributing imports shipped into Liverpool a standing grievance. The crisis had been sharpened by the opening of the Manchester Ship Canal two years before. Now that ships that had turned round on the Mersey increasingly did so at Manchester, Liverpool was losing business. Motor transport promised a two-thirds reduction in costs over railway rates, with the added advantage that goods could be transferred from shipboard to customers' warehouses direct, without transhipment to and from railway wagons.

The credentials of the Liverpool S.P.T.A. were of the highest: its first President was none other than Frederick Stanley, sixteenth Earl of Derby, Mayor of the city, Lancashire's most eminent citizen, and one of Britain's leading racehorse owners. He had a history of interest in self-propelled vehicles, having been a co-sponsor of the 1873 Locomotives on Roads Bill and a member of that year's select committee on the subject. No suitable lorries had yet been designed, as William Worby Beaumont had pointed out to the Liverpool Chamber of Commerce. The Liverpool S.P.T.A. took upon itself the encouragement and development of such vehicles, running a series of annual trials from 1898. Even more remote from the noisy vicissitudes of everyday motoring than its parent, the association had much in common with such bodies as the Royal Agricultural Society.

So it was that Sir David Salomons and his Self-Propelled Traffic Association finally parted company with the motor car's main line of evolution. The *Engineer*, first in the field to promote the new generation of machines in 1894, formally signalled its own rejection of what the motoring scene had become in a leading article in September. Entitled "The Horseless Carriage of the Future", it was the *Engineer's* statement of faith in purist engineering principles, and a defiance of practical engineering and commercial realities: "We have no hesitation in saying that the light oils, petroleum spirit, benzole and the like, will play a very second-rate part in the future of self-propelled vehicles, in this country at all events." The heavier oils such as kerosene made too much smell and smoke; even the petrol engine was better in those respects. The future lay with steam, generated by oil fuel in a burner, and in electricity for town use.

After the early spring of 1896 the activities of the entrepreneurs monopolised attention, and most of the motor vehicles running on British roads were doing so under the aegis of commercial concerns. Private motorists, other than Salomons, faded from the public eye. They continued to motor, but having discovered the hard way that the law did not, after all, accept their machines as carriages, they avoided confrontations and let the big commercial battalions with more at stake fight their battles for them. Although imported motor cars were now available, few newcomers joined the ranks of private motorists, put off by the vehicle's drawbacks, or preferring to wait for the apparently imminent change in the law. Some potential buyers may have disliked the prospect of being associated, however indirectly and unjustly, with the exhibitionist and disreputable company promoters who dominated the motoring scene. In the absence of harder proof, this picture is inferred from circumstantial evidence; but it seems a likely one.

References to new recruits to private motoring are few and ambiguous. In February a three-wheeled Jeantaud electric with aluminium body was building in France for Queen Victoria. It had been ordered by Prince Henry of Battenberg, the Queen's son-in-law. But it was for use on the royal estates, not on public roads, so was more a sign of the motor car's rising status than of any growing popularity with private buyers. The prince died, in any case, before the car was completed, and the Queen never took delivery.

Her Irish subjects saw their first example of the new generation of motor cars in March, when John Brown of Belfast imported an iron-tyred Serpollet. He was careful not to drive it outside the jurisdiction of local magistrates who were known to him. In August the arrival of the first petrol car in Dublin, a Benz, was noticed with favour locally. In England, meanwhile, a Hildebrand & Wolfmüller motor bicycle was in use in March by William Cross, a Newcastle steam engineer and a member of the council of the S.P.T.A. Still more enterprising, perhaps, was any reader of the *English Mechanic* who followed its serialised instructions for building his own kerosene-fuelled motor car.

A revival of interest among the wealthy amateurs who were the most likely potential buyers appeared only when the new Act was about to come into force. Frank Hedges Butler, a rich and much-travelled wine merchant, saw and drove a Peugeot in France, witnessed the Paris–Marseilles race at the end of September, and visited the Paris Salon du Cycle in December. He later owned a Benz, and became the treasurer of the Automobile Club of Great Britain and Ireland.

A more significant figure altogether was Charles Stewart Rolls, whom we have already met. An early member of the S.P.T.A. and an energetic collector of signatures for the *Autocar* petition, he had experienced his first British car ride in February 1896 when visiting Sir David Salomons at Broomhill. It is not known exactly when Rolls bought a car of his own. He still lacked one in September, and at Kelso in October he inspected T.R.B. Elliot's Panhard. Rolls certainly owned a car before the Act came into force, for he told of being fined for not having a flagman and for exceeding the speed limit. He made two trips from London to Cambridge before 14 November. He has left us a detailed description of one, made in a newly acquired Peugeot while the full rigours of the old law were still in force.

To accomplish this he had first to win over the Chief Constables of Hertfordshire and Cambridgeshire. As often happened, these gentlemen told their officers to look the other way; but they only could do this so long as no member of the public lodged a complaint. Rolls made the journey by night to avoid attracting attention and, perhaps, to avoid breaking local by-laws restricting hours of operation. On the way a policeman asked for a ride; an experience that so overcame him that he begged Rolls to go down one hill as fast as he could. The news got about, and at midnight in Royston a crowd was awaiting the car. Delays from various causes meant that the Peugeot's average speed was only $4\frac{1}{2}$ m.p.h., and that the journey took $11\frac{3}{4}$ hours.

From early summer trade interests and promoters were running more and more vehicles on the roads, and with ever-growing frequency; but at first prosecutions were few. After February 1896 motorists had left off challenging the law so provocatively, and between then and August only three summons are recorded. In May Walter Bersey was prosecuted for motoring in Parliament Street, London, at over 2 m.p.h., outside permitted hours and without a man in front. He was fined £2 and costs.

In the same month A.G. New of New & Mayne was in trouble. This prosecution brought out the full absurdity of the existing Acts. New's Hildebrand & Wolfmüller motor bicycle was defined by the Kingston-on-Thames bench as a locomotive, as was inevitable in strict law. New was convicted of driving his machine on the Cobham road in the forbidden daylight hours, and also of having no locomotive licence. New was aware that his machine was likely to be classed as a locomotive, for he had been preceded by cyclist outriders with red flags; but this did not help him. He was fined 15s on each of the two charges. At the end of July a Miss Mannington Sladen of Albury in Surrey was prosecuted for driving an unidentified vehicle – probably an Arnold – within prohibited hours on the road between that village and Shere, and was mulcted of a 5s fine. She was, perhaps, Britain's earliest woman driver.

The absence of other prosecutions suggests that while their Bill was going through Parliament, the motor car's partisans generally refrained from actions that might harden public opinion against them. We have seen several instances of motorists both professional and private asking the authorities for permission for specified runs in this period, and their action may have been typical.

In August the picture changed dramatically. In the last week of the month Charles McRobie Turrell, Lawson's secretary, was summoned before the Margate magistrates for having driven Lawson's Léon Bollée in the town on the last day of July at more than 2 m.p.h. It was alleged that along the Parade, he had been doing 14 m.p.h. The Locomotives on Highways Bill had received the royal assent on 14 August. This was before the summons was issued – a fact which Henry Chaplin communicated to Turrell in court by telegram – and the case was dismissed.

In the same week the magistrate at Westminster took a different line with Walter Bersey, fining him £2 with costs for exceeding the 2-m.p.h. speed limit in Parliament Square, and failing to have a man in front. He made it clear that the new law must not be anticipated: the old one still held good for the next three months. From now on, most of his fellow-magistrates agreed with him – as had happened before, they would stand by the strict letter of the law. Within a week Alfred Cornell was up before the Tonbridge bench for travelling at 5 m.p.h. in the town, and for failing to have three people in charge of his vehicle, one in front with a red flag. The complaint came from a private resident of this anti-motoring town, not from the police. Cornell, too, received a telegram in court in support of his case, this time from his M.P., Arthur Griffith-Boscawen. Cornell pleaded that a conviction would result in loss of orders to a local manufacturer – Walter Arnold of East Peckham – but to no avail. He was fined 1s and 9d costs on each of the charges.

Even so, the new confrontation continued. At Epsom early in September l'Hollier Gascoigne & Company were prosecuted for running a car at Leatherhead without a locomotive licence, and for exceeding a 4-m.p.h. speed limit. The second charge was dropped, but on the first a fine of 10s and costs was imposed. A little over a month later, at the Mansion House, Felstead & Hunt, clothiers of St Paul's Churchyard, were summoned in their turn. They had been running a delivery vehicle in the City, deliberately provoking the law as a means of advertisement, and were fined for it.

At Birmingham magistrates' court shortly afterwards, Harry Lawson and Harvey du Cros answered a charge that was not, for once, based on the existing Locomotive Acts – it was one of furious driving, by which they allegedly frightened a horse with their Mulliner-bodied Daimler. The magistrate was sympathetic. He described the motor car as "a useful invention", and found that the charge – which had been brought privately – was without foundation. It is possible that the prominence of the du Cros and Lawson "presence" in the Midlands had something to do with his decision.

As the date of the motor car's enfranchisement drew close, increasing impatience on the part of motorists collided more often with the courts' resolve to curb it. Turrell found himself in hot water again early in November, this time at Haywards Heath in Sussex. The magistrate "threw the book at him". He was accused of driving the Léon Bollée at Slaugham on 14 October without the legal minimum of three people in charge, without a man in front, without displaying his name and address on his "locomotive", and without sufficiently wide wheels. However, all but the first charge were withdrawn, and Turrell was fined £1 with 25s costs.

Early in the month James Roots was summonsed for driving his "steam car" – as the law described it – on London streets at more than 2 m.p.h., and with fewer than three people in attendance. Roots admitted to motoring at between 6 and 7 m.p.h. The court imposed what it called a nominal fine, of 10s with 2s costs. Walter Bersey was again prosecuted for driving outside approved hours. He was not alone in drawing attention to motor cars as close as possible to the Houses of Parliament: on 9 November William Marshall was fined 10s and costs for driving the Radcliffe Ward electric dogcart in Victoria Street at over 2 m.p.h. As we shall see, the police brought a prosecution against a car that took part in the Lord Mayor's Show on the same day, without success. The last recorded prosecution under the old Acts – a successful one – was for driving in London two hours before the new Act came into force on 14 November.

4

Triumph and Anti-Climax, 1896–7

The Lawson camp had been long planning a demonstration on a scale to eclipse all previous displays. Its ostensible purpose was to celebrate the passage of the Locomotives on Highways Act and the emancipation of the motor car in an appropriately splendid manner. Its main function, however, was to turn the occasion of emancipation into an unprecedentedly elaborate publicity exercise for motor cars in general, and for Lawson's business interests in particular.

The great event had a chequered history. The idea was first broached as early as July 1896, when Frederick Simms suggested a procession of vehicles through the streets of London, starting at Westminster, when the Act had come into force. It would be followed by a banquet, and the whole celebration would be run by the Motor Car Club. A few weeks later the planned route was altered, to run from the Imperial Institute to Westminster. Predictably, the *Engineer* attacked the idea on the grounds that the motor car was still too defective for such a public exhibition, the result of which would be a reaction against it.

By early September the Motor Car Club's plans had changed, and become much more ambitious. The Act that had received the royal assent a fortnight earlier would be coming into force in three months. The first date on which cars could use the freedom it gave was Saturday, 14 November. On any earlier date a run would be effectively illegal, unless special dispensation were obtained from the police, and the courts had made it clear that any anticipation of a change in law would be unwise. The idea for a procession confined to central London was dropped; instead, on 14 November there would be a grand "tour" of motor vehicles from London to Brighton and back. That Brighton should be chosen is not surprising. It had been a favourite resort of Londoners since Regency days, and the London–Brighton road was the busiest in the country, not just with ordinary traffic but with record-breaking four-in-hand drivers, cyclists and walkers. It was the natural place to hold an event designed to attract the widest possible public notice.

The *Engineer* regarded the tour as "scarcely less objectionable" than the London procession, but the Motor Car Club had the bit between its teeth. It next proposed to run a preliminary demonstration over the same route on 24 October. Since the old law would still be in force, it would be necessary to ask the local authorities concerned for a waiver. The aim of the first run, according to the Club's letter to the Chief Constable of Sussex, was "to give the officials of the Local Government Board engaged in framing the rules governing motor traffic and representatives of public bodies a practical demonstration of the capabilities and characteristics of the new vehicle". The London County Council and Metropolitan Police had already given their authorisation, added the letter.

Accompanying these blandishments was the text of the Club's instructions to participants in the run. These drew attention to the responsible attitude of the organisers by stressing the good behaviour expected of the motorists: "Owners and drivers of motor vehicles . . . should remember that motor cars are on their trial in England, and that any rashness or carelessness might injure the industry in this country." They should "use the greatest care as to speed and driving, so as not to endanger ordinary traffic, [and] treat the police and other authorities on the route with polite consideration".

The Chief Constable of Sussex passed the Club's letter to the Home Office, saying that he himself favoured the request, but was in need of advice. The Home Office then put the cat among the pigeons by referring the letter to the Metropolitan Police. Although it was true that the London County Council had given its dispensation, the police denied that they had even been asked for theirs. Either there had been a breakdown in communication, or the Motor Car Club – recalling, perhaps, earlier favours – had anticipated agreement. The Metropolitan Police reacted adversely to what they no doubt regarded as a liberty; they said that the Local Government Board was against the idea of a preliminary run, and that they, too, opposed it.

In the end the Home Office told the Chief Constable of Sussex to exercise his own discretion, and he gave permission for the cars to pass through his jurisdiction; but the Surrey police and Surrey County Council refused theirs. With two out of three police forces and one of the county councils on the route hostile to a demonstration on 24 October, the Motor Car Club's enterprising attempt to influence the Local Government Board's decisions broke down. There would be a run on 14 November only.

By the first week in November arrangements were complete. The

Central Hall, Holborn, could be used to store cars prior to the event. The run would start at the Whitehall Place entrance of the Metropole Hotel, Northumberland Avenue, where breakfast would be available from 9.30 at 10s a head, including wine. The first car would leave at 10.30. The approved route would follow the most direct route to Brighton, except for a diversion to Reigate. It would go by Croydon, Merstham, Reigate, Crawley, Bolney and Pyecombe, finishing at Preston Park, Brighton. Taking Whitehall Place as the starting point and Preston Park as the finish, the length was a little under 52 miles.

Participants were asked to travel slowly and keep close order as far as Brixton, $3\frac{1}{2}$ miles from the start. Beyond that point they might travel as they pleased, so long as they kept behind the "pilot" car of Harry Lawson, President of the Motor Car Club. Lunch would be laid on at the White Hart Hotel, Reigate, at 12.30. There, too, petrol and oil would be on hand. Cars would re-start together at 1.30 and arrive at Preston Park from 4 o'clock. They would then proceed in convoy to the Metropole Hotel on Brighton front. Cars could be stored in Dupont's stables in Waterloo Street. A special train would be chartered to carry non-participants to Brighton at 15s a head. It would stop on the way at Redhill to enable its passengers to meet the motorists at nearby Reigate during their lunch halt. A dinner, costing £1 1s 0d a head including wine, would be provided at the Brighton Metropole that evening.

Such was the detailed, careful organisation of the run. Nothing seems to have been overlooked. It remained to be seen how well it worked in practice – if the plan had a weakness, it lay in the punctual and orderly progress expected of the motorists.

Five days before the big event, the Lawson interests arranged a "curtain-raiser" to focus attention on motor cars in London. In the now well-established tradition of participation in street carnival processions, the Daimler Motor Company entered a German-built machine in the Lord Mayor's Show, held on 9 November. It was of the old type, and was variously described as a barouche and a landau. On its rear was hung a violet banner bearing a gold inscription reading "Present Times", to point up the contrast with the vehicle in front of it in the procession, the stagecoach *Old Times* similarly draped. Since 1888 this coach had held the record for the fastest double run to and from Brighton by a horsedrawn vehicle – 7 hours 50 minutes, with 16 changes of horses – so the message on the Daimler, which was entered in the Brighton run, was doubly significant.

Harry Lawson and Charles McRobie Turrell were in charge. They were wearing what was described as "yachting" dress, but was in fact the uniform of the Motor Car Club, unveiled to the public this day.

The *Daily Telegraph* correspondent was told that the resemblance was deliberate – "travelling by motor car is the nearest approach to that pastime". Full rig consisted of a white-topped navy blue cap with a shiny peak and the Motor Car Club badge in front, and a dark blue serge suit with brass buttons. Both cap and suit were adorned with gold or silver braid. There was plenty of precedent for more or less elaborate club uniforms – cycling and other sporting clubs frequently wore them – but this one, when exposed to the full glare of publicity on the day of the Brighton run, was regarded as flamboyant, vulgar and ridiculous; just what might be expected of company promoters, in fact. According to the *Engineer*, it was "not exactly the garb of a German band, and not exactly the dress of an excursion steamer steward, but something between the two, only more pretentious". Léon Bollée put it more succinctly: to him its wearer resembled "*un amiral Suisse*".

In other respects the *Present Times* Daimler and its crew generally drew kind words from the press, if not invariably from the public. The car was said to be handsome, quiet and easily controlled in thick traffic. According to the *Daily Telegraph* its progress was a "triumph" – the only notes of dissent were such remarks as "Wot about the poor 'osses?" and "You've done me out of a job", from those whose livings depended on horses. The *Morning Post* alone seems to have disagreed – it was "an unattractive-looking landau . . . which wended its weird and silent way amidst the jeers of the spectators. It was quite evident from the reception it met with yesterday that whatever career of usefulness and economy may be in store for the motor car, many a long year will elapse before it will become a popular feature in the Lord Mayor's Show". The City police brought a summons afterwards, but it was dismissed.

Britain's motorists converged on London for the great day. For many, their first big problem lay in reaching the start, let alone the finish; and some failed to accomplish even that much, at least with their motor cars. The day of the run was for J.A. Koosen the day on which his case against the buyer of his first Lutzmann was heard in London. Charles Rolls had entered his Peugeot, but in Hatfield, on his way to London the night before the run, he turned the car over and broke an axle.

In the Lawson and Arnold camps mechanical breakdowns produced disorder. Three Léon Bollées, to be driven on the run by Léon and Camille Bollée and H.O. Duncan, were imported for the occasion. True to their new form, the Metropolitan Police refused to allow them to be driven from Victoria Station to the Central Hall in Holborn. They had to be towed through the streets by horses, and on the way the rope attached to Duncan's car snapped. Walter Arnold's contingent decided to motor up from Kent less than 24 hours before the first car's departure time, which was risky, but was thought to be good publicity. Five cars – four $1\frac{1}{2}$-h.p. Sociables, including the prototype of a British-built car, and a big 6-h.p. victoria – together with a van acquired by the Sunlight Soap Company left Tonbridge at 10 a.m. on Friday the 13th, which was hardly a good omen. A man with a red flag accompanied them, for decanting in "dangerous places". During a demonstration of "marvellous control" at Sevenoaks, the van hit a wall and bent an axle, but continued. The victoria, which Hewetson had been driving, was abandoned and Hewetson joined Cornell's car. It was 11 p.m. before the surviving Arnolds reached Bromley, a mere 13 miles from their starting-point. There they spent the night. As soon as midnight was past, there were cars running freely about the London streets, for the Act was now in force.

On the following morning the scenes were still more frantic. The *Autocar*'s "Special Red Letter Day Number" and a special but more sedate supplement to the *Automotor and Horseless Vehicle Journal* were on sale in the streets. These were foul, cold, dark and slippery under a weeping, lowering sky. In the Metropole Hotel's Whitehall Rooms, celebrations began early over the elaborate breakfast (with wine). In front of the Duke of Teck,[1] the Duke of Saxe-Weimar, Gottlieb Daimler, "a number of French drivers"[2] and upwards of 150 others, the Earl of Winchilsea tried to tear up a red flag. The hem baulked him and had to be cut with a knife before the badge of oppression could be satisfactorily rent. This was the only act for which history remembers the Earl of Winchilsea. It was more than merely symbolic, for until a matter of hours before some local authorities had still required a flagman; but to future generations who would henceforth believe that a red flag had been statutory, the deed guaranteed confusion.

Those present greeted the gesture with enthusiasm, but Bertram van Praagh sobered them up. Ominously, he made excuses in advance for the shortcomings of the cars, and emphasised the drivers' lack of experience. Anything could happen, he implied. What followed is best described in the words of Jerome K. Jerome, who, in his capacity as editor of the weekly journal *To-day*, was due to ride to Brighton in one of the cars: "Upon this, one or two gentlemen, who had been worrying Mr Lawson's life out of him for seats, became suddenly less ardent. They told Mr Lawson not to mind them; they could see how difficult it was to provide seats for everybody. They would sacrifice themselves, and go down by train."[3]

Outside, the weather conditions had not discouraged the gathering of "a crowd such as even London rarely sees".[4] Nine or ten deep, it caught both organisers and police completely unawares. Even after Sir Edward Bradford himself rode up and summoned reinforcements, traffic was at a standstill. Women were fainting in the crush, and children in danger of being trampled. Once the police line broke, and spectators surged forward out of control. J.A. Koosen, in the thick of it, struggled to reach court in time for the hearing of his case. In the end he cleared a path by stationing himself in front of an ambulance that was in the same predicament, and shouting "Cholera! Cholera!"

Fortunately, the crowd was in a happy mood. Most of the hostile comment came from those whose livelihoods would be affected by the new machine. They either feared it, or affected to despise it. "I don't think much on them", said a bus conductor. One cab driver called a car a "baked potato can", and another declared that "when a couple of dozen lives have been lost in the streets, people will be glad to get even a broken-down growler"; but an American onlooker disagreed, and the crowd taunted a third cab driver with the threat of imminent unemployment. There were other diversions, too. Cyclists in their thousands flocked to accompany or watch the cars, and among them were ladies in "rational dress", always good for a jeer.

As car crews fought their way through the press to their vehicles, "Mr Lawson's horn sounded the charge, and the horse police trotted into the crowd ... the people scattered right and left."[5] The Paris–Bordeaux-winning Panhard moved off with Lawson and Otto Mayer. The Brighton run was on. Behind Lawson, the largest assembly of motorists so far seen on Britain's public roads attempted to sort itself out. Since the course was a public road, the Motor Car Club had neither the authority nor the ability to prevent any vehicle from taking part, even those "unfinished and badly-considered",[6] and *Engineering* rightly regarded many of the participants as "crude and experimental". But the fact was that there had been a total of 58 entries, and the number of actual starters was 32 or 33; a commendably high proportion bearing in mind British motorists' lack of experience and the ratio of entrants to starters in early overseas events.

As a publicity operation for Lawson's business interests the event promised well, for they contributed by far the largest proportion of starters. To its important guests, the Motor Car Club allocated the most impressive motor cars belonging to the Lawson camp. In the *Present Times* barouche rode Gottlieb Daimler, in the care of Frederick Simms. In addition to the Paris–Bordeaux winner, Lawson had bought from the manufacturers the Panhards that had come first and second in the Paris–Marseilles race, for their promotional value. On the Brighton run Colonel Sir Vivian Majendie rode on the winning machine, chauffered by Mayade, the man who had driven the car in the race. The Panhard that had come second, also driven by its driver in the race, Merckel, carried in its capacious wagonette body Lord Winchilsea, Jerome K. Jerome and the representatives of the *Daily Telegraph* and *Pall Mall Gazette*. This was an unusually comfortable car, with its windshield and roof; which is possibly why it was so popular.

On board the Panhard victoria that had been driven by Emile Levassor in the Paris–Marseilles, and was now in charge of Charles McRobie Turrell, were Jack Dring and Charles Jarrott. Dring was official timekeeper of the Stanley Cycle Club, and was performing the same function today. A Daimler charabanc carried another load of newspapermen. Evelyn Ellis was there with his Panhard, and a *Daily Graphic* artist as passenger. The sources are frequently contradictory or vague about who rode in which car. It is possible, too, that some drivers and passengers changed cars *en route*. The attribution of people to cars given here represents the general consensus of opinion on the subject.

Lawson employees were given the job of taking the less glamorous vehicles to Brighton. Charles Crowden drove a Panhard dogcart. H.O. Duncan had a Léon Bollée, with Charles McRobie Turrell's father William in the passenger seat. Charles Bush of the Daimler company was in charge of a Daimler delivery van belonging to Peter Robinson's store, doubling that day as a breakdown vehicle.[7] At the wheel of a Panhard van was J.S. Critchley. The number of motor vans entered showed that the companies involved had taken the forecasts of the pundits to heart, and had observed the popularity of these vehicles in Paris. Harrods stores was represented by a small Daimler bus, with room for four inside passengers.[8] There was a De Dion tricycle ridden by Samuel Gorton, the young son of the general manager of the Quinton Cycle Company; and two Mulliner-bodied Bersey electrics, one a landau full of ladies with Walter Bersey in charge. Edward Joel Pennington drove a "torpedo" tricar, and one of his motor bicycles may also have started. Three Britannia electrics certainly did – a carriage, a cab and a bath-chair, the last driven by a lady.

Overseas entries reflected strong foreign interest in the Brighton run – the tricars of Léon and Camille Bollée, and still more notable, J. Frank Duryea with two of his latest cars all the way from Peoria, Illinois. The name Duryea was familiar in British motoring circles, after its well-publicised victory in the Chicago *Times-Herald* race a year earlier. It had remained the best-known American petrol car. In the 30-mile New York *Cosmopolitan* race on 30 May, from New York to Irvington, four Duryeas and two Roger-Benzes had started, and a

single Duryea finished. At the Rhode Island State Fair races at
Narragansett Park early in September, a Duryea made third best
performance against two electrics. The holder of the European
licence, J.L. McKim, was in England, and rode to Brighton on one of
the cars. Also on board the "Brighton" machines were Charles
Harrington Moore of the Motor Car Club, and the coachbuilder and
electric car pioneer George Thrupp. [9]

Although Lawson's cars dominated the starters' list, the rest of
Britain's tiny motor trade was well represented. There were four
Roger-Benzes from the Anglo-French Motor Carriage Company, and
Cornell's and Hewetson's Arnold. This and the Sunlight Soap van
were the only representatives of the East Peckham team to reach the
start in time. There was at least one Lutzmann from Julius Harvey &
Company. One rather unlikely starter was a coke-fired Lormont steam
bicycle from Paris. There were no other motor bicycles apart from the
problematical Kane-Pennington; perhaps the weather and the
Paris–Mantes fiasco had put them off. Appropriately, Magnus Volk
– the pioneer electric vehicle operator of the 1880s, whom we have
met – found a seat on a car, and so did Charles Rolls, but their vehicles
were not identified. Other personalities of the motoring world were
not so lucky: Claude Johnson and S.F. Edge went to Brighton by
bicycle.

One or two of the machines that were said to have reached the start
remain unaccounted for. There may have been duplication in the
published lists, no two of which agreed. Since they involved the same
patents and systems, Daimlers, Panhards and Peugeots were often
confused by the British press, and Lawson licence-holders and their
friends would call a Panhard or a Peugeot a Daimler, after the original
patent. If the doings of these misty vehicles were not chronicled, or
their crews named, it is hard to give them substance, let alone
differentiate them from other participants. New & Mayne and Petter
entered vehicles, but none started.

At least the spectators on bicycles and on the special train were
moving towards Brighton; which could not be said for some of the
motorists outside the Metropole Hotel. An unidentified motor cyclist
was observed "lying prostrate in the road with the machine on top of
him, helpless and unable to move."[10] This may have been the motor
cyclist seen by someone else disconsolately looking for a hansom cab.

Still greater entertainment was offered by "a French mechanic,
stranded with his car, in misery and rage, and keeping off the crowds
with the aid of a particularly vicious and formidable-looking starting
handle".[11] The representative of the *Cycle and Motor World* found
the rider of the Lormont steam bicycle complaining bitterly of the

obstructive curiosity of spectators. Thrupp's Duryea got going, only to suffer from "loafers" hanging on to it: "progress was thereby much impeded."[12] Navvies were recruited to push-start one car, and another, which the driver tried to push-start alone, was last seen running away with him in pursuit.

As and when they were able, the rest made their way down Whitehall Place, along Northumberland Avenue and the Embankment, and across Westminster Bridge – a spasmodically advancing "snake" of motor vehicles, cyclists, carriages and horse riders, with here and there four-horse coaches anxious to show their paces on the famous Brighton road against their latest rivals. Among them were the *Old Times* and *Excelsior* coaches, the latter filled with journalists. The cars inched forward like ships at sea, parting waves of spectators that closed fast behind them. There were no sign of Sir David Salomons or his friends. His absence said everything needful of his relationship with the contemporary motor car movement.

The destruction of the red flag had been an appropriately confusing start to a day of chaos, during which effective control and supervision were absent, and everyone did as they pleased, in so far as crowds and recalcitrant machinery allowed. Each witness saw only his own little part of the action, and no one, then or later, could say for certain what had happened elsewhere. This left the gates wide open not just to error, but also to deliberate deception and bitter controversy.

Public enthusiasm extended unabated further down the route. It was estimated that at least half a million people were watching the run, among them 10,000 cyclists. In Croydon shop windows had been cleared to make room for spectators; there was no real break in the crowds until after this point, nine miles from the start and on the edge of open country. At Reigate, the streets were again jammed. "Reigate Welcomes Progress", proclaimed a banner. Another at Crawley read "Success to the Motor Car", and at Albourne Green, near Sayers Common, an enterprising blacksmith put out a sign saying that motor cars would be repaired "while you wait". The banner at Preston Park – from which the Brighton council had excluded motor cars four months before – announced that "Centuries Look Down upon This, Your Immortal Ride".

Some of the immortals did not get to see it. Beyond the London streets the rain brought mud that coated cars and occupants alike, and the cold was sharpened by high winds. Constant stopping and starting in heavy traffic caused engines to boil, as did steep and muddy hills. One of the first casualties was the Kane-Pennington victoria. It "got lost in the crowd at the start, and had to join the procession at a later point", reported the *Autocar*. Then (not for the first time) it burst one of its unburstable tyres, and finally retired. Car and driver completed their journey to Brighton by rail. H.O. Duncan and Turrell senior were running down a hill near Patcham when a restive horse turned a carriage across their path. Duncan avoided a collision by swerving off the road, nose-diving the Bollée into a wet ditch. Duncan stayed with the car, but Turrell was catapulted into the ditch. The Bollée finished its journey to Brighton behind a horse and cart, at the end of a tow rope.

Other participants disappeared from the run more discreetly. The first few miles, where congestion was greatest, were the most destructive. Brixton was the scene of wholesale retirements. Among others, a Roger-Benz fell out here, and some of the electrics were seen making for the railway station. These town cars were not suited to long journeys on the open road, even if spare batteries were available, and the appalling conditions must have made the task almost impossible. Both Berseys, a Britannia and the Pennington all, however, reappeared at the finish. Contact was lost with many other participants because, seeking to avoid the Reigate crowds and shorten the journey, they took the direct Redhill road, which cut about 2 miles off the distance. Some others – the Bollée brothers and Merckel among them – stayed on the Reigate road but drove straight through the town without stopping for lunch.

Many of the participants ignored the Motor Car Club's appeal for restraint. The *Daily Graphic* correspondent estimated speeds to be higher than 25 m.p.h.; though his own car took four hours to cover the 21 miles to Reigate, and he took the train on to Brighton "not wholly sorrowing". Charles Harrington Moore's Duryea averaged better than the legal limit in spite of stopping to help another car, and keeping to the speed limit in built-up areas. The *Daily Telegraph* representative wrote of "the exhilaration of travelling at 25 miles an hour in a motor car", passing the *Excelsior* coach, and pelting full tilt down Handcross Hill. The *Pall Mall Gazette* man on the same car gave its speed as 30 m.p.h. going down the hill, while his fellow-passenger Lord Winchilsea boasted publicly at the dinner that evening of the pace Merckel's racing car had achieved. The Mayade Panhard took Handcross Hill nearly as fast, both drivers ignoring the "Dangerous to Cyclists" sign at the top. Some drivers, even, admitted to speeding – Charles Crowden said with pride that his Panhard had exceeded 16 m.p.h. on the level. There were no prosecutions – clearly the police and magistrates along the route had decided on a day of grace.[13] The first car through Croydon, a Daimler, went by at 11.44 hotly pursued by two mounted policemen. It was estimated to be doing at least 18 m.p.h., and to the delight of the crowd, who showered the passing cars with rice and flowers, the police were left behind. All they were trying to do, however, was escort the car through the town.

Given such speeds, and a public totally unused to them – including children who treated empty country roads as playgrounds – it is astonishing that only one serious accident occurred. At Crawley Frank Duryea's car ran down the small daughter of a Three Bridges publican, fracturing her skull. At the time the Duryea was said to be speeding, but its driver was later exonerated – the regulations had been observed, and no one was to blame. Rumour said that the petrol tank of one car had "blown up", killing the driver, but there were no other disasters, real or imagined.[14]

Close shaves were, however, unavoidable and innumerable. The *Pall Mall Gazette* car missed a tram in Brixton "by at least three inches, bringing upon us the cheers of the populace", and a pedestrian by an inch and a half, "bringing upon us his curses". Horses were very restive, not always on account of the motor cars. At Smitham Bottom near Coulsdon an animal in the midst of cyclists knocked over half a dozen of them, and Mayade had to drive up a bank to avoid another horse crossing the road. The cyclists themselves were scarcely less troublesome. The *Daily Telegraph* correspondent watched as one fell off and was nearly run over by the car behind. Another ran into the back of the Panhard, tumbled, caught hold and was dragged along at 10 m.p.h., only to let go and fall again. Only half in jest, one feels, Jerome K. Jerome took note of the cheerful professional interest shown in the passing cars by the medical students of Westminster Hospital, and by a hearse-load of undertakers' men on Brixton Hill.

A connoisseur of ironies would have had plenty to amuse him. Charles McRobie Turrell's Panhard – with the official timekeeper Jack Dring on board – arrived in Brighton two hours after the four fastest cars did so, while Rush's breakdown van itself broke down so thoroughly that it eventually crawled into Brighton at 3 o'clock the following morning. Lawson's "pilot" Panhard reached Preston Park at 4.30. At least three cars had preceded it, disregarding the Motor Car Club's injunction to keep behind the president. Only three others had come in by 5 o'clock, and as the weather was so bad, the plan for a procession into the town centre was abandoned. The Mayor boarded Lawson's car, and all – councillors, mounted police escort and such cars as had appeared – hurried dripping down to the front.[15]

With the organisation so dislocated, there was total confusion over who finished first. The Motor Car Club's official results, which timed cars to the Metropole Hotel, gave the honour to the two Bollée brothers. The faster tricar was said to have passed through Brixton at 11.30, and to have arrived in Brighton at 2.25; an average speed between the two places, given that it did not stop at Reigate, of 16½ m.p.h. Although the Motor Car Club, representing Lawson interests, had every reason to press the case for the Bollées, Brighton newspapers, with reporters on the spot, confirmed that they arrived first. The Frenchmen arrived 95 and 65 minutes before any motorists were expected, and neither checked in at Preston Park, so controversy was almost certain to arise.

George Thrupp, however, insisted that Frank Duryea's car deserved the palm. He issued a sworn statement to the effect that this machine started at 10.40 and arrived at 3.45, having stopped for 1 hour 5 minutes at Reigate; an average running speed of just under 13 m.p.h. No other cars had preceded it, claimed Thrupp, thus implying that if the Bollées were in Brighton first, they did not arrive on their own wheels. Henry Sturmey, for his part, claimed that the Duryea carrying Charles Harrington Moore had led the field. The official results placed one of the Duryeas third and a Panhard fourth. The arrival time they gave for the Duryea agreed to within a minute with Thrupp's; about the only common ground that existed between any two independent sets of results.

There was equal disagreement over which vehicles finished, and when. *The Times*, having initially given the number as only 13, later said that 22 vehicles left Brixton, and 20 of these completed the course; a praiseworthy result, it remarked.[16] According to the *Autocar*, 15 had checked in at Preston Park by 5.45 p.m., and 22 by 9 p.m. The *Engineer* compounded confusion with known inaccuracies. It listed the arrivals up to 6 o'clock – the time when the finish control officially closed – as two Léon Bollées, two Daimlers, three Panhard cars and a "Panhard" bus, one Roger-Benz of the Anglo-French company, the two Berseys and a Britannia – a total of 12. Several others, mostly unidentified, came in afterwards. One was Hewetson's and Cornell's Arnold; other survivors of the East Peckham contingent, far behind, had stopped for the night on the road. The *Engineer*'s account included electrics that were known to have come by rail from Brixton, and while noting that a Duryea made good time, mentioned neither of them among the early arrivals. The "Panhard" bus may have been any similar Daimler-engined machine. Evelyn Ellis arrived too late for the dinner, but when is not known.

The available data is too fragmentary and contradictory for any significant conclusions to be safely drawn from it. It was natural that the cars of the most experienced drivers – Duryea, the Bollée brothers, Mayade, Merckel, Otto Mayer – should figure most prominently. It was no accident, either, that all these names were foreign. Although very greatly outnumbering the overseas visitors, the only British drivers on the run with a respectable mileage under their belts were Ellis, Simms, Turrell, Hewetson and Cornell, and Duncan (who crashed); none had known such long, punishing competitions as the foreigners.

The Lawson interests were quick to dissociate themselves from the failures, disingenuously making a virtue out of necessity. The report of the Motor Car Club claimed that originally, only cars that had been "officially tested and duly passed" had been allowed to enter. When the event had perforce been thrown open to all, not only the "20 efficient cars entering as pre-arranged" took part, but also "all kinds of experimental machines".

But on the evening of the run nothing, it seemed, marred the general euphoria. Although the weather was worse than ever, the crowds in Brighton were immense. Over 200 participants and guests sat down to dinner, to see Gottlieb Daimler, "quite overcome" by his reception, presented on behalf of the Panhard company with the Motor Car Club's trophy for the firm's victory in the Paris–Marseilles race. On Monday the cars paraded informally in Brighton, and by the following day they were gone. The Arnolds returned to East Peckham via Tunbridge Wells, where they stopped for the night. Crowden drove back to London via the very long and steep ascent of Reigate Hill. Harrington Moore returned with Mayade aboard the Paris–Marseilles winner, reaching nearly 30 m.p.h. on the way. Lawson drove back on the Panhard that had come second in the race: his time from Brighton to the Metropole Hotel in Northumberland Avenue was 4 hours 14 minutes, representing an average speed of almost exactly the legal limit. According to the *Sun*, the two Panhards were racing one another.

Such speeds as these had convinced the press – not without reason – that the London–Brighton "tour" had been a race. The fastest cars had, after all, been driven "flat-out" at racing speeds. Mayade's Panhard was capable of 32 m.p.h. and had averaged 15.7 m.p.h. in the Paris–Marseilles event. These figures should be compared with those relating to the performance of cars in the Brighton run, remembering, too, that in the Paris–Marseilles, high speeds could be attained more easily and kept up far longer. In spite of its advertised good intentions, the Motor Car Club had been as responsible as anyone, with its stress on the importance of arriving first – which it compounded by awarding gold medals to the first eight to finish.

Moreover, in plain disregard of their club's expressed policy, its own members – its officials, even – had been among the worst offenders. The cars in which Harrington Moore rode – of which, admittedly, he was not in charge – had flagrantly violated the new speed limit going to and coming from Brighton. He saw nothing wrong in this, though saying in the same breath how much he disapproved of racing. To

Engineering, the event was not only a race, but "last week's Saturnalia". The *Pall Mall Gazette* refused to take the run seriously and was completely uncensorious, but still called it a race. As much as anything else, the gulf between principles and practice on the Brighton road showed up the Motor Car Club in its true colours as a body dedicated entirely to short-term commercial convenience. With the Act safely won, the desire for publicity for members' motor cars, which speed would provide more surely than anything else, overrode all considerations of diplomacy or public spirit. A feeling of *esprit de corps* and a respect for discipline would have prompted most members of a true club to obey the competition rules: the absence of the qualities is fair proof of the non-existence of the institution.

Yet, amazingly, the national press did not disapprove of the run, nor of the way in which it was handled – rather the reverse. To *The Times* the event was generally well executed and good for the motor car's image; a long leading article concluded that "enough had been done to show that motor cars . . . are destined to play a great part in the future transport both of people and of merchandise". To the *Daily Graphic*, which ran a long report, the run was "a brilliant success" in spite of breakdowns, chaos and the absence of "the best inventions", whatever that meant. The motor car was underpowered for mud and steep hills, but it had shown itself "already a workable vehicle . . . speedier than any method of road locomotion yet existing". Even the *Engineer*, usually so critical of the doings of the company promoters, could scarce forbear to cheer. This "epoch-making event", equal in significance to the opening of the first railway, would "live in the memories of those who were fortunate enough to witness the procession for many long years". In the wake of the Brighton run, the *Engineer* even withdrew, with reservations, from one of its most cherished positions. "At the present moment the spirit-propelled motor car is first and the rest nowhere" – though this could not last, it added. The *Sun*, already known for its support of Lawson, was the most fulsome of all, if not the most accurate: "The event of Saturday will be an everlasting memorial to the man who has, with such an amount of pluck and daring, secured the monopoly of this great trade in the British Isles."

Doubts were expressed, but they did not concern the organisation of the run or the conduct of the participants; nor was the ultimate success of the motor car usually questioned. The more cautious commentators differed from the enthusiasts only on the point of how long that success would take to manifest itself, bearing in mind the motor car's imperfect state The *Globe* was full of doubts, but even the poor best of which motor cars were capable was "sufficiently good to demonstrate their practical utility". To the *Standard*, the verdict on the vehicles demonstrated on the Brighton road was that they were ugly and uncomfortable, and smelt and vibrated badly – "they may be, and probably will be, the vehicles of the future, but not of the immediate present." Summing up a leading article and report, the *Daily Telegraph* declared that although it was "in its raw and clumsy infancy . . . the motor car has come to stay". According to *The Economist* on the day of the run, it was too early to say if the motor car would be successful, but "the industry possesses great potentialities".

For all the reservations, this was heady stuff, and the Lawson machine appeared unstoppable. Certainly Lawson and his partners seemed to have no doubts. To them, the Brighton run was not an isolated publicity exercise, but the centrepiece and main support of a new series of financial firework displays designed to dazzle investors while they were robbed. Here was conclusive, spectacular proof that motor cars – specifically those that Lawson's companies advertised – had finally "arrived"; that they were now both legal and demonstrably practical, and therefore good business. There was some excuse for this. In desperately adverse conditions of weather and traffic, with only one accident involving a member of the public, more than 20 vehicles – two-thirds of the field – had completed a journey as long as any made by a car in Britain within a day, in a time that equalled or bettered that of any ordinary horse-drawn carriage.

Lawson's new "spectacular" was timed for the moment when the Locomotives on Highways Act at last became law; when the great public procession that celebrated it was in all the newspapers. Not a trick was missed. Early in November the bait was laid: the British Motor Syndicate, as it was still generally known, announced a third interim dividend of a handsome 110 per cent, payable in Great Horseless Carriage Company shares, and making a grand total for the year of 150 per cent.

On the Monday following the Saturday of the run, the prospectus of a new Lawson promotion was announced: the London Electrical Cab Company. The public were invited to subscribe for shares to a total value of £150,000. The company would operate the British Motor Syndicate's Bersey patents. Its directors included Evelyn Ellis, H.H. Mulliner and J.H. Mace.

A week later a much more ambitious operation was set in train: the "reorganisation" of the British Motor Syndicate[17] as a new company. This manoeuvre enabled the Lawson interests to ask the investing public for another £1 million. The prospectus, dated 23 November, was lavishly produced, and its language was as extravagant, and as familiar, as ever. The new Syndicate, already the "sole owner of all the principal British motor car master patents of known and admitted value" would, like the old Syndicate, use its capital to buy still more patents, and make its shareholders' fortunes by selling licences in these patents. All builders or importers of motor cars constructed under the Daimler, Panhard, Peugeot, De Dion, Bollée and other patents concerned would have to buy a licence or pay a royalty. As for the effect on shares, "fabulously high prices are certain to be reached in the near future".

The prospectus was adorned with artists' impressions of the Motor Mills and the premises of Humber & Company, the New Beeston Cycle Company, and Coulthard of Preston, all in the imaginative style beloved of estate agents. The directors were the usual mix of Lawson's satellites and impressive public names, reshuffled for the occasion: Lawson himself; Thomas Robinson; H.J. Mulliner; Thomas Humber; Lord Norreys; and the famous young cricketer Prince Ranjitsinhji, who was up at Cambridge with a Daimler. Frederick Simms occupied his usual niche at consulting engineer. The nominal £1 shares of the new company were sold at a premium price of £3 from the beginning.

Lawson did not let the momentum of the Brighton run die away while his new companies were launched. The Stanley Show was a fine "shop-window", as always, and it fell conveniently between 21 and 28 November. The Lawson presence at the Agricultural Hall was overwhelming, numbering over two dozen vehicles. They included many of Lawson's Brighton run cars, among them the *Present Times* Daimler and both the leading Paris–Marseilles Panhards, six New Beeston tricycles, and no fewer than nine or ten "Coventry Motettes" – the name for the British-made Léon Bollée. The implication was that at least as many of each vehicle had been built in England; but the *Engineer*[18] and other papers called them De Dions and Léon Bollées respectively. There was also a Britannia electric bath-chair and a Gladiator motor tricycle.

Among the exhibits at the rival National Cycle Show at the Crystal Palace immediately afterwards were four Penningtons of different types, including the Brighton run torpedo, Holden's four-cylinder motor bicycle, and a newcomer – a tricar designed by Herbert Austin, manager of the Wolseley Sheep Shearing Machine Company of Birmingham. This was Austin's second car; the first had been an abortive copy of the Léon Bollée. The new machine was a light experimental dogcart with a tubular frame and wire wheels, one of them at the front, and pneumatic tyres. The engine was water-cooled, and had two cylinders and electric ignition. There were two forward speeds. The weight was 4 hundredweight, and top speed was 10 m.p.h.

In another bid to keep the publicity ball rolling, Charles Harrington Moore announced the Motor Car Club's next extravaganza, "a great motor car competition" for May 1897, in which speed would be the main consideration. Offers of the use of a private track were solicited, and there would be a special prize for the vehicle to cover one mile in one minute. Such a proposition, at a time when the fastest competitors in the Paris–Marseilles race had been capable of little more than half this speed, was a typical Lawson gesture, oblivious to practical considerations but shrewdly aware of the sensational properties of high speed. Harrington Moore put it more tactfully: "Speed . . . affords the most satisfactory test . . . of a mechanical vehicle."

Going above and beyond the enthusiasm of the press for the Brighton run, a minority of far-sighted journals expressed the opinion that it was the passing of the Locomotives on Highways Act that had been the truly epoch-making event. The *Morning* recognised this as early as July. Referring to two Bills in the pipeline that had been monopolising Parliament's attention[19] at the expense of measures such as the motor car Bill, it said of the latter that it was "likely to be immensely greater in its effects than either". At the end of August the *Westminster Gazette* described the Act as "the measure that will be remembered when all others [passed in the session] are forgotten"; it was "only second in the importance of its results to the construction of the first railway" – an analogy that others drew. Interviewed in the United States early in October, Joseph Chamberlain – influenced, perhaps, by his shareholding in the New Beeston Cycle Company – commented that the motor vehicle "promises to assume great importance".

With the benefit of hindsight, we can agree with all these sentiments, for indeed, the motor car had achieved a vital, if restricted, freedom of operation. The Act had its positive side. Motor vehicles had won Parliamentary recognition as a species of private carriage, and were no longer classed with traction engines. The lighter vehicles – a category into which all private cars could be made to fit without hardship – were allowed to travel at a speed comparable with that tolerated of other private vehicles on the road, if not at one that permitted it to realise its full potential. Only one person need be in charge, and adequate supplies of fuel could be carried. Motorists would no longer require separate licences for every county in which they drove; nor would they be subject to arbitrary local regulation of the hours during which they could motor and of the roads they could use, for such by-laws had to have Local Government Board approval.

In the short run, however, the general euphoria did not appear to be justified by events. The expected motoring boom did not come. Though people could now use motor cars, they showed no signs of doing so in significantly greater numbers than before. One reason was that home-built cars were simply not becoming available. No boom on the scale envisaged could be sustained by imports alone. The man from whom the public hoped and expected the most – Harry Lawson – was also the source of their biggest let-down. The two weeks or so on either side of the Brighton run were for Lawson a sort of grand Wagnerian apotheosis: he would never rise higher, and already as he enjoyed his triumph, enemies were multiplying about him, reaching to pull him down. Prompted, perhaps, by the start of a new display of Lawsonian business pyrotechnics, a press that had mostly been uncritical quite suddenly rounded on him, pouring scorn on all who had fallen for his blandishments, and warning off potential investors.

The *New Saturday* was an early assailant. A week before the Brighton run, it set a tone that promised no quarter. "This 'horseless carriage' boom . . . is a gross fraud upon the investing public . . . . Every patent of value . . . has expired, so that the world is now open for the production of self-propelled vehicles without let or hindrance" – not quite true, but a fair reflection of what Salomons had been saying for nearly a year. *The Economist*, on Brighton Saturday, was more restrained but hit the nail on the head with deadly precision. Motor car advertising was "designed much more with the view of attracting capital from the public . . . than purchasers for the vehicles themselves". Investors were advised to "pay less attention to the promises of profits held forth in prospectuses than to the business capacity and reputation of the men to whom the employment of the capital is to be entrusted". Still more lethal in its own way was the minute analysis of Lawson's business ventures which the *Statist* published on 21 November. Rosorting hardly at all to overt criticism, it let the facts speak for themselves.

The *Engineer* felt that the very success of the Brighton run was itself a danger to the investing public. "As an advertisement for the Motor Car Club and Mr Lawson [it was] an unqualified, even a magnificent success", yet because motor car design was far from perfect and constantly evolving, the promoters' patents, on which they set so much store, conferred no monopoly and had no value. *Engineering* unleashed the most savage invective of which it was capable. "A little ready cash to the needy inventor, a sweetening of the Press, and a cunningly-worded prospectus with lying promises to tempt the cupidity of the ignorant public" were the stock-in-trade of "the company-monger, with his blatant self-advertisement, slimy persuasiveness, and cozening ways". The Lawson interests did not normally answer criticism, but even they complained of this particular attack.

The issue of the new British Motor Syndicate prospectus brought another flood of protest. The *Engineer* called it "impudent", and denied once more the existence of any "master patents" – there was "absolutely nothing . . . to fetter any manufacturer". *The Economist* returned to the attack. The prospectus was "striking enough in the boldness of its statements, but it is even more remarkable in what it leaves unsaid". There was no word of how many shares had been subscribed, which was suggestive. And if the shares really were easily saleable at a premium, why was it necessary to invite purchasers from among the general public, in a lavish prospectus? The only explanation was that members of the Syndicate already holding shares wanted to get rid of them – but why, if their prospects were so brilliant? Could it be that these shareholders were in fact doubtful of the value of their "master patents"? Lawson "has the reputation of great shrewdness, and a distinct capacity for looking after the main chance".

The highly respected *Economist* and *Statist* used the scalpel rather than the hatchet, but to anyone with eyes to read, Lawson and his partners were now totally exposed. The *Pall Mall Gazette*'s comments on the prospectus were more earthy. That paper listed several reasons why "not a shilling should be entrusted to those who are responsible for it". The document was full of mis-statements – claiming, for example, that its shares were at a premium when in fact they were already selling at less than their face value. The over-capitalisation was "absurd" in relation to what was offered in return – a share in patents of "very questionable value". The last reason for not buying shares was simply that "the Syndicate is under the auspices of Mr Harry J. Lawson".

As usual, Lawson used eminent names in the prospectus in order to give it a bogus respectability, and as in the case of his Daimler promotion, drew fire for doing so. William Worby Beaumont's name was mentioned merely as the vendor of patents to the Syndicate in its former incarnation, together with the fact that he worked for the *Engineer*, yet such was the odium in which Lawson's name was now held that both the man and the journal objected strongly.

If the *Pall Mall Gazette* was right about British Motor Syndicate share values, the Lawson edifice was, indeed, starting to crumble even as its last bricks were set in place. A small slide had been noted as early as the beginning of October, when Daimler £10 shares were changing hands at £7–£8. A buyer who had paid only £3 each for 25 shares in the Great Horseless Carriage Company – issued at £10 – told *Pall Mall Gazette* readers early in December how they had just slumped even more: he had sold them for less than two-thirds of the price he had given. The whole complex, elegant structure was collapsing with extraordinary speed, and at the least expected moment. Within a little more than two weeks of the flotation of the reorganised British Motor Syndicate, Lawson made what was for him an unprecedentally frank and low-key admission on behalf of his manufacturing concerns: "We do not expect to be able to place motors in any quantity on the streets until next spring – say May or June – and even then we shall have been at the business only a few months." With these words he gave the lie to his own representatives' claims to have been in production earlier; but he or they had done this before. They counted on the public having a short memory, so had never worried about consistency. More significant was the absence of Lawson's habitual, overweening "bounce" and optimism – a sinister sign for shareholders. This uncharacteristically sober mood was short-lived; by the time of the British Motor Syndicate's company meeting in January 1897, it was gone. The remarkable thing was that Lawson allowed it to show at all.

By the end of 1897 the empire built up by Lawson and his associates had fallen apart. Of all the companies with which they had been linked, only one or two offered even a trace of comfort to their shareholders. Those least concerned with manufacture and most with pure speculation went first, and none collapsed faster than the newest, the reconstituted British Motor Syndicate. As early as January rank-and-file shareholders were agitating successfully for the return of their subscriptions; by March they were organising against their management. In April Lord Winchilsea resigned from the chair of the Great Horseless Carriage Company, and in September a shareholders' committee with the support of over half their number was formed to take joint action. The committee complained that although the British Motor Syndicate had bought some up-to-date patents, their own management had not gained the use of these; and that the licences the company had acquired from the Syndicate were non-exclusive. Their directors, claimed the committee, were not working in shareholders' interests at all, but in those of the other Lawson companies on whose boards they sat.[20] In January 1898 the Great Horseless Carriage Company was reconstructed as the Motor Manufacturing Company. By then, Lawson was no longer in control.

Three months earlier the New Beeston Cycle Company, too, had been reconstructed. The ailing motor side of the business was divorced from the more successful cycle side, and £110,000 extra working capital was sought for the former. At the same time, all the company promoters on the boards were bought out, to their considerable profit.

The Daimler Motor Company had an equally hard time. The first production vehicle was turned out early in March 1897: only at this point did its trading start, as a manufacturer of motor cars, and as late as May, deliveries had yet to begin. By June Lawson had been replaced as chairman by Henry Sturmey. Simms and Daimler left the board next; by October Lawson was not even a director. This fact probably helped the company, which by then was performing slightly better than most other Lawson concerns. It was producing motor cars consistently, albeit with painful slowness and in penny packets. Sturmey rather than Lawson was by now responsible for public statements, and these, while still inconsistent, were less irresponsible in tone than hitherto, and rang more true. By July a total of 20 vehicles, all of them of the modern Panhard type, had been completed and sold, and 200 men were turning out three vehicles a week – a miserably low level of productivity. By November the number was four a week, and 24 were in course of construction.[21] In other words, there was virtual stagnation.

The less prominent enterprises with which Lawson and his colleagues had been associated were suffering, too. In September New & Mayne went into receivership, and by December 1897 the Britannia Motor Carriage Company was in financial trouble. As for Edward Joel Pennington, he was still at work in the Motor Mills in April, at the same time as he and Lawson were floating a new concern called the Motor and Cycle Company of Ireland. This made nothing, and was wound up in September. Two months later Pennington was trying unsuccessfully to arouse interest in his patents in Paris. His vehicles were no longer being offered from the Motor Mills; his association with Lawson was over. His nearest approach to a production car had been his torpedo, of which five were made.

The British-built Léon Bollée, or Coventry Motette – the other tenant of the Great Horseless Carriage Company – departed from the Motor Mills also, after about four examples had been made there.[22] It had come only because of the Humber fire, and around the end of 1896 Charles McRobie Turrell, on Lawson's instructions, found other premises for its manufacture at Parkside, Coventry. Turrell resigned from his position as Lawson's secretary to run the new works, and by early 1897 production of the Coventry Motette had begun. It was made by the Coventry Motor Company, which had been established in October 1896. The company was said to have been wholly owned by the British Motor Syndicate. This is supported by the fact that its capital was initially only £10,000. No appeal to the public for funds can be traced. Confusingly, in February and March 1897 the Coventry Motor Company and the Great Horseless Carriage Company simultaneously offered what was basically the same machine – the first advertising it as the Coventry Motette and the second as the Léon Bollée. Those offered by the Great Horseless Carriage Company may have been the four vehicles made at the Motor Mills, and still unsold.

Falling share prices reflected crumbling public confidence. In February 1897 Great Horseless Carriage Company £10 shares had sunk in value to £3 15s 0d, and those of the Daimler Motor Company to £4, while New Beeston Cycle Company shares were "practically unsaleable".[23] In October Daimler shares were holding their depleted value, but Great Horseless Carriage Company stock stood at £1 2s 6d.[24]

The Motor Car Club, an integral part of the Lawson machine in its role as promotional organisation, declined with the companies it served. The great "Motor Derby", as Salomons disapprovingly called the speed trials scheduled for May, never took place. Instead, about 20 cars took part in a "tour" from Coventry to Birmingham. Tame though it was, this event had to be thrice postponed. Towards the end of November about twice as many cars started from the Metropole Hotel in London for a run to Sheen House, Richmond, by way of commemorating the first full year of freedom; but more than 100 had been expected, and it was remarked that in design, the participants showed no progress over 1896 – the sole improvements were in detail.

In May the *Autocar* had urged the need for an independent organisation on the model of the Automobile Club de France, devoted to the collective benefit of all motorists, rather than a body dominated by a single individual or financial interest. It is clear from the sequel that the *Autocar* was voicing a widely held view. Two months later Charles Harrington Moore resigned as secretary of the Motor Car Club, and in August Frederick Simms inspired and organised a meeting of all those interested in forming a new club on the lines suggested. Evelyn Ellis was elected as its first chairman, and Harrington Moore appointed as its secretary. Others present at the meeting included Walter Arnold, Alfred Cornell, James Roots, P.W. Petter and William Worby Beaumont. These names illustrate the breadth of support that existed for the new club. Such were the beginnings of Britain's first national motoring organisation, the Automobile Club of Great Britain and Ireland; later the Royal Automobile Club. In 1898 the A.C.G.B.I. and the moribund Self-Propelled Traffic Association amalgamated, bringing about the union of all major motoring interests. Discredited, shrunken and supplanted, the Motor Car Club now visibly represented no more than a rump of business interests – the remains of what had been the Lawson empire.

One company alone, of all those created by Lawson and his associates, showed the form hoped of it. In August 1897 the London Electrical Cab Company at long last put Bersey cabs on the streets of the City and West End – a dozen of them. Some plied for hire; others could be engaged by the day. Smooth, quiet, comfortable, reassuringly manageable, they were a modest success with the public, and former horse cab drivers found them easy to learn and handle. Seventeen were running by September, and 25 by the end of the year. Another 50 were commissioned in 1898. Eventually they proved an economic failure, but of all the representatives of the "new locomotion" in Britain, they were most fit for their purpose, so for two years the Mulliner-bodied Berseys in their smart black-and-yellow livery were the most successful.

As his other enterprises fell in ruins about him, Lawson fought back hard, trying to shore them up with the familiar, tawdry magic. He issued on behalf of his companies a publicity brochure of unparalleled grandeur and elaboration, entitled *The Coming Motor Traffic*, resuscitating all his old arguments and visions. As if aware of the crisis, he made a great show of protecting his licences and patents – essential policy if he wanted to prop up public confidence. Already, the British Motor Syndicate had taken action when Herbert Austin had built his close copy of the Léon Bollée, forcing him to abandon the design in favour of the tricar he showed at the 1896 National Cycle Show.

This encounter had not been publicised. It was different when in January 1897 the Syndicate sought an injunction against Charles Rolls for running his Peugeot without one of its licences. This episode showed up more than one of the weaknesses in the gimcrack Lawson edifice. Rolls had, in fact, tried to obtain his car through the Syndicate, but had failed. This demonstrated that whatever the advertised intentions of Lawson's businesses, they were not interested in delivering goods. Moreover, although the Syndicate won its case, and prominently advertised a great "victory" in the *Autocar*, the weakness of its patent claims was betrayed by the fact that Rolls was in no way penalised. He paid £15 by way of a licence fee, as he had been happy to do from the beginning, and each party paid its own costs. Two months later the Syndicate tried again, threatening Roots & Venables with legal action for breach of certain of its patents; but when the company called for details of the alleged violation, the Syndicate did not pursue the matter.

Lawson really did seem to believe that he could keep his monumental confidence trick going indefinitely. But public confidence in him had disappeared; nothing would now convince even the most gullible investors that his motor car shares had any value. The cycle boom, too, had collapsed in July 1897, and the value of shares in Lawson's over-capitalised cycle companies fell as well. The drop in share values in the one commodity no doubt accelerated the drop in the other. Lawson would still float motor companies, but his days of domination were over. The basis of his power – his patents and licences – passed to others. Even this vanished in 1901 when the validity of one of the major patents held by the British Motor Traction Company – successor to the British Motor Syndicate – was successfully challenged by the Automobile Mutual Protection Association, a manufactures' organisation set up to fight patent monopolies.

The possibilities of the motor car had not occupied Lawson's entire attention even in the boom days of 1896 – as we have seen, he speculated in cycles and tyres at the same time – and he had earlier experience of company promotion in still other fields. So, having exhausted the potential of the motor industry, Lawson turned his hand readily elsewhere. He continued his association with Ernest Terah Hooley, and the two men finally ran foul of the law. They floated the Electric Tramways Construction & Maintenance Company, which was, as usual, simply a device for funnelling investors' money into their own pockets. In 1904 they stood trial for conspiracy to defraud the company's shareholders, with Sir Edward Carson prosecuting. Full of virtuous condemnation of Lawson as "a slippery card", and brilliantly defended by Rufus Isaacs, Hooley was found not guilty. Lawson defended himself, with all his old cocky confidence. He tried to enlist the sympathy of the court, and distract it from more relevant considerations, by describing himself as the inventor of the safety bicycle (and thus father of the modern cycle industry), as the founder of the British motor industry, as a large-scale provider of employment, and generally as a public benefactor. None of it worked; Lawson went to gaol for 12 months, with hard labour. The great charade was over.

There was a grain of truth in Lawson's claims for himself, as there was in most of his assertions, for this helped to give them verisimilitude. His bold company promotions, backed by barn-storming self-confidence and a limitless capacity for ballyhoo, created an interest group of investors of which he was the self-appointed spokesman, and powerfully reinforced the idea – put about in a more gentlemanly fashion by others – that like it or not, the motor car was "the coming thing". The actual number of people involved was modest, and the sums of money they invested smaller than the promoters made out, but promotional skills conjured up a more impressive picture. It is true to say that Lawson and his fellow promoters did more than anyone else to create public opinion on the motor car; a machine in which the public had earlier had little interest, in either sense of the word. Government ministers felt themselves under a new kind of pressure – one quite different from the backstairs persuasions of Salomons – to bring in and push through a Bill to emancipate the motor car; a pressure whose presence and influence they acknowledged.[25] Without Lawson and his example an Act would have been passed, but failing the pressures he called into being, it would probably not have come so soon.

Viewed in historical perspective, the Lawson episode brought another benefit: "It was a valuable purgative period . . . the way was now clear, for neither the swindles of financiers nor the claims of patent holders were ever to trouble the industry seriously again."[26] This was in marked contrast with the experience of the movement in the United States.

The fraudulent character of the companies linked with Lawson and his colleagues explains why those businesses did not produce or import more than a handful of cars, after these vehicles had been granted their qualified liberty. It does not explain why other firms, honestly run and offering a good product, failed to do so. The grossly under-powered, dirty-running kerosene cars of Petter, Hill & Boll and Roots & Venables did not and could not succeed commercially, but the Benz design was a different proposition. The *réclame* of the Brighton run caused the Arnold Motor Carriage Company to lay down 11 more cars in 1897–8, in addition to the prototype that had run on 14 November,[27] but that was the extent of its manufacturing effort. These cars were basically Benz, but the engines were Arnold-made, with a different bore and stroke and bronze castings in place of iron. James Tuke, Arnold's agent, was active. By the end of 1897 he was running the Yorkshire Motor Company, a flourishing sales organisation which introduced to Britain the marketing of cars on hire purchase, and rented them out as well.

The Anglo-French Motor Carriage Company advertised "Lurries, Vans, Broughams, Cabs, Victorias, Coaches, Dogcarts and Char-a-bancs" in the "Red Letter Day" issue of the *Autocar*. But promises of manufacture came to nothing until 1897; the factory at Digbeth, Birmingham, was not even equipped until March of that year. Three months later the premises were in business and working, employing about 70 hands. In March, too, Radcliffe Ward's London Electric Omnibus Company still had only one bus running experimentally on the streets, yet was asking the public for another £50,000 working capital. The prospectus had promised 125 buses, with the original capital. New company promotions in 1897 were legion, but all were modest by Lawson standards, both in intent and in capitalisation. They resembled the promotions of 1896, however, in their general lack of success.[28]

The universal inertia was reflected in the disappointing turnout of motor vehicles at the year's exhibitions. There was no longer such a pressing need to influence Parliament or the Local Government

Board, and elaborate publicity exercises on the part of company promoters were things of the past; but these factors were not the whole answer. Most of these displays were originated by exhibition promoters anxious to cash in on the novelty of the motor car, rather than by motor trade interests. Better things might have been expected of exhibitions put on by the more responsible, disinterested and established organisers of such affairs, but they met the same fate.

The biggest disappointment was the long-heralded *Engineer* competition, held in May at the Crystal Palace. Out of 72 entries, just five materialised, and only one of these, an Arnold, could be considered as other than experimental. The organisers declared the competition void. The lack of support proved, they said, that there was no Coventry motor industry, and that the Daimler Motor Company in particular had been afraid to submit its vehicles to testing. Critics of the competition pointed out that its conditions put would-be entrants off: notably the requirement for six sets of blueprints with each vehicle, and the fact that petrol cars, though admitted, were banished to a class of their own, where they could not compete directly with other types of vehicles, nor try for the most prestigious and valuable prizes.

Much was expected, too, of the Royal Agricultural Society's Manchester Show in June, but this also was regarded as a damp squib. Four of the Anglo-French company's Roger-Benzes turned up, and a Leyland Steam Motor Company's van. The Yeovil Motor Company and the Wolseley Sheep Shearing Machine Company had stands, but no cars. Only the Leyland van undertook the road trial, from Crewe to Leek.

As for Charles Cordingley's engineering exhibition in September, "as an exhibition of motor cars it must be pronounced a failure": most companies ignored the occasion.[29] The Stanley Cycle Show in November was better supported, with entries from the Daimler, Great Horseless Carriage, Humber and Beeston companies; but as with the year's other exhibitions nothing new, no sign of progress, was discernible. At the National Cycle Show, Holden's motor bicycle alone was visible.

Very suddenly, the steam had gone out of the entire motoring movement. Charles Jarrott noticed the difference in atmosphere. Before the Brighton run, "horses were to be superseded forthwith"; afterwards, "everybody . . . relapsed into placid contentment, and felt secure that the good old-fashioned animal used by our forefathers was in no danger of being displaced." The unexpected lack of motor vehicles on the roads was very noticeable. Undoubtedly, some would-be manufacturers suffered in investors' eyes, however illogically, from association with the Lawsonian image of the company promoter. Lack of financial support from the public may well have contributed to their failure to produce vehicles in significant quantities. In November 1896 *Engineering* drew attention to the way in which inventors were damaged by the notoriety attaching to Lawson and his associates, but its words applied equally to other companies trying to raise capital from the investing public: "The honest inventor who came after, having laboriously perfected a system of real value, finds the money market as bare for him as a field of sprouting wheat after a flight of locusts." A month later the *Automotor and Horseless Vehicle Journal* described shares in motor car companies – all of them, not just Lawson's – as "almost unsaleable" on the Stock Exchange.

But with these non-Lawson companies, it is at least equally likely that failure to build cars in quantity was due to a lack of sufficient demand for them. They had their appeal, for reasons already stated; but this was not enough, in the face of their manifold drawbacks, to bring about the sort of boom that most people had been expecting after all the ballyhoo of 1896. Their faults of design and construction, conspiring with bad roads and layman's ignorance to cause unreliability; the difficulty of driving the more complicated vehicles; the fact that motor cars had entered a highly competitive field against a powerful, entrenched rival in the shape of the horse carriage; their high first cost; a feeling, perhaps, that they were vulgar machines associated with company promoters, raffish high society and mechanics; and finally, the heavily qualified nature of the freedom they had won – all these factors conspired to ensure that the new machine gained ground slowly and hesitatingly in its early years in Britain.[30]

Conclusion
Why Recovery?

The recovery of the British motoring movement from the effects of the artificial boom of 1895–6, its struggle with its enemies, and the first stages in the formation of the modern motoring scene are no part of this story. The tale has already been most ably picked up and recounted by others.[1] Nevertheless, the fact of recovery, after so unpromising a start, is interesting in itself. It provides one obvious question that remains to be asked: why did the motor car as defined in the opening words of this study take root after 1896, when it had failed to do so at two other junctures when the auguries seemed equally favourable – in 1831–2, and especially in 1861, when the first and second generations of vehicles had their best chance of establishing themselves? The explanations customarily offered beg this question. Certainly the ground was made ready by the gradual replacement of fraudulent promoters by businessmen who truly wanted to make motor cars; by the establishment of a single, disinterested, fully representative motoring organisation; and by the revival of confidence among investors that such developments as these encouraged.

But this answer is incomplete even as an explanation for recovery after 1896; and it does nothing to explain the second half of the apparent paradox. In particular, one is left wondering why success did not come after 1861, instead of 1896. After all, at each of these points the self-propelled road vehicle had just been given legal recognition; severely limited, but sufficient to allow it to develop. Socially, too, its position was similar; people tended to dislike it when they saw it, but most had not seen it, outside carefully stage-managed demonstrations; and comment in the media was generally friendly. Public opinion was still largely unformed. There was therefore no obvious reason for public acceptance, and the business confidence that founded an industry, to manifest itself after 1896 rather than after 1861.

The full answer is complex, lying partly in the special weaknesses of

479

the vehicles of the first two generations, and partly in the strengths of those of the third. After Walter Hancock's gigs or phaetons and Frank Hills's *britzka* had given such a powerful and promising lead in the late 1830s, why did the private self-propelled carriage fail to establish itself? William Bridges Adams's colourful and graphic attack on the steamer's anti-social qualities was justified, and furnished only part of the answer: there were more subtle discouragements. Even if the steamer had been better behaved, there was no good reason for the potential customer to buy one. With technology's aid the horse carriage was approaching a peak of elegance and comfort, and the roads it ran on had never been so good. The carriage, furthermore, was the prime symbol of social status.

Then there was the fact that steam on the road was already dead on its feet by the time private steamers were built – indeed, they were one symptom of its decline, in that Gurney and Hancock turned to them only when their ventures into commercial public service had foundered. The sources of cash that might have financed improvements in all types of passenger steam carriage had been impoverished or frightened off the whole subject by the failure of the steam coach and bus operators. Investment money was going into railways instead. Parliamentary attitudes were vital indirectly, as a prime cause of the defeat of the commercial operators, but in a direct sense they were irrelevant, for high turnpike tolls would probably not have discouraged the rich enthusiast who would have bought a private steamer.

The same was true of the period after 1861: equitable tolls, as granted by the Locomotives Act of that year, meant little to operators of private steamers, who had been running about enthusiastically for nearly three years without its benefit. The horse carriage had attained that position of entrenched strength towards which it had been moving 30 years before. Steam had, indeed, returned to the road, but in no way that helped the private self-propelled vehicle. This second generation of private steamers had disadvantages all its own. The typical machine, based solidly on railway locomotive practice, was socially even more objectionable than its predecessor of the 1830s. Not without justice, it was equated in the public eye with that perambulatory nightmare, the traction engine, and suffered accordingly. Having no strong interests to fight for it, it had its prospects blighted by the Act of 1865, which prevented it from using the one necessary attribute of a private vehicle that it possessed – speed. The fact that later private steamers were in general more civilised was unimportant – the damage had been done by 1865.

What, then, was special about the state of affairs in Britain after

1896? First, an alternative to the horse carriage that was more acceptable than the steamer had been found, in the shape of the petrol motor car. Its drawbacks were many and various, but were of a kind that could be overcome by technical improvements, whether to vehicles, fuels or roads, and by the spread of knowledge of how to build and drive cars that would come with time. With all its daunting disadvantages, it was, in any case, more acceptable than the steamer.

In addition, the motor car of the turn of the century offered positive, and absolutely crucial, benefits over horse carriages and over steam carriages of the post-1861 period. Since there was no need to change tired horses, it could keep going indefinitely. It could cover unprecedented distances in a day, aided in this by its potential for high speed, and by the fact that constant and prolonged halts for topping up water tanks were unnecessary. It could be prepared for a run easily and quickly; and cars based on the Benz or early Daimler formulae – which were in the majority – were relatively simple to drive. Neither point could be made for horsedrawn or steam carriages. In short, the petrol motor car was the nearest approximation that had so far appeared to "instant" self-propelled transport, ready to go at short notice, and able to keep going. As reliability improved and drivers gained experience, these qualities became more apparent.

When petrol cars had been running long enough for realistic figures to be produced, it was discovered, too, that their friends' claims for economy over horsedrawn vehicles were to some extent justified, in that the more intensively they were used, for example by doctors, the greater the advantage over the horse. In 1900 running 30 miles a day for 200 days a year in a one-horse, two-seater carriage, using two horses in relays, cost 6.5d a mile, and in a light two-seater car with pneumatic tyres, 4.75d a mile. A one- or two-horse, four-seater carriage, with three horses in use, cost 12.06d a mile, and a four-seater car on pneumatics, 7.39d a mile. Such differences might seem little to the rich, but they were vital to the winning of a wider market among middle-class professional men and commercial users.

The new machine, furthermore, was more or less ready-made. Manufacturers did not need to wait upon research and development, which had already been done on the Continent. There was not even a necessity, as it turned out, for total reliance on expensive foreign licences, since the most important relevant patents had expired. If British manufacturers were slow in providing cars, they could be imported, as soon as foreign constructors could fill orders. If a would-be owner bought a car of established make, he could be reasonably confident that he would not be used as an experimenter's guinea-pig.

A second factor new in the 1890s was the popularisation of the idea of investing in public limited companies; of having "a piece of the action", however small it might be. This created a huge reservoir of capital, consisting of the savings of many small men, that became available to finance industry and trade, and was attracted particularly to innovative enterprise. The wealth of the nation was so great, and the desire to participate in the wealth-making process so strong, that money flowed back even into an industry that had let millions run to waste. It did so precisely because the petrol motor car was so promising.

There was a third element, less easily definable than the others – the fact that the idea of self-propelled private transport was much stronger in the 1890s than in the 1860s. The multiplication of private steamers between the two dates, in defiance of the 1865 Act, was one symptom of this; another was the recommendation in both the 1873 select committee report and the 1874 Bill that light private vehicles should be free from speed restrictions – a suggestion remarkable for the fact that in those years there were few such machines on the road, and no lobby campaigning for them.

It is rightly said that the popularisation of the bicycle helped to promote the idea of personal mobility, but any extension of this to argue that the ground was thus prepared for the motor car must be treated with care. It is true that an engineer with a bicycle, or an employee in the cycle industry, might easily turn his thoughts to a motor cycle or car, but he would tend to use one as an employee, not as an owner – at least until a second-hand market was established – or else he would build one himself. Car ownership was for carriage folk, and bicycles for the masses. Carriage folk were not given the idea by riding bicycles, for by and large they did not do so. Carriage folk could imagine owning a motor car, because they could afford it, but the average bicycle owner, a shop assistant or City clerk on his £2 a week or less, could never seriously contemplate it.

The spread of the idea of private self-propelled transport was part of a much broader picture, the theme of which was the gradual acceptance by people of machines into their everyday lives; their growing familiarity with and acclimatisation to technologies they did not understand, but welcomed or at least tolerated. The world of 1861 knew the steam engine, the railway, gas light, the electric telegraph, the sewing machine, the camera. That of 1896 had been given, in addition, mains electricity, electric light, trains and trams, the telephone, the gramophone, the typewriter, the dirigible airship, the oil engine, and most recently the cinema, wireless telegraphy and the X-ray machine. Indeed, although Britain was still a fundamentally conservative society, the virtue of progress in a variety of directions –

social, political and economic as well as technological – was increasingly accepted by all shades of opinion; a process exemplified by the programme of the Conservative administration of 1895–1902. The acceptance of new technology was just one aspect of this trend.

Again, we must not overstress this factor, for there is no way of proving that it made the idea of owning a motor car more natural at the end of the century than it had been 30 or 40 years earlier; but it provides a reasonable hypothesis. Britain was on the way to becoming the technology-oriented society familiar today, in which the motor car – almost as much a "part of the furniture" as the clock on the mantelpiece – is one of the many machines we take for granted. In this process, the motor car has played a bigger part than any other machine.

To understand what happened to the British motor car in the 19th century, it is not enough to study only, or even mainly, the vehicles themselves and the careers and reminiscences of their builders. To do so is to gain an impression of a lonely, persecuted band of visionaries defeated not merely by technical problems, but by the determined, relentless hostility of a united front of all-powerful enemies – commercial rivals, turnpike trusts, friends of the horse and of the agricultural interest in general, and simple, blinkered conservatives. Such a picture is quite misleading. It is necessary – and a beginning has been made in these pages – to look carefully at social, political and economic conditions in Britain, among them the evolution of Parliamentary institutions, of political philosophy and morality, and of the machinery of national and local government. The condition of agriculture, the price of food, the fear of revolution; the state of industrial technology and patent law; the development of roads administration; the growth of the popular technical press – all these are relevant. So, too, is the state of other forms of transport: stage coaches, railways, canal passage boats, steamboats, the design and economy of horse vehicles and cycles. All these help to throw light on events, trends, human motives and practical consequences.

Most important, a close study must be made of Parliamentary debates on Bills, of the content of those Bills, and of the evidence given to select committees. Equally keen attention must be given to the composition of committees, and the interests and backgrounds of committee members, witnesses, and participants in debate inside and outside Parliament. The lay, non-technical Press both national and local must be examined; so must those company prospectuses and turnpike trust minute books that are available. In all these matters, the present work has tried to point the way.

At the end of the day, the student will not only have acquired a rounded picture of a substantial segment of 19th century British life and society; he or she will have arrived at something much nearer the truth of what happened to the British motor car – and self-propelled road vehicles in general – than can be obtained through a narrower approach to the subject.

The revelations will be many. It will appear, for instance, that in the battle over steam coaches in the 1830s, on the result of which the fate of contemporary motor car builders depended, the issues were far from cut and dried. The truth is that not many more than half of the new turnpike trust Bills introduced in the 1830s discriminated against steam even in the worst years; that not one, even of the most notorious, can be said with certainty to have had lethal designs on it; and that even when the trusts blocked roads, the action was not always necessarily motivated by malice. It will turn out that the steam coach's two most dangerous potential rivals – the coachmasters and the railways – either despised or ignored it.

Conversely, steam vehicle builders had great reserves of strength – at various times, they were offered a lot of money by rich speculators, and they were backed by famous engineers and prominent statemen and politicians. It transpires that the House of Commons, in spite of being still dominated by the landed and agricultural interest, consistently supported steam on the road in the 1830s; the Lords alone, aiming to favour the horse and trust interests, opposed it.

The picture that emerges is one of ill-judged and tactless pro-steam propaganda influencing the trusts to take action against steam in a small number of well-publicised cases, and inducing the Lords to keep on rejecting Commons Bills. The outcome is that capital is frightened away from a nascent industry already burdened by intractable technical and economic problems and unbusinesslike constructors, going instead to the more promising railways. The relevance of this failure to the motor car is very clear: the builders may or may not have made more motor cars if they had survived in business – overcoming, perhaps, the social drawbacks of private steamers – but they failed to survive as motor car constructors because they failed to survive as coach and bus constructors.

Coming to the 1860s and 1870s, an equally unfamiliar scene unfolds. In spite of the propaganda put forth by motor car interests in the last stages of their battle for recognition, in the 1890s, there is little evidence of public or Parliamentary resentment towards motor cars as such, or even acknowledgement of their existence. The legislation and debate of the time is concerned almost exclusively with the traction engine: its friends try to secure legislation in its favour, its enemies try to curb it. The unregarded motor car wins or loses – generally it loses – incidentally to the gains or losses of the traction engine, to the fate of which it is firmly tied. Ironically, the only overt malice towards motor cars comes from the traction engine builders, who might have been thought sympathetic, but who are in fact responsible for thinking up the red flag, that notable symbol of oppression to the motor car lobby of the 1890s.

It turns out, furthermore, that the three locomotive Acts that became law in the period – those of 1861, 1865 and 1878 – were not devised by anti-traction engine interests to restrict these machines, but were inspired, or at least supported, by vocal and increasingly strong pressure groups of engine manufacturers and progressive landowners, with the idea of protecting them. By and large these groups succeeded in their aim – at the expense of motor cars – even if they had to make concessions to do so. The friends of the traction engine gained a little more from each Act, even though it was the period of greatest hostility towards self-propelled road vehicles, and even though traction engines were responsible for creating most of that hostility. From each Act, at the same time, the friends of the motor car lost; sometimes a little, sometimes a lot.

Looking at the third and final act of the drama – the coming of the petrol-driven motor car to Britain – the surprises that reward a broad rather than a narrow view mount up. We see little or nothing of that favourite scenario of the motor-car lobby and of reminiscing pioneers – motorists and their friends as a tiny, beleaguered band of enlightened philanthropists battling against serried ranks of selfish horse, carriage and railway interests, and of senseless reaction. It is an image very much like that propagated by the steam partisans of the 1830s.

Instead, there appears a picture of several disparate groups of opinion-formers, each intent on freeing the motor vehicle from restrictions for its own, frequently differing reasons. Their weaknesses are not those to which they admit. They suffer because they are constantly fighting one another instead of together; because their propaganda is frequently inept and counter-productive; because the machine they espouse falls so far short of the public expectations they have aroused. All this has a very familiar ring to a student of the 1830s.

The friends of the motor car are shown to have strengths which – again – will not be acknowledged. Some groups are skilled, experienced, more or less unprincipled, and very aggressive practitioners of the art of public relations and the "hard sell". The full and startling extent of Harry Lawson's "empire" (or rather empires) and influence – not always appreciated – becomes clear. Some operators have a lot of money behind them; and there is a significant segment of the investing public with a stake in their schemes. These are new strengths. Other groups with more elevated motives have friends in high places, and the motor car now has government backing, whether that government is Liberal or Conservative. The most vocal opposition in Parliament is more likely to be motivated by political expediency than by any genuine interest in the controversy.

There is nothing heroic about the struggle, as it turns out, for the foe hardly exists in any identifiable form. The railway interests see no enemy and perhaps a friend in the motor vehicle; many farmers feel the same way; the progressive coachbuilders hail it as a new source of custom; and to many of the keenest and most eminent horsemen the motor car is a new and sporting experience, not a menace. Nor, at this time, are most magistrates "anti-motorist", in spite of the provocation they receive. They rightly observe the letter of the law, but they usually criticise it, implicitly or explicitly.

The outcome is, indeed, "touch and go" right up to the end, but not for the reasons suggested by the motor car lobby, and there has been no dramatic confrontation, no divided nation. Initially the friends of the motor car – those little groups of dedicated publicists and promoters – have the field entirely to themselves. Then they provoke the appearance of an even smaller group of convinced, organised anti-motorists; the two tiny armies fight it out in front of a public at first massively indifferent to the issues, and never more than marginally involved. Though weak in numbers, the opposition is dangerous because it works on the other camp's weaknesses. Finally the contest turns into a race between public opinion that is showing signs of hardening against the motor car as it takes shape, and the urgent efforts of the vehicle's partisans to wring useful concessions from an increasingly reluctant administration and local government apparatus.

The friends of the motor car win, by a whisker; but to the objective onlooker it has been a disjointed, hasty, unedifying and undignified scramble. This is a truer picture than the struggle of light with darkness conjured up by propagandists and the reminiscences of the pioneers.

Notes

1 Albert M. Hyamson, *David Salomons*, 119; Lord Montagu of Beaulieu (ed.), *History of Ten Years of Automobilism, 1896–1906*, 3–4.
2 Later, another journal agreed: *La Vie au Grand Air* gave generous space to motoring.
3 Beaumont became a vice president of the Society of Engineers, vice chairman of the Roads Improvement Association, and consulting engineer to the Automobile Club of Great Britain and Ireland on its foundation in 1897.
4 *Engineer* (24 Apr. 1896) 425.
5 The significance of this comparison, which sounds comical today, lay in the fact that, given a good surface, the pneumatic-tyred safety bicycle was the fastest vehicle on the road, in the sense that a normally strong and healthy cyclist could keep up 12 m.p.h. for hours on end: a speed that quickly exhausted a horse in harness. Its average speeds were therefore much higher. Twenty or thirty miles in a day, commonplace for a keen cyclist, was double the capacity of a horse drawing.
6 See pp. 335–6.
7 Because the same men might have different interests, the figures add up to considerably more than the total of Conservative and Liberal M.P.s in Parliament.
8 That is, all owners of land, irrespective of other interests. See J.D. Chambers and G.E. Mingay, *The Agricultural Revolution 1750–1880*, 158.
9 The royal commission, set up by the government of the day, was an instrument of inquiry into major public issues that was increasingly used as an alternative to the select committee, set up by Parliament.
10 W.J.K. Davies, *Light Railways: Their Rise and Decline*, 7.
11 The Bill passed into law, but was a failure, as its opponents predicted. By 1918 less than half of the mileage authorised by the Board of Trade had been built, and only £203,000 in Treasury subsidies had been taken up.
12 It was estimated that out of the 8000 engines in use in 1896, only about 600 were licensed for road haulage. See Report and Minutes, Select Committee of the House of Commons on Traction Engines (1896) 218.
13 Later first Baron Eversley. He was the nephew of Charles Shaw-Lefevre, first Viscount Eversley, a friend of steam on the road in the 1830s.
14 To allow legislation to be amended easily to suit changing circumstances without recourse to the cumbersome procedure of obtaining new Acts, Parliament was increasingly delegating authority to government departments. Thus the Board of Trade was given powers in connection with light railways.
15 Hansard (30 July 1896).
16 It had been a weak administration, in that it had commanded no absolute majority in the Commons, and had been forced to depend on Irish Nationalist support.
17 *Engineer* (21 June 1895) 527–8.
18 He was not the only American newspaper tycoon to feel thus. James Gordon Bennett, proprietor of the *New York Herald*, had watched the Paris–Rouen trials,

and had sent a reporter to follow it on a bicycle. Bennett was a financial guarantor of Paris–Bordeaux, and put up a trophy for the Gordon Bennett international motor races, first run in 1900.

19 *The Times* (13 Aug. 1895); the *Engineer* (16 Aug. £895), from *Scientific American*.
20 *Engineer* (22 Nov. 1895) 495–6.
21 So says the most scholarly American reference book on the period: The Editors of "Automobile Quarterly", *The American Car since 1775*, 58 *ff*. The *Engineer* said at the time (3 Jan. 1896, 1–5) that the competing Duryea still had belt-and-chain transmission, and that a new car was to have gear final drive.
22 *Engineer* (3 Jan. 1896) 1–5.
23 The earliest government department to be set up to look after agriculture, dating from the 18th century.
24 Salomons claimed to have written 56,000 letters in the course of his campaign on behalf of the motor car. See A. Hyamson, op. cit., 121.
25 Walter Arnold claimed $\frac{1}{2}$d a mile for the Benz derivatives that he later imported – see *Automotor and Horseless Vehicle Journal* (Dec. 1896) 85 (advertisement).
26 Henry Sturmey, the editor of the *Autocar*, agreed with Salomons' reasoning – see letter, *Daily Graphic* (16 Oct. 1895).
27 George Smith, *Concise History of English Carriages and Motorcars*, 91.
28 The organising committee of the Paris–Bordeaux race had been kept in being, reconstructed as the world's first automobile club.
29 The Earl had moved the 1880 select committee on the Highways Acts. By the 1890s the agricultural depression had created a class of needy peers only too willing to forget the traditions of their forefathers and become associated with business. See F.M.L. Thompson, *English Landed Society in the 19th Century, passim*.
30 The Humber, Raleigh and Dunlop figures come from Geoffrey Williamson, *Wheels Within Wheels*, 116–42; those for Singer and Swift from an anonymous contemporary *exposé, The Hooley Book*, 15–17. Hooley's own figure for his Humber profit was £300,000 (*Hooley's Confessions*, 73).
31 Hooley himself, in *Hooley's Confessions*, 49, 293, gives two different figures.
32 Geoffrey Williamson, op. cit., 116–42. Finding out the truth about who raised how much in what promotions, and on what terms, is full of difficulties. For example *The Hooley Book*, 15–17, suggests that Hooley was responsible for the Humber flotation, which may be a way of saying that he financed Lawson; but the *Saturday Review* (22 Feb. 1896, 200), another almost contemporary source, attributes the promotion solely to Lawson, making no mention of a Hooley involvement. The boom year for cycle company promotions was 1896. At the end of 1895 the capital invested in public companies engaged in manufacture was less than £6 millions. By November 1896 the figure was over £11 millions. Turnover was running at the rate of £12 millions per annum. See *Automotor and Horseless Vehicle Journal* (Nov. 1896) 59.
33 *Saturday Review* (22 Feb. 1896) 200; ibid. (18 Apr. 1896) 399. Lawson tried to make out (*Saturday Review*, 11 Apr. 1896, letter) that of seven companies he had floated in ten years, he had failed with only one; but he did not convincingly refute the figures quoted against him.
34 £250 in the case of the Daimler Motor Company.
35 Thus the cycle manufacturers Humber & Company were advertised as builders of the Kane-Pennington.
36 For example, the British Motor Syndicate bought a part of the premises previously acquired by the Daimler Motor Company, then sold it to the Great Horseless Carriage Company. See p. 415.

37 For instance, the Daimler Motor Company, a Lawson "manufacturing" concern, paid him £40,000 for the use of the Daimler patents held by his British Motor Syndicate. In the 12 months to November 1896, the Lawson promotions that owned patents had been paid £200,000 by other Lawson promotions.

38 *English Mechanic* (18 Oct. 1895) 202. This journal did not name the makes, but obviously those for which the Syndicate held the licence were meant.

39 In Apr. 1896.

40 The Great Horseless Carriage Company.

41 The Daimler Motor Company, the Great Horseless Carriage Company, and the London Electrical Cab Company.

42 The Universal Electrical Carriage Syndicate (a subsidiary of the Great Horseless Carriage Company), and the London Electrical Carriage Company.

43 The Great Horseless Carriage Company.

44 Edge and Jarrott became Britain's most renowned racing drivers of the early 1900s. Edge's genius for salesmanship made the Napier the nation's leading make until the coming of the Silver Ghost Rolls-Royce, and later galvanised the A.C. concern. Jarrott & Letts was a major name on the distributive side of the industry.

45 *Birmingham Daily Gazette* (23 Nov. 1895).

46 Sturmey wrote authoritatively on cycling, photography and, later, motoring – a very common combination of interests.

47 Iliffe "nursed" a more famous journalist than Sturmey. In 1885 he bought *Bicycling News*. For the next three years one of its sub-editors was a keen young cyclist called Alfred Harmsworth, who left to start his own paper, *Answers*.

48 Patent no. 22650, 1895. Sturmey is best known today for his part in the invention of the Sturmey-Archer epicyclic three-speed gear system, but he patented many other inventions too, including a power attachment for horsedrawn vehicles, and a loading crane driven from the engine of a self-propelled goods vehicle.

49 The Great Horseless Carriage Company. See Kenneth Richardson, *The British Motor Industry 1896–1939*, 11–19.

50 The Daimler Motor Company.

51 It was not, however, until early 1897 that a steam brake with body by Atkinson & Philipson was actually on the road. The motive power was provided by Toward & Company of Newcastle.

52 See p. 51 *ff.*

53 H.H. Mulliner was also on the board of the Dunlop Pneumatic Tyre Company. It is clear that he was as heavily involved with Lawson as he was with the motor car movement – a common combination.

Different branches of the numerous Mulliner family ran separate coachbuilding businesses and sales organisations. The picture was a complicated one, but here, fortunately, we need be concerned only with the Mulliners who dabbled with the motor car in 1896. There were five of them, all of the same generation. Four were brothers. Arthur Felton Mulliner became Chairman of Mulliners Ltd of Northampton. His younger brother Herbert Hall Mulliner was Chairman of Mulliners Ltd of Birmingham. In association with another brother, Francis, Arthur and the fourth brother, A.G. Mulliner, founded Mulliners (London) Ltd as a subsidiary of the Northampton business. Mulliners (London) Ltd was a sales outlet with a showroom. Francis was involved with another Mulliner coachbuilding concern in Liverpool, of which A.G. Mulliner was managing director.

Henry Jervis Mulliner, a first cousin of the four brothers, joined Mulliners (London Ltd) in 1896, and four years later founded H.J. Mulliner & Company, the first coachbuilding firm in Britain to specialise in motor car bodies.

During 1896 Arthur, H.H. and H.J. each made at least one car body, but who built what is in most cases difficult to determine, because contemporary sources usually referred simply to a "Mulliner" body. Francis Mulliner owned a car during the same year.

54 As bus operators had discovered, nothing – except sustained high speed – reduced the working life of a horse so fast as constant stopping and starting.

55 In 1895 one London jobmaster alone kept 1200 horses.

56 See comment from *The Country Gentleman*, quoted in Harold Nockolds (ed.), *The Coachmakers: A History 1677–1977*, 117–19.

57 See p. 421.

58 Lord Montagu of Beaulieu (ed.), *A History of Ten Years of Automobilism 1896–1906* (1906) 18–19; Alfred Harmsworth (ed.), *Motors and Motor Driving* (1902) 366; *Autocar* (18 Jan. 1896) 143. Other motorists came to the same understanding with their local police forces and magistrates: see the *Autocar* (8 Feb. 1896) 170.

59 According to one source, Carr designed this tricar himself: see the *Autocar* (16 Oct. 1897) 659–61. It was practical, if not very lively, long-distance transport for two.

60 This firm was a subsidiary of the Britannia Lathe & Oil Engine Company, which at the same time offered kerosene engines for road vehicles and other purposes.

61 C.E. Venables.

62 Also described as a wagonette and a phaeton: possibly different bodies were fitted.

63 *Glasgow Weekly Herald* (28 Dec. 1895); *Autocar* (23 Nov. 1895) 47. In November 1896 Johnston bought T.R.B. Elliot's Panhard, perhaps in order to learn from it.

64 The *English Mechanic* (6 Sept. 1895, 63) disapproved of deliberate provocation of the police: "The immediate effect of the French trials has been to stir people up against the law."

65 As noted, it was usual for cyclists – and later motorists – to be dedicated amateur photographers.

66 *Engineer* (29 Nov. 1895) 524; *Autocar* (7 Dec. 1895) 68–71. Parkyns's Bateman tricycle, that had passed to Sir David Salomons, was shown working at the meeting.

67 It has been calculated that every year, Britain's city streets were swamped in about 10 million tons of horse manure (F.M.L. Thompson, *Victorian England: The Horsedrawn Society*, 10–12). London alone had 80,000 horses in 1897. To the stink and dirt were added the din from horses' hooves and iron tyres on the stone setts that still surfaced most streets, and acute congestion. The motor car was widely expected to remedy all these ills, once it had become general. Since the motor car or van occupied only half the space of a horsedrawn vehicle, the streets would become much less crowded. It all makes ironical reading nowadays. See Sir David Salomons, *The Horseless Carriage*, 20–21.

68 A body founded in 1892 to organise the farming interest for mutual aid.

69 The Great Horseless Carriage Company. The family was chronically short of money. The eleventh Earl had gone bankrupt, and the thirteenth Earl was later compelled to sell off large estates.

PART 2

1 *Engineer* (20 Dec. 1895) 611–12.
2 *Engineer* (20 Dec. 1895) 617.

3 Holborn Viaduct was the centre of the cycle distribution business, and a logical place for Lawson to establish himself.

4 Claude Johnson, *The Early History of Motoring*, 36. Johnson was writing 30 years later, and did not produce evidence, but he was very close to the people and events involved: see p. 411. In 1897 he became first secretary of the Automobile Club of Great Britain and Ireland, Britain's first independent national motor club.

5 *Engineer* (7 Feb. 1896) 146.

6 See p. 411.

7 *Autocar* (19 Dec. 1896) 718. Others had called self-propelled road vehicles "motor cars" before the new club named itself in Jan. 1896. *Engineering* referred to "petroleum motor cars" in June 1895. The magazine *Cycling* is said to have proposed the term in the latter part of the year (George Smith, op. cit., 76), and in November Frederick Simms himself recommended either "motor car" or "motor carriage" (*Engineer*, 1 Nov. 1895, 434). Properly, it was the name already given to railcars; that is, self-contained driving and passenger-carrying rail units, driven by steam or electricity. "Car" usually signified a railway wagon or carriage, or a tramcar, while "motor" simply meant "driving". But the term was used thus only in technical circles, and the vehicle it described was almost as new and unfamiliar as its road-bound contemporary, so there was no good reason why it should not be "borrowed".

   "Motor car", as one word or two, was only one of many names given to the machine in its earliest days. Not surprisingly, a French derivation was the most popular – the clumsy "horseless carriage", or *voiture sans chevaux*. Among the runners-up were "automobile carriage" (the French *voiture automobile*, from which the first word was already being dropped: *Kent and Sussex Courier*, 7 Feb. 1896). The host of names that never caught on included "autocar", as canvassed by Sturmey's journal, and fleetingly popular outside its columns.

   "Motor car" came up from nowhere at the same time as the Motor Car Club's name was in every newspaper as the organiser of Lawson's spectacular exhibitions and demonstrations. It is not too fanciful to suggest that the prominence achieved by the club settled the name by which the new machine was known in Britain.

8 In February the police near Catford in Kent were known for their tolerant attitude: see the *Autocar* (22 Feb. 1896) 196–7.

9 George Johnston was still motoring in mid-March 1896: see *Coach Builders', Harness Makers' and Saddlers' Art Journal* (Apr. 1896) 46.

10 There was a link between the Prince of Wales and Evelyn Ellis – and thence with Simms and the Lawson camp – through Ellis's cousin Major-General Sir Arthur Ellis, an aide-de-camp to the Prince. General Ellis accompanied the Prince to the opening of the next Imperial Institute exhibition in May, and advised on the foundation of the Automobile Club of Great Britain and Ireland in the following year.

11 The Bill was not printed.

12 The Commons Standing Committee on Law.

13 The volume of business in the Commons was so heavy that Parliament adopted this resort to relieve the pressure on its time. It was not unusual – see vol. 2 p. 251. Why George Robert Canning Harris, fourth Baron Harris, should speak for the Local Government Board is not clear. His father had served on the 1865 Lords Select Committee on the Locomotives Bill of that year, and he himself had experience of administration in government, but Harris's main claim to fame was as the most outstanding amateur cricketer of his day.

14 *Engineering* (15 May 1896) 644–5; *Engineer* (19 June 1896) 607. *Engineering* had

commented favourably on the Daimler car's handling at the Crystal Palace display already described.

15 Quoted in the *Autocar* (6 June 1896) 374–5.
16 *Westminster Gazette*, quoted in the *Autocar* (28 Aug. 1896) 224–6.
17 *Engineer* (8 May 1896) 467 (letter).
18 *Autocar* (4 July 1896) 427. Maidstone seems to have been a notably "anti-motoring" town, perhaps because of a concentration of activity in the area on the part of Walter Arnold, l'Hollier Gascoigne and their friends. Tonbridge produced the only two recorded exemplary punishments of motoring offenders in our period. Opinion in Tunbridge Wells veered to the opposite extreme, under the influence of Salomons. Kent was running true to form as the battleground between supporters and opponents of the self-propelled road vehicle.
19 The Anglo-French Motor Carriage Company.
20 *English Mechanic* (1 Nov. 1895) 250.
21 *Engineer* (5 July 1895) 12.
22 A used car trade took root in Britain during 1897, when the first cars turned out by British factories started to change hands, and it became worth while to deal in them. See advertisements of the Motor Car Company in the *Autocar* (28 Aug. 1897, 560; 2 Oct. 1897, 640; etc.).
23 *Automotor and Horseless Vehicle Journal* (Oct. 1896) 35.

PART 3

1 Reviving a term first used in the report of the Select Committee of the House of Commons on Locomotives on Roads (1873).
2 "It fell to my lot to suggest the clauses of the whole Bill in its first crude form": Lord Montage of Beaulieu (ed.), op. cit., 8.
3 There is no hint of its identity. It was probably an electric vehicle; these were comparatively numerous in London, and Clifden had shown an interest in them, asking Harris on the occasion of the Bill's first reading if it covered electric propulsion.
4 Flood-Page, an electrical engineer who had worked for the Edison & Swan Electrical Company, would soon be Chairman of the London Electric Omnibus Company, formed to operate Ward's buses.
5 Another such was Colonel A.W. Brookfield (Conservative, Sussex East).
6 The Tunbridge Wells Farmers' Club wanted both trailers and a 4-ton limit.
7 The standing committee was a new Parliamentary instrument – that on law dating only from 1888 – designed to expedite the conduct of Parliament's business. Lords and Commons had their own standing committees, which, as the name implied, were permanent bodies. Bills that were comparatively non-contentious, and did not go to a select committee, would go to the standing committee rather than be discussed solely in a committee of the whole House; or it might not go before the whole House at all. The smaller, more easily managed body would consider a Bill in detail, and move and pass amendments in the same way as other committees. These decisions then went back to the House for approval. Standing committees were a symptom of the increasing complexity of Bills, of the growing number of members wanting to speak, and of the determination of some Irish Nationalist M.P.s to wreck every measure. See W. Ivor Jennings, *Parliament*, 269.
8 *Engineering* (15 May 1896) 644–5; *Engineer* (19 June 1896) 607; *Autocar* (9 May 1896) 326.

9 Louis Delmer of Malines, in Belgium, showed a Benz-type car at the 1895 Paris Salon du Cycle. Sir David Salomons must have seen it there and been impressed, for he later ordered one.

10 Sir John Thornycroft was another example of an eminent marine engineer who had interested himself in self-propelled road vehicles as a young man, having designed one in the 1860s. The 1896 van was the first in a long line of Thornycroft steam goods vehicles.

11 Hewetson was happy to do so, since he received three-quarters of the takings. By now he was importing Benzes in association with Arnold; they had three cars at the Crystal Palace at various times, and sold them all. See Lord Montagu of Beaulieu (ed), op. cit. 54–6.

12 *Autocar* (25 Jan. 1896) 154.

13 Johnson later made his mark as Secretary of the Automobile Club of Great Britain and Ireland, and as the business partner of Charles Rolls and Henry Royce.

14 *Autocar* (18 Apr. 1896) 299.

15 S.F. Edge, *My Motoring Reminiscences*, 27

16 *Engineer* (8 May 1896) 472–3; *Daily Graphic* (2 May 1896). The *Autocar* added l'Hollier Gascoigne & Company's Roger-Benzes to the makes represented. According to the same source, by the time the exhibition opened to the public on 15 May, the ageing Garrard & Blumfield electric was also present. By mid-July a Britannia electric had put in an appearance, too. See the *Autocar* (18 July 1896) 453.

17 Alfred Harmsworth (ed.), op. cit., 365. In this source the diary entry is dated 11 May, but there is no record of another preview between 1 May and 14 May, and it likely that 11 May is a misprint for 1 May.

18 *Daily Graphic* (2 May 1896).

19 *Engineer* (8 May 1896) 472–3. The arrangement, though unmechanical in the extreme, was not quite as hilariously "Heath Robinson" as this implied. According to one account, the purpose of the bands, which were under tension, was to help the pistons to move against the compression when the machine was being push-started, and before the ignition fired – a sort of elastic-powered starter motor.

20 A few years later, Newnes was a car owner and a founder-member of the Automobile Club of Great Britain and Ireland.

21 Lord Montagu of Beaulieu (ed.), op. cit., 14.

22 New had arranged to import the Hildebrand & Wolfmüller: see p. 419.

23 *Autocar* (16 May 1896) 343, 355. Cycle tracks in London and the Midlands henceforth became favoured places for testing motor bicycles and tricycles, and ultimately for racing the latter. By early June a De Dion tricycle had followed the example of the Hildebrand & Wolfmüller: see *English Mechanic* (12 June 1896) 369.

24 Otherwise one of his own Kane-Penningtons.

25 The licence seems to have passed into the hands of Harry Lawson and Martin Rucker personally, rather than belonging even technically to the British Motor Syndicate. See prospectus, Great Horseless Carriage Company.

26 See p. 471.

27 Such figures were much bandied about, so are quoted here; but they meant little. It is not known whether the £500,000 included sums spent on all patents and licences bought to date; how much of it was paid in shares; or how much of the £750,000 was actually subscribed at the time. In any case, all sums paid by the Lawson "manufacturing" concerns to the British Motor Syndicate were simply circulating within the Lawson camp.

28 *Autocar* (6 June 1896) 374. This was presumably the machine demonstrated to the press on 8 June.

29 Humber may have been sold a non-exclusive licence; most of the planned Coulthard vehicles were buses. Coulthard later became known for their steam goods vehicles.

30 Quoted in the *Autocar* (27 June 1896) 411. By Oct. 1897 only half of the subscription – which was then £600,000 – had been taken up by the public.

31 *Engineer* (5 June 1896) 569.

32 *Industries and Iron* (22 May 1896) 410. This versatile firm also made an electric outboard motor.

33 *Autocar* (12 Sept. 1896) 542.

34 *Autocar* (18 July 1896) 453.

35 Claude Johnson, op. cit., preface, 2.

36 The last remark suggests that Chaplin was well aware of the voting strength of the railway interest in the House.

37 Hansard (30 June 1896). Strangely, Chaplin – who should have known better – perpetuated the myth that statute still required a red flag.

38 Set up in Mar. 1896.

39 Among others, the London Chamber of Commerce had opposed the increase to 4 tons. See the *Engineer* (22 May 1896) 516.

40 This sentiment had nothing to do with protecting motorists. It was shared by men as different as Chaplin and Parker-Smith, and was concerned with the unsuitability of a single speed limit for all road conditions.

41 It is interesting to note that Sidney Gedge later "changed sides", acquiring – like his colleague on the Road Safety Association, Lord Lonsdale – a financial interest in the motor industry.

42 The *Engineer* (7 Aug. 1896, 143) agreed that the duty would hinder the growth of the new industry.

43 Lord Montagu of Beaulieu (ed.), op. cit., 8.

44 Alfred Harmsworth (ed.), op. cit., 364–5.

45 *Autocar* (18 July 1896) 447–8.

46 Lord Montagu of Beaulieu (ed.), op. cit., 20; *Autocar* (1 Aug. 1896) 478. An earlier Marquess of Breadalbane had been a supporter of traction engines: see vol. 2, p. 209.

47 The first agencies to be instituted in the British motor trade were those of Cornell and Clark (for Daimlers).

48 *Autocar* (11 July 1896) 434.

49 Lord Montagu of Beaulieu (ed.), op. cit., 34. The first British-built Daimler of modern, Panhard type is said to have been completed by mid-November.

50 See a notably bumptious performance, even by Lawson standards, in the *Hornsey and Finsbury Park Journal* (29 Aug. 1896).

51 *Engineer* (2 Oct. 1896) 341.

52 *Engineer* (13 Nov. 1896) 504.

53 *Autocar* (14 Nov. 1896) advertisement. A year later the British Motor Syndicate's directors stated that up to November 1896, no cars of any description had been built in Britain under its patents. J.S. Critchley's date for the completion of the first was October. See *Automotor and Horseless Vehicle Journal* (Nov. 1897) 53.

54 When the firm was involved with the courts, it was as l'Hollier Gascoigne.

55 *Automotor and Horseless Vehicle Journal* (Nov. 1896) 63; *Engineer* (6 Nov. 1896) 480. As we have seen, some racehorse owners favoured the motor car.

56 A local government expert and an exceptionally able administrator; formerly an

M.P. and Parliamentary Secretary to the Board of Trade.

57 In 1899 Cordingley founded the *Motor Car Journal*, Britain's first really cheap, popular motoring magazine. At 1d a week it sought a wider, less technically oriented market than the *Autocar* at 3d or the *Automotor and Horseless Vehicle Journal* at 6d. Cordingley was also later the organiser of Britain's first motor shows – that is, trade exhibitions in which motor cars were not incidental to pedal cycles.

58 *Autocar* (24 Oct. 1896) classified advertisement.

59 See p. 452.

60 *Autocar* (24 Oct. 1896) 619. The British Motor Syndicate considered buying the licence at one time, but decided against it. Wisely on the whole, Lawson avoided involvement with steam. See *Pall Mall Gazette* (16 Nov. 1896).

61 *Automotor and Horseless Vehicle Journal* (Nov. 1896) 57.

62 *Automotor and Horseless Vehicle Journal* (Nov. 1896) 160.

PART 4

1 This German prince was married to a cousin of Queen Victoria. He was the father of the future Queen Mary, and father-in-law since 1893 of the Duke of York, the future King George V.

2 *Autocar* (21 Nov. 1896) 666–73.

3 *To-day* (21 Nov. 1896) 81–3. It was widely said that £50 was being offered for a seat.

4 *Daily Graphic* (16 Nov. 1896).

5 *Sun* (14 Nov. 1896).

6 *Engineer* (13 Nov. 1896) 499; *The Times* (16 Nov. 1896).

7 Or, according to some sources, carrying parcels for delivery to customers in Brighton. Perhaps it was doing both.

8 This and the press charabanc may have been Peugeots or Panhards.

9 Thrupp bought the car on which he rode, and by the spring of 1897 Thrupp & Maberly held the British licence for Duryea.

10 Charles Jarrott, *Ten Years of Motors and Motor Racing*, 2nd edn (1912) 4.

11 ibid.

12 *Cycle and Motor World* (25 Nov. 1896) i–ii. This was a glossy society journal, formerly the *Cycling World Illustrated*, that launched a motoring supplement after the Brighton run.

13 The next recorded prosecution, and the first under the new Act, was of a Birmingham motor car agent who was alleged to have driven at 20 m.p.h. and refused to stop on request. The court was lenient, imposing a fine of 10s and costs, accompanied by a warning, when £10 was in order. See the *Engineer* (25 Dec. 1896) 665.

14 *The Times* (14 Nov. 1896).

15 *Globe* (16 Nov. 1896); Charles G. Harper, *The Brighton Road*, cheap edn (1922) 54–60. Harper, a journalist and professional artist, witnessed the start and finish of the run.

16 *The Times* (17 Nov. 1896). The figure of 22 leaving Brixton is plausible. The London streets are known to have taken a heavy toll, and several cars had by then been consigned to the railway.

17 For the new concern, the original name was revived: few had used "British Motor Company".

18 *Engineer* (27 Nov. 1896) 546. It is highly unlikely that any production versions of

these machines yet existed. The *Wheelman and Motorcar Weekly* spoke of five French and four English Bollées. This is plausible, since it was said that about four Coventry Motettes were made at the Motor Mills.

19 The Education Bill and the Agricultural Land Rating Bill. The latter was one of the measures taken to abate the effects of the agricultural depression.

20 *Automotor and Horseless Vehicle Journal* (Oct. 1897) 19. The rank-and-file shareholders were only now realising that the company was not what it claimed to be: a manufacturing concern.

21 *Automotor and Horseless Vehicle Journal* (July 1897) 412; *Autocar* (20 Nov. 1897) 739. Henry Sturmey blamed the company's low rate of output on the exigencies of the production process. First, all of a vehicle's components had to be brought together. It took two weeks to "erect the motor", which was then tested for between two and three weeks. "Quite as much work" – concurrently, one imagines – was required to put together the frame and running gear, and "about three weeks" to "put the motor into its frame". In the coachbuilding shop, 16 coats of varnish were applied, each being separately dried and rubbed down. This was standard carriage practice; but the time taken in assembling the mechanical parts bears out the picture of a company that had not, when in Lawson's control, planned to manufacture more than token numbers of vehicles, at most, and was therefore ill-equipped for serious manufacture. See *Automotor and Horseless Vehicle Journal* (Nov. 1897) 55; Daimler Motor Company report.

The British motor industry had been slow in getting into production, said Sturmey (*Autocar*, 13 Mar. 1897, 174), because of its ignorance of how to make cars, but as far as the Lawson companies are concerned, this begs the question. The reason for ignorance in that quarter was lack of will to learn, under a regime that put quick profits from fraudulent company promotions before all else. It can be no coincidence that Daimler deliveries began when Lawson left. There is no reason to suppose that ignorance delayed production in non-Lawson companies: there were other factors (see pp. 475–7) in play that probably affected all companies equally. No companies other than Lawson's gave ignorance as a reason for hold-ups, and if it had been one, it is hard to see why, being an obvious and plausible excuse, it should not be used.

22 Coventry Motettes were often referred to as "Léon Bollées", so it is difficult to say exactly when manufacture under the new name began. In Jan. 1897 the Coventry Motor Company is said to have sold a Léon Bollée: see the *Autocar* (11 Sept. 1897) 584.

23 *Automotor and Horseless Vehicle Journal* (Feb. 1897) 204.

24 Kenneth Richardson, op. cit., 119. In July Great Horseless Carriage Company shares had slumped for a while to 17s 6d.

25 See pp. 408, 425.

26 S.B. Saul, "The Motor Industry in Great Britain to 1914", *Business History*, v, 22.

27 The prototype was sold to H.J. Dowsing, an electrical engineer who fitted it with the world's first electric starter. Dowsing was an ingenious and prolific inventor of electrical aids to motoring, including Dowsing's Electric Socks for winter wear.

28 One of the exceptions is of interest, as it represented a much-needed boost for the Daimler Motor Company, as well as being a modest success story in itself. The coachbuilders J. & C. Stirling of Hamilton, North Berwick, began buying modern Daimler-type chassis from the Daimler company and fitting them with their own bodies. The first Stirling was on the road in Jan. 1897, and by April the company was accepting orders. By October, more than a dozen vehicles had been sold. T.R.B. Elliot's second car was a Stirling. He disliked it until he substituted rubber

tyres for the iron tyres supplied, which had been shaking the car to pieces. In Dec. 1897, Stirling's Motor Carriages Ltd was floated for £100,000. See the *Autocar* (23 Jan. 1897) 61; ibid. (11 Dec. 1897) 800; the *Automotor and Horseless Vehicle Journal* (Feb. 1897) 182; ibid. (Oct. 1897) 21.

29 *Automotor and Horseless Vehicle Journal* (Sept. 1897) 496.

30 Until the Motor Car Act of 1903 was passed, and motor vehicle registration became obligatory, it was no one's business to count up all the motor cars in Britain – nor, indeed, was there any means of doing so. Production figures were so fragmentary or subjective as to be useless, and no tally of motor car imports was kept until 1902.

Traditionally, goods and chattels are counted in order to tax them, but even this does not help us in the case of the motor car in its earliest days. The annual returns of carriage duty payable under the Customs and Inland Revenue Act of 1888 do not distinguish between horse carriages and horseless. The returns of excise duty levied under the Locomotives on Highways Act of 1896 did do so, but were concerned with passenger vehicles only, not with goods carriers; and only then with those weighing between 1 and 3 tons (the upper limit for vehicles covered by the Act). These were a small minority of the "light locomotives" on the road. The expensive, complicated Panhards and Panhard-derived Daimlers scaled 21 hundredweight or a little more, their exact weight depending on their bodywork. Most cars were much lighter. The Lutzmann was not small, yet weighed only $16\frac{1}{2}$ hundredweight. The Duryea weighed up to about 10 hundredweight. As for the Léon Bollée, it turned the scales at 4 hundredweight or less.

The figures for vehicles covered by the 1896 Act show uneven growth up to March 1901 – two of the years actually showing a drop – and thereafter a consistent and rapid advance. We may suppose that the rate of increase for lighter vehicles was faster, since they were more popular.

Number of passenger vehicles, 1–3 tons, paying excise duty at end March

1897	1898	1899	1900	1901	1902
16	75	61	230	198	334

Figures from Reports, Commissioners of Inland Revenue.

The Local Government Board reports are still less useful, as they give the excise duty receipts alone, and then only to March 1900.

One other relevant set of figures is available: that illustrating the growth in numbers of the membership of the Automobile Club of Great Britain and Ireland in the period. But these figures can do no more than suggest the rate of change in number of vehicles – they are not much of a guide to the numbers themselves. Not every Club member necessarily owned a vehicle, though no doubt most did so; a few owned more than one; and a few doubtless owned commercial or public service vehicles instead of, or as well as, private cars.

Number of members of A.C.G.B.I. at end of year

1897	1898	1899	1900	1901
163	380	586*	710	1203†

*Early 1900
†Early 1902

At the end of 1901, the Motor Union – a body on the lines of the Cyclists' Touring Club, organised that year to protect the interests of motorists as individuals, at local level – had 1154 members, all probably owning vehicles.

No very detailed conclusions can be drawn from these sets of figures. It is possible only to see a general growth in the numbers of vehicles regardless of weight, and confirmation that lighter cars were considerably more popular than heavier ones.

CONCLUSION

1   S.B. Saul, op. cit.; Kenneth Richardson, op. cit.; William Plowden, *The Motor Car and Politics 1896–1970*; F. Lesley Cook, *Effects of Mergers*.

Select Bibliography

BOOKS, PAMPHLETS ETC.

Apart from the first nine works listed, only contemporary or other first-hand sources are given here. These include memoirs, letters, private papers and collections of personal reminiscences in essay form that may have been published some time after the events they concern, but which are no less original sources for that. Typical is the misleadingly titled *History of Ten Years of Automobilism 1896–1906*, edited by Lord Montagu of Beaulieu. Some histories are classed as first-hand material because they were written in the midst of a developing scene and were involved in it; for example Robert Stuart's *Historical and Descriptive Anecdotes of Steam Engines* (1829). Other histories are omitted because although equally contemporary they were remote and "historical" in tone; for instance William Fletcher's two catalogues of steam carriages.

It is difficult to single out the secondary sources old and new that are indispensable to an understanding of the background, but they include the following:

Albert, W., *The Turnpike Road System in England and Wales*, London, 1972.
Beer, S.H., *Modern British Politics*, London, 1969.
Chambers, J.D., and Mingay, J.E., *The Agricultural Revolution 1750–1880*, London, 1966.
Clark, R.H., *The Development of the English Traction Engine*, Norwich, 1960.
Deane, P., and Cole, W.A., *British Economic Growth 1688–1959*, Cambridge, 1967.
Jackman, W.T., *The Development of Transportation in Modern England*, Cambridge, 1916.
Thompson, F.M.L., *English Landed Society in the Nineteenth Century*, London, 1963.
Thompson, F.M.L., *Victorian England: The Horsedrawn Society*, Inaugural Lecture, Bedford College, London, 1970.
Webb, Sidney and Beatrice, *English Local Government*, v, London, 1913.

Adams, William Bridges, *English Pleasure Carriages*, London, 1837.
Adams, William Bridges, *Roads and Rails*, London, 1862.
Anon., *The Coming Motor Traffic*, London, 1897.
Anon., *A Concise History of Steam Carriages on Common Turnpike Roads*, n.d.
Anon., *Connection of Sir David Salomons Bt with the Development of Self-Propelled Traffic in the United Kingdom*, 1896.
Anon., *The Hooley Book*, London, 1904.
Anon., *Observations on Railways with Locomotive High-Pressure Steam Engines*, 1825.
Anon., *The Roads and Railroads, Vehicles and Modes of Travelling of Ancient and Modern Centuries*, etc., London, 1839.
Bateman, John, *The Great Land Owners of Great Britain and Ireland*, London, 1878.
Beaufort, Duke of, *Driving*, Badminton Library, London, 1890.
Beaumont, W. Worby, *Motor Vehicles and Motors*, London, 1900.

Bradfield, J.E., *The Public Carriages of Great Britain*, London, 1855.

Cary, John, *Cary's New Itinerary*, London, 1828.

Clark, D.K., *The Exhibited Machinery of 1862*, London, 1864.

Cracroft, Bernard, *Essays Political and Miscellaneous*, London, 1868.

Crompton, R.E.B., *Reminiscences*, London, 1928.

Cruchley's New Plan of London, London, 1831.

Cundy, N.W., *Inland Transit*, London, 1833.

De Bachaumont, Louis Petit, *Mémoires secrets*, London, 1777–89.

Defoe, Daniel, *A Tour through the Whole Island of Great Britain*, London, 1724–7.

Duncan, H.O., *The World on Wheels*, Paris, 1926.

Edge, S.F., *My Motoring Reminiscences*, London, n.d.

Faden, W., *New Pocket Plan of the Cities of London and Westminster*, London, 1803.

Galloway, Elijah, *History and Progress of the Steam Engine*, London, 1831.

Gerland, Ernst, *Leibnitzens und Huygens' Briefwechsel mit Papin*, Berlin, 1881.

German Prince, A, *Tour in England, Ireland and France*, Zurich, 1940.

Gordon, Alexander, *A Historical and Practical Treatise upon Elemental Locomotion*, London, 1836.

Gordon, Alexander, *Observations Addressed to Those Interested in either Railways or Turnpike Roads*, London, 1837.

Gordon, Alexander, *Observations on Railway Monopolies*, London, 1841.

Grand-Carteret, John, *La Voiture de demain*, Paris, 1898.

Gurney, Goldsworthy, *Mr Goldsworthy Gurney's Account of the Steam-jet, or Blast*, London, 1859.

Gurney, Goldswrothy, *Observations on Steam Carriages*, London, 1832.

Hancock, Thomas, *Personal Narrative of the Origin and Progress of the Caoutchouc or India-Rubber Manufacture in England*, London, 1857.

Hancock, Walter, *A Narrative of Twelve Years' Experiments*, London, 1838.

Harmsworth, Alfred (ed.), *Motors and Motor Driving*, Badminton Library, London, 1902.

Hebert, Luke, *Engineers' and Mechanics' Encyclopedia*, London, 1836.

Herapath, John, *A Letter to the Duke of Wellington upon Mr Gurney's Steam Carriage*, 1829.

Homer, Henry, *An Enquiry into the Means of Preserving Publick Roads*, Oxford, 1767.

Hood, Thomas, *The Comic Annual*, London, 1830.

Jarrott, Charles, *Ten Years of Motors and Motor Racing*, 2nd edn, London, 1912.

Johnson, Claude, *The Early History of Motoring*, London, 1926.

Knight, J.H., *Notes on Motor Carriages*, London, 1896.

Leupold, Jacob, *Theatri Machinarum Hydraulicarum*, Leipzig, 1724–5.

Lockert, Louis, *Petroleum Motor Cars*, London, 1898.

McAdam, J.L., *Remarks on the Present System of Road-Making*, London, 1827.

Maceroni, Francis, *A Few Facts Concerning Elementary Locomotion*, London, 1834.

Maceroni, Francis, *Propositions and Illustrations Interesting to All Concerned in Steam Power*, London, 1835.

Maceroni, Francis, *Memoirs*, London, 1838.

Medhurst, George, *A New System of Inland Conveyance*, London, 1827.

Mogg, Edward, *Survey of the High Roads of England and Wales*, London, 1816.

Montagu of Beaulieu, Lord (ed.), *A History of Ten Years of Automobilism 1896–1906*, London, 1906.

Napier, David, *David Napier, Engineer, 1790–1869: An Autobiographical Sketch*, Glasgow, 1912.

Parnell, Henry, *A Treatise on Roads*, London, 1833.

Paterson, Daniel, A New and Accurate Description of All the Direct Roads, etc., London, 1826.

Postlethwayt, Malachy, *Universal Dictionary of Trade and Commerce*, London, 1751.

Preston, P.D. (ed.), *Papers Read Before the Institute of British Carriage Manufacturers 1883–1901*, London, 1902.

Rickman, John (ed.), *Telford: Written by Himself*, London, 1838.

Ritchie, Leitch, *Turner's Annual Tour*, London, 1834.

Salomons, Sir David, *The Horseless Carriage*, Tunbridge Wells, 1895.

Sennett, A.R., *Carriage Without Horses Shall Go*, London, 1896.

Smiles, Samuel (ed.), *James Nasmyth, Engineer: An Autobiography*, London, 1883.

Smith, George, *Concise History of English Carriages and Motor Cars*, 1896.

Stuart, Robert, *Historical and Descriptive Anecdotes of Steam Carriages*, London, 1829.

Tangye, Richard, *One and All*, London, 1890.

Tangye, Richard, *The Rise of a Great Industry*, London, 1905.

Taylor, Lt. Gen. Sir Herbert, *The Taylor Papers 1775–1839*, London, 1913.

Warter, J.W. (ed.), *Selections from the Letters of Robert Southey*, London, 1856.

Young, Arthur, *A Six Months' Tour through the North of England*, London, 1770.

Young, Arthur, *A Six Weeks' Tour through the Southern Counties*, London, 1768.

Young, C.F.T., *The Economy of Steam Power on Common Roads*, London, 1861.

JOURNALS, NEWSPAPERS AND PERIODICALS

Only contemporary or otherwise first-hand sources are given here. These include memoirs, obituaries and so forth that may have been published some time after the events they concern, but which are no less original sources for that. Obvious examples are articles in the *Autocar* for 1895–6, and in the *Engineer* for 1894–6, covering events of earlier periods.

Académie de l'Industrie, *Journal*, 1835.

Académie des Sciences, *Comptes Rendus*, 1839.

Ashton Reporter, 1867, 1899.

Australian, 1836.

Autocar, 1895–7.

Automotor and Horseless Vehicle Journal, 1896–7, 1899.

Banffshire Journal, 1860.

Bell's Life in London, 1827.

Bicycling Times, 1881.

Birmingham Advertiser, 1833.

Birmingham Daily Gazette; Birmingham Gazette, 1832, 1834–5, 1895.

Brighton Gazette, 1896.

British Association, *Reports, Transactions*, 1860, 1896.

Cambridge Chronicle, 1843.

Cassell's Family Magazine, 1879, 1888.

Cheltenham Chronicle, 1831.

Coach Builders', Harness Makers' and Saddlers' Art Journal, 1896.

Cornwall Gazette & Falmouth Packet, 1802.

Coventry Times, 1896.

Courier, 1827, 1834.

Coventry Mercury, 1835.
Cycle and Motor World, 1896.
Cyclist, 1881, 1894.
Daily Chronicle, 1895.
Daily Graphic, 1895–6.
Daily Mail, 1896.
Daily Telegraph, 1894–6.
Design and Work, 1879.
Devizes Gazette, 1827.
Economist, The, 1896.
Edinburgh Journal of Science, 1828.
Edinburgh Observer, 1828, 1834.
Edinburgh Weekly Journal, 1828.
Engineer, 1856, 1858–61, 1864, 1866, 1869–72, 1874, 1877–9, 1881–3, 1886–9, 1891,
     1893–6.
Engineering, 1866, 1871, 1886, 1891, 1894–6.
English Mechanic, 1882, 1889–92, 1895–6.
Essex Standard, 1832.
Evening Argus (Brighton), 1896.
Farmer's Herald, 1861.
Field, 1878, 1896.
Financial News, 1896.
Financial Times, The, 1896.
Folkestone Chronicle, 1857.
Foreign Quarterly Review, 1832.
France Automobile, La, 1896.
Gentleman's Magazine, 1821–2, 1829, 1834–5, 1837.
Glasgow Argus, 1834.
Glasgow Chronicle, 1829–30.
Glasgow Courier, 1834.
Glasgow Free Press, 1828, 1834.
Glasgow Herald; Glasgow Weekly Herald, 1829, 1834, 1872, 1895–6.
Globe, 1834–5, 1896.
Gloucester Journal, 1829.
Great Eastern Railway Magazine, 1911.
Greenwich & Deptford Chronicle, 1881.
Halifax Chronicle, 1830.
Hornsey and Finsbury Park Journal, 1896.
Illustrated London News, 1857, 1860.
Implement and Machinery Review, 1895.
Industries; Industries & Iron, 1887, 1896.
Institution of Civil Engineers, *Proceedings*, 1873, 1876–7, 1890.
Institution of Mechanical Engineers, *Proceedings*, 1853, 1856.
Iron and Steel Institute, *Journal*, 1879.
John o'Groat's Journal, 1860.
Journal Militaire et Politique, 1772.
Journal of Elemental Locomotion; Journal of Steam Transport and Husbandry,
     1832–3.
Kent and Sussex Courier, 1895–6.
Kent and Sussex Mercury, 1833.
Kentish Mercury, 1881.

Lancet, 1896.
Leicester Daily Post, 1896.
Literary Chronicle, 1827.
Literary Gazette, 1829.
Liverpool Mercury, 1862.
Locomotion Automobile, La, 1895.
London Journal of Arts and Sciences, 1825–9.
Maidstone Gazette, 1835.
Manchester Guardian, 1821, 1830
Mark Lane Express, 1855–8.
Mechanics' Magazine, 1825–6, 1828–41, 1846–7, 1849, 1855–7, 1859–61, 1865, 1867–8, 1871.
Mining Journal, 1858.
Mirror, 1829.
Mirror of Literature, Amusement and Instruction, 1823, 1827.
Morning, 1896.
Morning Advertiser, 1840.
Morning Chronicle, 1832–4.
Morning News and Public Ledger, 1834.
Morning Post, 1860, 1896.
New Saturday, 1896.
Newcastle Daily Chronicle, 1896.
Observer, 1827, 1833.
Oxford Chronicle and Bucks & Berks Gazette, 1860.
Pall Mall Gazette, 1896.
Practical Engineer, 1889–90.
Punch, 1896.
Quarterly Review, 1848.
Railway Times, 1843.
Register of Arts and Journal of Patent Inventions, 1827–9, 1832.
Royal Agricultural Society, *Journal*, 1841, 1849, 1856, 1859, 1871, 1895.
Saddlers', Harness Makers' and Carriage Builders' Gazette, 1896.
St James Gazette, 1896.
Saturday Magazine, 1832.
Saturday Review, 1895–6.
Scotsman, 1825, 1827, 1834, 1867.
Scots Times, 1829.
Sickle, 1828.
Society of Arts, *Journal, Proceedings*, 1888, 1895–6.
Society of Engineers, *Transactions*, 1862.
Southampton Echo, 1896.
Southampton Herald, 1827.
Sporting and Dramatic News, 1896.
Sporting Times, 1896.
Standard, 1838, 1896.
Star, 1896.
Statist, 1892, 1896.
Sun, 1894, 1896.
Sussex Daily News, 1896.
Sydney Gazette, 1836.
Times, The, 1824–5, 1827–34, 1838, 1840–42, 1851, 1855, 1859–61, 1864, 1867.

Times of India, 1896.
To-day, 1896.
Tricycling Journal, 1881.
True Sun, 1833–4.
Tunbridge Wells Gazette, 1896.
Westminster Gazette, 1896.
Wheelman and Motorcar Weekly, 1896.
Windsor and Eton Express, 1895.
Wolverhampton Chronicle, 1859.
Worcester Herald, 1831.
World, 1896.

COMPANY PROSPECTUSES, TURNPIKE TRUST MINUTES, COLLECTIONS

The largest single collection of relevant company prospectuses discovered by the writer – five in all – is at Pressmark 1881.b.23 (Prospectuses of Joint Stock Companies, 5 vols) in the British Library. Other prospectuses are bound in with, or published in, relevant journals at around the time when subscriptions were being solicited – for example, the *Journal of Elemental Locomotion* and *Journal of Steam Transport & Husbandary*, 1832–3, the *Mark Lane Express*, 1857–9, and the *Autocar*, 1895–7. In some cases extracts were published.

The major collection of turnpike trust minutes books consulted is kept at the Archives Office, County Hall, Maidstone, Kent. The Gloucester, Cheltenham and Tewkesbury trust minutes are held by the Gloucestershire County Council Record Office, Shire Hall, Gloucester.

Anglo-French Motor Carriage Company, 1896.
Bray's Traction Engine Company, 1859.
British Motor Syndicate, 1895, 1896.
Common Road Steam Conveyance Company, 1839.
Daimler Motor Company, 1896.
Endless Railway Traction Engine Company (Boydell's Patent), 1861.
General Steam Carriage Company, n.d.
General Steam Coach Company, n.d.
Great Horseless Carriage Company, 1896.
London & Birmingham Steam Carriage Company, 1832.
London Electrical Cab Company, 1896.
London, Holyhead & Liverpool Steam Coach & Road Company, 1833.
New Beeston Cycle Company, 1896.
Patent Steam Carriage Company, n.d.
Steam Carriage Company, n.d.
Steam Carriage & Waggon Company, 1833; Report, 1841.
Traction Engine & Endless Railway Apparatus Company, 1857.

Minutes, Gloucester, Cheltenham and Tewkesbury Trust, 1831.
General Committee Minutes, Greenwich and Woolwich (Lower Road) Turnpike
    Trust, 1860.
Minutes, Home and Blean Highway Board, 1870–90.
General Minutes, New Cross Turnpike Trust, 1860.
Minutes, Rochford Highway Board, 1871.

British Transport Historical Records.
The Archives of Arnolds (Branbridges) Ltd, East Peckham.
The Frederick Simms Papers, London School of Economics Political Science.
The Salomons Papers, David Salomons House, Broomhill, Southborough, near Tunbridge Wells, Kent.

STATE PAPERS: ACTS, BILLS, REPORTS AND MINUTES, PARLIAMENTARY JOURNALS

Customs and Inland Revenue Act, 1888.
Hawking of Petroleum Act, 1881.
Highways Act, 1835.
Highways and Locomotives (Amendment) Bill, 1878.
Light Locomotives on Highways Order, 1896.
Local Government Act, 1888.
Locomotive Act, 1861.
Locomotives Act, 1865.
Locomotives Bill, 1859.
Locomotives Bill, 1860.
Locomotives Bill, 1871.
Locomotives on Common Roads Bill, 1877.
Locomotives on Highways Act, 1896.
Locomotives on Highways Bill, 1895.
Locomotives on Roads Bill, 1872.
Locomotives on Roads Bill, 1873.
Locomotives on Roads Bill, 1874.
Petroleum Act, 1871.
Petroleum Act, 1879.
Stage Coaches Bill, 1832.
Tolls on Steam Carriages Bill, 1836.
Toll Relief Bill, 1832.
Turnpike Tolls (Scotland) Bill, 1831.
Report and Minutes, Select Committee of the House of Commons on Mr Goldsworthy Gurney's Case, 1834–5.
Report and Minutes, Select Committee of the House of Lords on the Highways Act, 1881.
Reports, Commissioners of Inland Revenue, 1897–1902.
Minutes, Select Committee of the House of Commons on the Liverpool and Manchester Railway Bill, 1825.
Report and Minutes, Select Committee of the House of Lords on the Locomotives Bill, 1865.
Report and Minutes, Select Committee of the House of Lords on the Locomotives Bill, 1871.
Report and Minutes, Select Committee of the House of Commons on the Locomotive Bill, 1859.
Report and Minutes, Select Committee of the House of Commons on Locomotives on Roads, 1873.
Abstract of Report, Ordinance Select Committee, 1858.
Report and Minutes, Select Committees of the House of Commons on Petroleum, 1894, 1896–7.

Report and Minutes, Select Committee of the House of Commons on Steam Carriages, 1831.

Report and Minutes, Select Committee of the House of Lords on the Tolls on Steam Carriages Bill, 1836.

Report, Select Committee of the House of Commons on Traction Engines, 1896.

Report and Minutes, Select Committee of the House of Commons on Tramways, 1877.

Report, Select Committee of the House of Lords on Turnpike Returns, 1833.

Report and Minutes, Select Committee of the House of Commons on Turnpike Trusts, 1839.

Report and Minutes, Select Committee of the House of Commons on Turnpike Trusts, 1864.

Report and Minutes, Select Committee of the House of Commons on Turnpike Trusts and Tolls, 1836.

Abstracts, Income and Expenditure of Turnpike Trusts, 1834, 1857.

Hansard.

House of Commons Journals.

House of Lords Journals.

Index